Compassionate Ministry

COMPASSIONATE MINISTRY

edited by
GARY L. SAPP

Religious Education Press
Birmingham, Alabama

Library of Congress Cataloging-in-Publication Data

Compassionate ministry / edited by Gary L. Sapp
    Includes bibliographical references and indexes.
    ISBN 0-89135-090-X
    1. Caring—Religious aspects—Christianity. 2. Sympathy—Religious
aspects—Christianity. 3. Pastoral counseling. 4. Christian eduction.
I. Sapp, Gary L.
  BV4647.S9C66   1993   93-37385
  253—dc20   CIP

Religious Education Press, Inc.
5316 Meadow Brook Road
Birmingham, Alabama 35242
10 9 8 7 6 5 4 3 2

Religious Education Press publishes books exclusively in religious education
and in areas closely related to religious education. It is committed to enhancing and professionalizing religious education through the publication of
serious, significant, and scholarly works.

PUBLISHER TO THE PROFESSION

CONTENTS

INTRODUCTION

Compassion has been a core construct in all major religions for thousands of years. In Western Christianity, the parable of the Good Samaritan is particularly revered as one of the quintessential acts of religiously committed individuals. More audaciously, the New Testament states, "Greater love hath no man than this, that a man lay down his life for his friends" (Jn 15:13). This conception of compassion assumes selfless behavior motivated by a compelling love which is altruistic. Religiously committed persons have little difficulty in accepting this assumption as correct prima facie. However, many proponents of Western philosophy and psychology are not so sanguine. They overwhelmingly contend that all compassionate behavior is ultimately self-serving and egocentric.

Since 1970, a small group of social psychologists in the United States has questioned this cynical view regarding the motivation of compassionate behavior. Using the term religious prosocial motivation, C.Daniel Batson and his associates have carefully examined the evidence supporting the role of altruism in motivating prosocial behavior. They have identified crucial relationships between how one manifests compassionate behavior and one's religious orientation. Batson's position is thus a "breath of fresh air" amid a large body of research which almost totally rejects the role of variables characterized as spiritual or transcendental.

Identifying altruism as a motivation for religious compassion may strike some readers as gratuitous. However, providing valid support for this contention from empirical studies may provide a rap-

1

prochement between writers across the religious spectrum. These individuals range from those who have decried the conceptualizations of religion as a set of beliefs with magical powers to those who find religious sentiments to be reaction formations or responses to fine-grained reinforcement schedules. It is hoped that those who seek motivation for good deeds in religious revelation may find some common ground with those who prefer more mundane explanations. Given the disintegration of historical and theological authority as the basis of cohesive moral values across Western societies and the concomitant ascendancy of science as an arbiter of values, it is imperative that religious individuals be able to justify their beliefs, both personally and professionally, as something more than personal whims or imperfectly formulated defense mechanisms.

The purpose of this book is twofold. First, this volume seeks to provide a comprehensive overview of compassion from both a theological and a social science perspective. These diverse viewpoints provide a relevant foundation and broaden the dialogue of questions that relate to religious compassion. These perspectives, however, are complementary in that the writings of these authors are informed by a religious faith. Their thoughtful expositions reaffirm the notion that compassion deserves its place as one of the central notions in contemporary religion. A second of the two purposes is to examine how compassion might best be manifested through different forms of pastoral ministry. The intent is that this book will be relevant and useful not only for scholars, students, and others who wish to expand their knowledge about religious compassion, but also for those persons engaged in pastoral ministry who may recommit themselves and their work to the daily sharing of religious compassion with others.

Compassionate Ministry is divided into two parts consisting of four and two chapters, respectively. Part I deals with the foundations of religious compassion, while Part II focuses more on application of the concepts enunciated in Part I to two central areas within the overall ministry of compassion. In order to give balance to the book, each of the last two chapters is somewhat longer than each of the first four. This arrangement gives religious counseling and religious instructional practice their due consideration.

Every effort was made in the planning and implementation of this book to provide linkages between scholarly investigations of compassion and pastoral practice. Thus all four chapters in Part I, though primarily devoted to a scholarly exploration of the topic at hand also deal with relevant pastoral implications of this scholarship. And the two chapters in Part II treat not only pastoral practices in counseling and education, but also incorporate the scholarship on compassion which illumines this practice, making it more effective in the long run.

In Chapter 1, Dianne Bergant outlines the biblical basis for being compassionate. She suggests that compassion begins with the awareness of the interdependence of all living beings. This notion of interdependence is an ancient one going back to God's covenant with Israel. Compassion is a divine attribute and its nature and evolution is traced linearly from the Old Testament to that manifested by Jesus and his disciples. Bergant conducts a careful textual interpretation of compassion analyzing pertinent words and their contextual meanings. She delineates the historical, reciprocal roles of the biblical theology of compassion and the communities that preserved this theology. She first focuses on the compassion of God in the Old Testament linking it to the compassion of Jesus in the New Testament. Jesus' compassion in turn serves as the pattern for the compassion of Christians and the standard whereby they can measure their lives.

In the second chapter, Wayne Whitson Floyd traces the origins of a theological interpretation of religious compassion in the Jewish and Christian traditions. He presents a constructive, theological interpretation of the meaning of compassion, particularly as it is influenced by Christian thought. In the latter section of the chapter he evaluates the implications of the constructive theological interpretation for a variety of ministries. He considers the influence of third world Christian liberation theologies on Christianity's practice of ministry. The influence includes feminist and black Christian liberation theologies and the theology of compassion in non-Christian religious traditions. Floyd concludes by suggesting that a fully developed Christian theology of compassion will require the fundamental rethinking of many complacent assumptions regarding the practice of ministry.

In Chapter 3, Gary Sapp provides an overview of relevant writings in philosophy and delineates research in psychology that has influenced current conceptions of religious compassion. Compassion is conceptualized as a multifaceted construct comprising three areas: affective, motivational, and behavioral. Once the construct of compassion is defined, the crucial issue of motivation of compassion is discussed and the role and significance of altruism in compassion is considered. The chapter then discusses religious compassionate behavior, what contemporary social psychologists refer to as religious prosocial behavior, suggesting that it is inextricably linked to different ways of being religious, namely, one's religious orientation. The chapter concludes by indicating that the religious orientation that might appear to be most closely aligned with compassionate behavior, i.e., religion as an open-ended quest may not directly lead to more compassionate behavior.

Donald Ratcliff opens his chapter by addressing the absence of religious compassion both individually and corporately. A major concern is to isolate the social forces that work against compassion and develop strategies to minimize their effects or eliminate them altogether. Four sociological theories are considered: functionalism, conflict theory, exchange theory, and symbolic interactionism, which, he believes, comprise nearly all sociological research and understanding. These four perspectives are interfaced with religious concerns and used to illuminate the understanding of why religious compassion does not occur more frequently. He concludes the chapter by addressing specific sociological topics: socialization, culture, small groups, and collective behavior, with an eye to applying religious compassion on a more practical level.

Anthony Headley, Joe Boone Abbott, and Gary L. Sapp, examine the role of compassion in the ministry of religious counseling. They begin by delineating the structural components of compassion and conclude that it is a complex multifaceted emotion. They then analyze the process of compassion and discuss whether it demands experiences similar to the one who is suffering. Since compassion is addressed to the suffering of others, suffering is considered also. In the second section of the chapter, the material on compassion and its structure and compassion's relation to suffering are considered as the bases for applying compassion to the field of the counseling profession. Specific examples from pastoral counseling are provided to illustrate effective techniques for manifesting compassion.

In the concluding chapter James Michael Lee discusses religious compassion as it relates to instructional practice. To introduce the chapter, he discusses the meaning and scope of religious instruction and the content of religious instruction for compassion. He then defines the construct of compassion and discusses the issue of whether compassion can be taught. Of particular importance is the overview of general principles relating to the structural content of compassion. These include a detailed outline of the instructional process and an emphasis on cognitive, affective, and lifestyle procedures. Lee concludes the chapter by discussing the limits of compassion in religious instruction.

The preparation of this book has occupied a substantial portion of the lives of several fine people. I wish to express my appreciation to these stellar collaborators for their excellent work and their patience as we have brought this book to fruition. A particular note of thanks is due James Michael Lee who is responsible for much of the conceptualization and motivation in bringing this project to life. To him I am deeply grateful.

GARY L. SAPP
Birmingham, Alabama

Part I

FOUNDATIONS OF
RELIGIOUS COMPASSION

1

Compassion in the Bible

DIANNE BERGANT

"Be compassionate as your Father is compassionate."
Luke 6:36

"The whole idea of compassion is based on a keen awareness of the interdependence of all these living beings, which are all part of one another and all involved in one another." At first glance, this excerpt from the last talk of the renowned Trappist monk Thomas Merton, given just two hours before his death in 1968, suggests a strong Buddhist influence in his thinking. In this Eastern tradition, interdependence flows from some type of common bonding, and compassion is the attitude one has toward all with which one is linked. *Prajna* or 'wisdom' and *karuna* or 'compassion' constitute the two pillars of this major world religion. Described as the reverence for all beings, such compassion is thought to be profoundly intimate and has often been especially characterized as the love of a mother for the child of her womb.[1] In his later years Merton was indeed immersed in Eastern religious thought, and this final lecture was given during a conference of international spiritual leaders

---

1. *The Encyclopedia of Religion* (New York: Macmillan, 1987), vol. 8, p. 269.

held in Bangkok. Still, there are at least two reasons why such a statement could well have originated from within his own Judaeo-Christian biblical tradition.

In the first place, within the First Testament of the Bible one finds *rah*ᵉ*mim*, one of the Hebrew words translated as 'compassion.' This word is derived from the same Hebrew root as is *rehem*, 'womb.' Although until recently this dimension of compassion, i.e., its relationship with 'womb,' seldom has been the focus of attention,[2] a careful study of the biblical passages wherein these related words appear should be beneficial in at least two ways. (1) It can illuminate the meaning of one of the most prominent characterizations of God present in the Bible. (2) It can provide insight into the reason for and the nature of compassion toward others as found within the biblical tradition.

The second reason that Merton need not have ventured beyond his own tradition in his understanding is that the notion of interdependence based on some form of bonding is not peculiar to Buddhism. The idea of covenant is central to biblical religion, both Jewish and Christian. Most people acknowledge the role played by this theological concept in describing the divine/human relationship. A closer look at it will show that it has a social dimension as well. Joined to God in covenant, we are also intimately related to each other, interdependent in this union.[3] We have not only come forth from the same divine womb,[4] but we have also been born anew as a people of God.[5]

While compassion is generally thought to be a human sentiment, the text chosen to introduce this chapter suggests that, from a biblical point of view, the disposition is first a divine attribute, and it is after this that the human expression of compassion should be modeled. This point does not diminish the element of common bonding with its sense of interdependence from which flows the human

---

2. Cf. Phyllis Trible, *God and the Rhetoric of Sexuality* (Philadelphia: Fortress, 1978), pp. 31-59; John F. Craghan, *Love and Thunder* (Collegeville, Minn.: The Liturgical Press, 1983), pp. 11f; Virginia Ramey Mollenkott, *The Divine Feminine* (New York: Crossroad, 1984), pp. 15ff; Samuel Terrien, *Till the Heart Sings* (Philadelphia: Fortress, 1985), pp. 56-59. Sallie McFague, *Models of God* (Philadelphia: Fortress, 1987), pp. 109-116.

3. This idea is captured in Paul's image of the body of Christ, 1 Cor 12:12-31.

4. Dt 32:18.

5. 2 Cor 5:17.

sentiment. On the contrary, grounding compassion in this way establishes it as a reality that is religious as well as emotional.

Until recently most theological conversation about divine compassion simply referred to those biblical texts that seemed to support the particular perspective being developed. Such discussion was seldom based on rigorous biblical analysis. The reason for this may have been the auxiliary role scripture usually played in theological development. Or it may have been that compassion was not considered as significant a divine attribute as were justice, holiness, transcendence, omnipotence, etc., and biblical theologians had not yet engaged in substantial investigation of pertinent passages.

This chapter is offered as an initial step in the direction of such investigation. It will begin with an examination of the references to divine compassion found in the First Testament and then proceed to an analysis of the compassion manifested in Jesus and exacted of his disciples. It is fundamentally a word study and, as is always the case with word studies, merely lays the ground for further investigation.

To claim that God is compassionate is to call into question the long accepted principle of divine impassibility.[6] This in turn raises an even more fundamental question, i.e., the metaphorical character of theological language.[7] Practically all of the language in the Bible that refers to God is metaphorical. Some metaphors have been drawn from the natural world (a rock, Ps 31:2-3; an eagle, Dt 32:11),

---

6. This is the doctrine that God cannot suffer. For a discussion of divine pathos and wrath see Abraham J. Heschel, *The Prophets* (New York and Evanston: Harper & Row, 1955), pp. 221-306. For further discussion of divine pathos see H.W. Robinson, *The Cross in the Old Testament* (London: SCM, 1955); Samuel Terrien, *The Elusive Presence: Toward a New Biblical Theology* (San Francisco: Harper & Row, 1978), pp. 245, 268, 289; Walter Brueggemann, *The Prophetic Imagination* (Philadelphia: Fortress, 1978), pp. 44-61.

7. The studies on the metaphorical character of theological language are too numerous to mention. Some of the more insightful are: James Barr, "Theology and Anthropomorphism in the Old Testament," *Vetus Testamentum Supplement,* 7 (1959), pp. 31-38; Terence E. Fretheim, *The Suffering of God: An Old Testament Perspective* (Philadelphia: Fortress, 1984); Sallie McFague, *Metaphorical Theology & Models of God* (Philadelphia: Fortress, 1982 & 1987); Virginia Ramey Mollenkott, *The Divine Feminine: The Biblical Imagery of God as Female* (New York: Crossroad, 1984); Phyllis Trible, *God and the Rhetoric of Sexuality* (Philadelphia: Fortress Press, 1978); David Tracy, *The Analogical Imagination* (New York: Crossroad, 1981); Walter Wifall, "Models of God in the Old Testament," *Biblical Theology Bulletin*, 9 (1979), pp. 179-186.

but most of them are anthropomorphic (a husband, Is 54:5; a mother, Is 66:14). Although a metaphor should not be taken literally (God is neither rock nor eagle nor husband nor mother), it should be taken seriously. It may not be a definition, but it does in fact describe (something about a rock and an eagle and a husband and a mother reveals something of God). As diverse as the biblical metaphors are, they all reveal God in some way in relationship with the world.

There are different kinds of metaphors used to characterize God. Some of them depict God in a particular role. Others are more descriptive of some divine quality. No one will deny the preponderance of the narrative form within the First Testament. There we find stories relating the deeds of the Creator, the Warrior-God, the divine Judge, etc. These various metaphors, as well as those mentioned above and many others besides, are all alike in that they are fashioned more in response to some perceived human need than a mystical insight into divine make-up. God acts in a particular way when something or someone outside of God requires such behavior. Divine activity is neither self-indulgent nor capricious. God acts for the benefit of the world and everything within it.

Still, it is not enough to say that God creates or saves or judges. Other ancient literatures depict other gods in similar fashion. What makes Israel's God unique is the kind of God that creates or saves or judges. A careful reading of the Bible will show that underlying each and every divine activity, whether creation, liberation, or judgment, is a God revealed as "compassionate and gracious, slow to anger, rich in steadfast love and faithfulness."[8] It is this fundamental character that informs all divine activity and, therefore, can be considered a controlling metaphor.[9] In the past, the First Testament has been interpreted from the perspective of controlling metaphors such as the unrivaled majesty of God or the inescapable judgment of God. Some of the most provocative developments in contemporary theology can be attributed to the dynamism of the metaphor

---

8. The only other phrase that occurs as often as this statement, or one of its various forms, is similar to it: "his steadfast love endures forever" (cf. Ps 136).

9. A controlling metaphor is one that can function as a hermeneutical key for interpreting the entire literary work. Cf. Max Black, *Models and Metaphors* (Ithaca, N.Y.: Cornell University Press, 1962); Ian T. Ramsey, *Models and Mystery* (New York: Oxford University Press, 1964).

of God as liberator. Only recently have scholars turned with renewed interest to the characterization of God as compassionate.

Before we look at the texts themselves, a few words about interpretation are in order. In even the most careful reading of the Bible we are limited in our ability to detect the contextual meaning of words. This meaning can be discovered only through careful interpretation of the biblical passages, first in themselves and then within their various contexts (literary and historical). Such interpretation can follow one of two basic approaches: historical-critical or contemporary literary-critical. Professional scholars engaged in contemporary hermeneutics span a wide spectrum of positions regarding these interpretive approaches. Those who hold that the real meaning is that intended by the original author employ historical-critical methods to discover it. Others contend that once a piece of literature leaves the hands of its author it enjoys a life of its own, independent of authorial intent. These interpreters favor literary methods.

Most contemporary hermeneutical methods include elements of each approach. Such will be the manner of interpretation employed here. It will include an analysis of pertinent words and their contextual meanings, an investigation of the role this theology may have played within the community that brought it forth or preserved it, and then a study of the development the theology seems to have undergone throughout the history of the community. It will conclude with a contemporary interpretation of the theology along with implications pertinent to our times.

The Compassion of God

As we examine the scriptures in order to discover the various characterizations of God found there, we must always remember that we are far removed from the original languages and patterns of thought, as well as from the original worlds of meaning. Conscious of this hermeneutical distance, we must exercise great caution as we engage in word study.

The Hebrew Language and Its Meaning

There are several Hebrew words that have been translated as 'compassion' or 'compassionate.' Although they frequently seem to be used interchangeably, slightly different nuances of meaning can be discerned.[10] This chapter will limit its investigation to only one of the four, *rhm*. The primary meaning of this root seems to be 'cherishing,' 'soothing,' or 'a gentle attitude of mind.' It is used to refer to the tender love of parents toward children, of God toward humankind. Of the almost fifty appearances of the verb, in all but five instances[11] the subject is God. In addition to this, the adjective *rahum* is used only of God,[12] and with few exceptions the noun *raḥᵃmin* denotes a quality of God.[13] This root seems to have expressed Israel's preferred way of understanding God's compassion.

As mentioned earlier, the root *rhm* also yields *rehem*, one of the two Hebrew nouns that can be translated 'womb.' The second word for womb, *beten*, derived from the root *btn* which means 'empty' or 'hollow,' can also be rendered 'belly,' 'abdomen,' or 'inmost being.' Although this noun is feminine in form, it does not always translate as 'womb.' It is also used to refer to the body of a man.[14] On the other hand, *rehem*, though masculine in form, is always translated 'womb.' It would appear that with *beten* the emphasis is on the spatial character of the womb, its ability to hold something. *Rehem*, however, besides conveying the general spatial meaning, carries the

---

10. Although there are four chief roots, the limitations of space preclude a careful analysis of three of them: (1) *hml* - Its primary meaning is 'softness.' Related words derived from this root include: nouns ('mercy' or 'gentleness'); and verbs ('to pity,' 'to have compassion,' 'to spare,' or 'to use sparingly'). (2) *hnn* - Meaning 'favor' or 'yearning,' its derivations include: 'to pity,' 'to give graciously,' or 'to compassionate.' From this root comes the word for 'grace' or 'favor.' (3) *hus* - This word is usually followed by the preposition translated 'upon,' thus yielding the meaning 'to look upon with compassion.' When this form is used, compassion is more frequently attributed to the eye that looks upon than to the person looking upon.

11. Babylon shows no compassion toward Israel (Jer 6:23; 21: 7) and subsequently will be treated without compassion (Is 13:18). In fact, it will endure the same torment that it previously inflicted on Israel (Jer 50:42). When the foreign king eventually does show compassion toward Israel, it is credited to God's compassion toward the nation (Jer 42:12).

12. A feminine form of the adjective does describe desperate yet compassionate mothers in Lam 4:10.

13. Joseph's compassion toward his brothers, especially the one born of the same womb as was he (Gn 43:30), is credited to God's compassion toward the sons of Jacob (Gn 43:14). Later all Israel had been told to be compassionate toward each other (Zec 7:9), a command that they disregarded. Other references are to the lack of compassion of Edom toward the northern kingdom of Israel (Am 1:11), of Babylon toward the southern kingdom of Judah (Is 47:6), and of a wicked individual (Prv 12:10).

descriptive connotation of sensitivity. This latter word suggests that there is a bond of profound emotion between a mother and the child of her womb or between those who come from the same womb.

It is important to note that the Hebrew word for 'compassion' is not derived from *btn*, the root that can be translated 'inmost being.' One might conclude from this that compassion is something more than an emotion, even a profound emotion that springs from one's inmost being. On the contrary, it comes from the root that yields the word with the exclusive meaning 'womb.' Hence, the word 'compassion' presumes a kind of intimacy and itself carries a fundamentally feminine connotation regardless of the subject of its attribution. It should be noted here that to state that there is a feminine connotation to this word is not the same as claiming a feminine dimension of the divine, a position held by some feminist thinkers. Rather, such a statement implies that certain characteristics attributed to God can best be represented by female metaphors.

In order to more fully understand the original meaning of *rhm*, 'to have compassion,' we must examine the passages wherein the verb or derivatives of it may be found. A contextual study of these passages suggests that they can be classified under four thematic categories: covenant renewal; mercy after wrath; repentance of sin; national restoration.

A. Covenant renewal

> Moses said, "I beseech you, show me your glory!"
> And God said, "I will make all my goodness pass
> before you, and I will proclaim before you my name,
> 'Lord'; I am gracious to whom I will be gracious,
> and I am compassionate to whom I will be compassionate."
> And God said, "You will not be able to see my face,
> for no one shall see me and live."[15]
>
> Exodus 33:18-20

> And the Lord passed before him and proclaimed, "Lord!
> Lord! mighty, compassionate, and gracious, slow to
> anger, rich in steadfast love and faithfulness."
>
> Exodus 34:6

---

14. Jgs 3:21.
15. All translations are by the writer unless indicated otherwise.

Biblical scholars agree that Exodus 32-34 comprises a literary segment which was originally independent. This passage recounts Israel's apostasy toward the God with whom it had covenanted itself;[16] the punishment God meted out as retribution for this infidelity; God's subsequent forgiveness; and the mediatorial role that Moses played in the restoration of the covenantal relationship.[17] The sin appears to have been occasioned by Israel's desire for some tangible sign of God's presence in its midst. Their constructing an image constituted a failure in trust that struck at the very heart of covenant relationship. This, then, is the narrative context within which we find the compassion of God proclaimed.

Chapter 33 is made up of several units that treat the question of God's presence. The people have been encamped at the base of Mt. Sinai. Here they have experienced both God's revelation and God's anger. Ancient peoples, it should be noted, frequently associated a deity with a particular place and they tended to limit the scope of divine influence and activity to that place. Israel was no different. They too wondered about the extent of God's influence. Would God be present to them should they leave the mountain? If so, how would this presence be manifested? The incidents recorded in chapter 33 address these questions.

Each of the units of the chapter depict God's presence with the people in a different way. In the first unit (vv. 1-6), the force of the divine wrath incited by the people's sin keeps the people from immediate contact with God, but God is still with them. An angel, a kind of divine manifestation found in several places in the tradition, will take God's place in leading them (v. 2). God was in the midst of the people in another way. The tent of meeting, referred to in the second unit (vv. 7-11), was a sacred and relatively permanent precinct which marked God's ongoing presence with Israel. In the third unit (vv. 12-17), Moses questions God about his need for assistance in leading the people, and he is reassured by God, "My presence will go with you" (v. 14).

The final unit (vv. 18-23) anticipates the theophany which is

---

16. The incident referred to is the fashioning and worship of the golden calf, Ex 32:1-6.

17. The movement of this narrative segment contains all four of the thematic categories that constitute this study.

recounted in chapter 34. Here, as in the preceding passage, the presence of God is promised to Moses as mediator of the covenant.[18] In asking to see God's glory, Moses is seeking an unmediated revelation of God.[19] Although this is denied him, he is granted a glimpse of God's goodness. Of special interest is the fact that the revelation of God accorded to Moses here is a manifestation of divine attributes rather than a kind of physical appearance. Along with this display of divine goodness is the proclamation of God's name, 'Lord.' Here God's name, which is a revelation of God's essential being, is explicitly identified with God's graciousness and compassion. This identification would suggest that compassion is constitutive of the very nature of God.

The revelation to Moses, promised in chapter 33, is described in 34:5ff. The covenant that had been broken by the people's sin was now restored through God's compassion.[20] This second giving of the law is clearly a revelation of a God who is "mighty, compassionate, and gracious, slow to anger and rich in steadfast love and faithfulness."[21] Although this statement appears to be a technical covenantal characterization of God, it is not found in the accounts that relate the initial covenant experience. It appears only after Israel's apostasy.[22] One might conclude, then, that the compassion of God is closer to divine forgiveness than to divine sympathy.

---

18. This is reminiscent of the account of God's initial revelation to Moses and the disclosure of the divine name (cf. Ex 3:4ff).

19. Moses is not unlike the people who sought some tangible sign of God's presence. The difference is that Moses petitioned God for a sign while the people took upon themselves the task of fashioning one.

20. Similarities between this passage and the account of the initial theophany, covenant encounter, and conferral of the law are obvious (cf. Ex 19).

21. Ex 34:6. The dyad "gracious and compassionate" appears in eleven other passages. It stands by itself in five of them (Pss 111:4; 112:4; Neh 9:31; 2 Chr 30:9 and in a slightly different form in Ps 116:5). It is linked with the second dyad, "slow to anger and rich in steadfast love," in five additional passages (Jl 2:13; Jon 4:2; Pss 103:8; 145:8; Neh 9:17). In only one other passage are both dyads joined with the final characterization "truth," (Ps 86:15). Actually, "steadfast love [a technical covenant term] and truth" are themselves frequently coupled (cf. 1 Sm 2:6; 15; 20; Pss 25:10; 40:12 [here also linked with compassion]; 57:4; 61:8; 85:11; 89:15; 115:1 and 117:2). Steadfast love and compassion are also joined in Ps 103:8.

22. We will see that this is the case with each appearance of a derivative of *rhm* when applied to God. The word is found neither in the account of the initial revelation of the name (Ex 3:13-15) nor in the one that relates the giving of the law (Ex 19).

God acts compassionately, not merely toward those who are weak and unfortunate, but toward those who, while in the past had been unfaithful to the covenant, now had turned again to God. God may have tender feelings toward the needy, but compassion is the disposition God shows toward repentant sinners. This may be Israel's way of admitting that it did nothing to deserve God's covenantal commitment. On the contrary, it did everything to disqualify itself from that privilege. The repeated reference to the steadfast compassion of God is an ever-present acknowledgement of Israel's own sinfulness and of God's constant love despite this sin. Although this characterization of God as compassionate later seems to become a standard way of describing God in contexts other than covenant renewal after apostasy, the earliest contextual meaning of compassion underlies all subsequent meanings and should never be absent from them.

B. Mercy after wrath

> Though in my wrath I struck you,
>   yet in my good will I have shown you compassion.
>
>   Isaiah 60:10

> In your wrath remember compassion!
>
>   Habakkuk 3:2

To claim that God acts compassionately only toward sinners is not to deny the fury of God that is inflamed in the face of human transgression. The scriptures are filled with descriptions of God's wrath which is best understood as offended love. This is a wrath of judgment, and not merely of temper. It is a wrath that does not persist; God punishes first, and then shows compassion.[23] Israel acknowledged its guilt and God's response in its prayers for mercy.[24] The tradition states that even before the people entered the land of Canaan, they were warned of God's wrath, yet they were also promised God's compassion if they followed God's decrees.[25] Even when the northern tribes separated themselves from the divinely appointed Davidic monarch, God was unwilling to permit their

---

23. Lam 3:22, 32; Dn 9:9.
24. Pss 77:10; 79:8.
25. Dt 13:18.

protracted oppression by a neighboring king. Instead, God remembered the covenant made with Israel's ancestors[26] and the blessings bestowed on them despite their own repeated unfaithfulness,[27] and looked with compassion on their rebellious descendants.[28] Even David, who sinned by conducting a census of the people and was told to choose the punishment to be exacted, chose the one wherein he felt that the compassion of God would be most evident.[29]

It is in the prophetic books that we find most of the references to God's anger giving way to compassion. The people's refusal to listen to the Holy One of Israel brings on their punishment. Still the Lord waits to show them favor and compassion,[30] treading their guilt underfoot in the process.[31] But this seems to be to no avail. Jeremiah announces that God's steadfast love (a technical covenant term) and compassion have been withdrawn and, therefore, it is pointless for the people to go to the house of mourning to lament.[32] Later one of the most moving images of God's compassion toward suffering sinners is found in that part of Jeremiah known as the Book of Consolations:

> Is Ephraim a precious son to me,[33]
> or a son in which I delight?
> for whenever I speak of him
> remembering I remember him again.
> Thus I yearn for him,
> compassionately I show him compassion,
> declares the Lord.
>
> Jeremiah 31:20

Chapter 31 deserves to be read in its entirety. The tenderness with which God speaks of this sorrowing repentant people is particularly noteworthy here. This poetry also highlights the role that repentance plays in moving God from anger to compassion.

---

26. Dt 4:31.
27. Neh 9:19; 27f; 31; Ps 78:38.
28. 2 Kgs 13:23.
29. 2 Sm 24:14 & 1 Chr 21:13.
30. Is 30:18.
31. Mi 7:19.
32. Jer 16:5.
33. Cf. 31:9c.

The same parental compassion expressed in Jeremiah is found in Psalm 103 and in the postexilic prophet known as Deutero- Isaiah. In the first passage we read:

> As a father has compassion on his children
> so the Lord has compassion on those who fear him.
>
> Psalm 103:13

In the prophetic passage, the restoration of the nation is described in imagery borrowed from the exodus tradition. As God had shown mercy to their ancestors and guided them through the wilderness, so now God has compassion on the exiles and leads them back to their own land.[34] Further in this chapter we find:

> Will a woman forget her suckling child;
> be without compassion toward the child of her womb?
> Even if these forget,
> I myself will not forget you.
>
> Isaiah 49:15

God is characterized as both a compassionate father and a compassionate mother. The loving attachment itself is explicitly related to the womb, probably not principally because of its female nature, but because of the generative properties of the womb. Like the womb, divine compassion is life-giving. Furthermore, compassion is the forerunner and enabler of restoration, of rebirth.

It is perhaps in the writings of the prophet Hosea that God's longing to be compassionate is most poignantly depicted. The domestic ordeal of the prophet becomes a sign of the turbulent relationship between God and the people. The unfaithful Gomer bears three children, all of whom are rejected by Hosea because they are illegitimate,[35] yet each child is given a symbolic name representing some aspect of the relationship between God and Israel. Hosea is told by God to name the second child, a daughter, Loruhama (not-receiving compassion) and the second son, Lo-ammi (not my people). God may be willing to show compassion to Judah (the southern kingdom) but the unfaithfulness of Israel (the north-

---

34. Is 49:10; 13.
35. Hos 2:6.

ern kingdom) has brought down God's wrath upon it.[36]

Although he is furious because of Gomer's betrayal, Hosea seems unable to sustain his anger indefinitely. So it is with God toward Israel. After the people have suffered for a time and have repented of their unfaithfulness, they are told:

> Say to your brother, "Ammi" (my people),
> and to your sisters, "Ruhama" (receiving compassion).
>
> Hosea 2:3

The covenant relationship is reestablished and depicted as marital intimacy:

> I will espouse you to me forever;
> I will espouse you to me in righteousness and justice;
> in steadfast love and compassion.
>
> Hosea 2:21

The notion of marital reconciliation which flows from God's compassionate forgiveness is found in Isaiah as well. It augments the Isaian description of the restored nation.[37] Here too we find a promise that, once reestablished, the covenantal relationship will endure:

> Though the mountains depart
> and the hills are shaken;
> My steadfast love will not depart from you,
> My covenant of peace will not be shaken,
> says the Lord who has compassion on you.
>
> Isaiah 54:10

We saw earlier in this study that compassion is the divine disposition shown toward those who were unfaithful to the covenant. The passages examined here demonstrate that God's compassion is not a sentimental emotion. It does not flow from some kind of divine tenderheartedness, a reluctance on God's part to see anyone suffer. On the contrary, it is a devotion that has survived the anguish of betrayal and has come through the fury of rage. It does not simply surrender justice for pity. Rather, while still clinging to

---

36. Hos 1:6f.
37. Is 54:7f.

justice, divine compassion moves beyond it to mercy. Israel was always reminded that behind any justifiable anger of God is God's readiness to enter again into an intimate relationship of love. The God of Israel, while just, is also forgiving.

C. Repentance of sin

> Let the wicked forsake the way of wickedness,
>   and the unrighteous their thoughts.
> Let them turn to the Lord,
>   and the Lord will be compassionate;
> and to our God, for God is rich in pardon.

Isaiah 55:7

The passages already examined have focused our attention on God's willingness and longing to show compassion. This representation would be a distortion if we failed to recognize that God's benevolence is dependent upon sinners' admission of their guilt and upon their conversion.[38] Since it was because of covenantal infidelity that the wrath of God was inflamed in the first place, those guilty of unfaithfulness must repent and return if God's anger is to subside. In several passages we discover that God refuses to withdraw the fury of divine wrath if there is no repentance on the part of sinners. This was true of the northern kingdom of Israel,[39] of Assyria, its conqueror,[40] and of the southern kingdom of Judah as well.[41] A third feature has now been added to our understanding of divine compassion: just as God's response to infidelity is wrath, so God's response to repentance is divine compassion. This is especially true of those people in covenantal relationship with God. A brief look at the dynamics operative within such a relationship will throw light on this feature.

A covenant is an agreement between two parties. It implies the strongest possible mutual pledge. It can be made between equal partners or between partners of unequal rank or strength. The agreement must be voluntary on both sides even though one party initiates the alliance and, in the case of unequal partners, the lesser of the two is bound by certain obligations. Israel always acknowl-

---

38. Prv 28:13.
39. Is 9:16.
40. Is 27:11.
41. Jer 13:14.

edged that God was the initiator of the covenant. The reason given for this choice on God's part was divine love toward Israel and God's promise made to their ancestors.[42] Inherently, a covenant is of limitless duration. Still, one of the partners can effectively break it. Should this happen, both partners must consent to repair the severed relationship and begin anew. The biblical tradition never portrays God as capriciously violating the covenantal bonds. It is always the human partner who is disloyal. While God may be enraged by this breach of pledge, it is wounded covenant love that breaks out in wrath and it is the same covenant love that disposes God to forgive and begin again. God's initial invitation to enter into the covenant was from the outset a mystery to Israel. The people always attributed their election to God's unqualified love. They were fully aware of their refusal to live up to their own responsibilities despite God's continual presence in their midst and God's provident care. They were humbly conscious of the depths of God's love as revealed in the reestablishment of the broken covenant. This love was ever inviting them to repentance and subsequent relationship. It may be that God's compassion was always within reach, but the errant human partners knew that they first would have to repent and return in order to abide in its embrace.

D. National restoration

> Then the angel of the Lord spoke out and said,
> "O Lord of hosts, how long will you be without
> compassion for Jerusalem and the cities of Judah
> that have felt your anger these seventy years?"
>
> Zechariah 1:12

> If you return to the Lord your God and heed God's
> voice in all I command you this day, you and your
> children, with all your heart and all your soul, then
> the Lord your God will change your captivity and will
> have compassion on you, and will turn and gather you
> from all the nations where the Lord your God had scattered
> you.
>
> Deuteronomy 30:2-3

---

42. Dt 7:6-8.

The greatest suffering that the nation underwent was the overthrow of the Davidic monarchy, the capture and destruction of the city of Jerusalem, and the exile to Babylon of a significant portion of the population of Judah in the sixth century B.C.E. (Before the Common Era). The extent of this catastrophe, perceived as the consequence of the consuming force of divine fury, became the measure of God's compassion once the nation had repented. The people were encouraged with the hope that God's compassion would take the form of compassion on the part of their captors, captors who would then deal mercifully with them.[43] Their prayer was filled with such confidence.[44]

Again it is primarily in the writings of the prophets that this trust in God's compassion is clearly articulated. Not only would the captives be forgiven and be returned to their own home land, but out of compassion for this people God would deal with other nations in ways that would benefit the returnees. Although the exile had decimated the people of Israel, in the future their numbers would swell, for aliens would join them and be counted as belonging to them.[45] Even those nations that once led Israel astray into false worship of Baal would be added to their number, if they would but repent and pledge their allegiance to the God of Israel.[46] The cities would be rebuilt,[47] leaders would be raised up,[48] and the nation itself would again prosper[49] as if it had never known misfortune.[50] God's compassion and a return to fidelity to God's law will bring new life.[51]

These last passages illustrate the ultimate goal of God's compassion—restoration. This restoration would include: reestablishment of covenant union; commitment to God and to all others in covenant with God; and a life of fullness that comes from restored harmony. Restoration would demonstrate that God's love is not defeated by human unfaithfulness. On the contrary, God's love is a vibrant creative force that is always straining toward some kind of

---

43. 1 Kgs 8:50; Ps 106:46; Jer 42:12; Dn 1:9; Neh 1:11; 2 Chr 30:9.
44. Ps 102:14.
45. Is 14:1.
46. Jer 12:15f.
47. Jer 30:18; Dn 9:18; Zec 1:16.
48. Jer 33:26.
49. Ez 39:25.
50. Zec 10:6.
51. Ps 119:77; 156.

union. The compassion of God is more than comforting, it is creative. As the womb brings to birth life with all of its possibilities, so divine compassion brings to rebirth life that was threatened or perhaps even lost.

The Greek Version and its Reinterpretation

A slight but significant shift in meaning occurred when the vocabulary of 'compassion' was transmitted from the Hebrew Scriptures to the Greek version and then later to the early Christian texts. We can examine this shift through comparing key passages as they appear first in the Hebrew version of the text and then in the Greek.

Translation, we should remember, seeks to bridge worlds that differ from each other. It does this by following methods developed within the translating society. Today we recognize that fundamentally this can be done in one of two ways. Following the principles of what is known as 'formal correspondence,' some translated versions are concerned primarily with accuracy of translation despite the presence of words and phrases that appear awkward to the reader. Other versions are more interested in what is called 'dynamic equivalence.' They seek to express the original meaning in language and patterns of thought more current to the translator. The latter approach seems to have been the predominant interpretive method used by the translators who produced the Septuagint.[52]

Several factors prevent a translation from being absolutely literal. In the first place, not all languages follow the same rules of syntax. Thus, a precise word-for-word translation, if possible at all, frequently will result in awkward sentence structure. Second, reality and experience may be perceived in diverse ways in differing cultures, and can be variously articulated even within the same culture. Words and phrases can have differing connotations in different contexts. Finally, living languages themselves often expand in the process of being used. Therefore, the richer the idea, the more diverse the connotations and the more possibilities there are for translation.

---

52. The name given to the Greek translation of the Hebrew Scriptures is derived from the Latin for 'seventy.' A tradition arose claiming that seventy-two scribes worked independently for seventy-two days and each produced exactly the same translation. This 'miracle' was considered evidence of the legitimacy of the translation and of its revelatory value.

In our concern to understand the Bible in a meaningful contemporary way, we may forget that frequently translation is a move
from one world of thought and perception to another. This is true
for us, and it was clearly the case when the Hebrew Scriptures were
translated into Greek sometime during the third century B.C.E. A
comparison of the Hebrew text with the Septuagint version shows
that not only did the Greek translation alter the meaning expressed
in the original Hebrew, but it also frequently translated words in a
number of different ways. For example, sometimes the Greek word
that translates *rhm* carries a meaning closer to that of *hds* (steadfast love) than to 'compassion.' This rather fluid use of language is
also found in the New Testament, thus making a precise tracing of
the theme very difficult.

The present linguistic analysis centers on "compassionate and
gracious," the first dyad in the technical covenantal characterization of God found in Exodus 34:6.[53] The Greek translation of this
verse has *oiktirmon* (a form of 'to be sympathetic') and *eleemon* (a
form of 'to be merciful'). This same translation is found in most of
the other passages where the phrase appears.[54] Although both
words denote sympathy, mercy, and compassion, *oiktirmos* refers
to the inward feeling that abides in the heart, while *eleos* manifests
itself chiefly in acts rather than words. Since there is no apprecia-
ble difference in meaning, the Greek renderings are used interchangeably in the translation of the Hebrew words. However, *oiktirmon* seems to be preferred when the referent is divine
compassion.[55] Neither Greek word carries the connotations of
'womb,' but *eleos* is the normal translation of *hsd*, the technical
Hebrew word expressing the steadfast love of the covenant. In the
language of later Judaism *hsd* and *rahᵃmim* can hardly be distinguished in meaning. Thus *eleos* eventually becomes the term most
commonly used to render the meaning of both of these Hebrew
words.[56]

---

53. Cf. n. 18 above.
54. Pss 111:4; 112:4; 2 Chr 30:9; Neh 9:17; 31; Jl 2:13; Jon 4:2. The rendering
is reversed in Pss 86:15; 103:8; 145:8. No form of *oiktiro* is found in Ps 116:5, but it
is used in Ps 103: 16.
55. Pss 102:8; 110:4.
56. Gerhard Kittel, ed., *Theological Dictionary of the New Testament* (Grand Rapids,
Mich.: Eerdmans, 1964), vol. II, pp. 479ff. Also, 1 Pt 2:10; cf. Hos 1:6; 2:25; 3:3.

The Compassion of Jesus

The New Testament writers may have preferred *eleos* when speaking of compassion, but they did not limit their use to that word. Forms of the verb *oiktiro* appear in several passages, notably the one from Luke that was chosen as the title of this paper: "Be compassionate (*oiktirmones*) as your Father is compassionate (*oiktirmon*)."[57] It is interesting to note that this word is used in referring to the compassion of God and to the compassion that Christians should have toward each other. However, it never refers to the compassion of Jesus, either historical or risen. Another word, *splanchnon*, is used there instead.

Perhaps one of the most significant appearances of *oiktiro* is found in Paul's Letter to the Romans. As he attempts to explain the relationship between God's promises to Israel and divine freedom, Paul quotes Exodus 33:19:

> For to Moses he says, I will show mercy (*eleeso*)
>   to whom I show mercy;
> and I will be compassionate (*oikteireso*)
>   to whom I am compassionate.
>
> Romans 9:15

The language is used here in the same way as it was used in the Septuagint,[58] that is, *eleos* translates 'mercy' (or in the Hebrew tradition 'graciousness') and *oiktiro* yields 'compassion,' although *eleos* is replaced by *splanchnon*. The same understanding of *oiktiro* is found in James 5:11. There we find a veiled reference to the covenantal dyad describing God as 'gracious and compassionate,' although *eleos* is replaced by *splanchnon*. God is further referred to as 'the Father of compassion,'[59] whose compassion is the inspiration for Christian sacrifice.[60] The sense of God's *rah'mim* lies behind this use of *oiktirmoi*.

Splanchnon, a word that essentially means the 'inward parts' of a sacrifice, almost always appears in the plural form. In early Greek it

---

57. Lk 6:36; cf. Mt 5:48.
58. The verb forms are different from the original Hebrew but identical to the Septuagint version.
59. 2 Cor 1:3.
60. Rom 12:1.

referred to the lower part of the body, especially the womb or the loins. Later it came to denote impulsive passions as distinct from the sensibilities of the heart. Since the word is rare in the Septuagint and seldom has Hebrew equivalents, it is difficult to discover its Jewish background. Apart from its use in the description of the tragic end of Judas,[61] *splanchnon* denotes profound feelings or emotion. Twice is it found in the New Testament in construction with *oiktiro*,[62] thus describing the kind of attachment Christians must have toward each other. It seems that for Paul emotions that might be regarded as personal inclinations are really expressions of being 'in Christ.'[63]

It is the use of the verb that is most interesting. With the exception of its appearance in three parables, its subject is always Jesus. It is used to describe the deep-seated emotion elicited in him by the desperate straits of others, and it seems to characterize the messianic quality of the actions that flow from this passion, thus giving the emotion itself messianic character.[64] Profoundly moved, he heals the blind,[65] the lepers, [66] the boy with a demon,[67] and unnamed illnesses of the crowds.[68] He multiplies loaves and fishes[69] and raises a boy from the dead.[70]

The verb appears in Jesus' parables that tell of a loving father who is overwhelmed to see his prodigal son returning,[71] of an unselfish Samaritan who is willing to care for one who otherwise would most likely spurn him,[72] and of an employer who, while exacting justice, is moved to pity.[73] The first parable is a characterization of the compassionate God. The second portrait of compassion is offered to Christians as an ideal after which they should

---

61. Acts 1:18.
62. Phil 2:1; Col 3:12.
63. Phil 1:8.
64. This use persists in one early Christian writing, the Shepherd of Hermas, where the reference is restricted to God alone, *Similitudes* 8.11.1; 9.14.3.
65. Mt 20:34.
66. Mk 1:14.
67. Mk 9:22.
68. Mt 9:36 (Mk 6:34); 14:14.
69. Mt 15:32 (Mk 8:2).
70. Lk 7:13.
71. Lk 15:20.
72. Lk 10:33.
73. Mt 18:27.

model themselves. The story itself ends with such an exhortation.[74] The third narrative both characterizes God as compassionate and exhorts Christians to act toward others with the same compassion that God has shown toward them.[75] Clearly, this deep-seated emotion is a profoundly religious sentiment.

Each time this verb appears it is within the context of the reign of God, supporting the claim advanced in this study, that it is used with messianic connotations. The miracles of Jesus have long been understood as signs of the inbreaking of God's reign. Each miracle in its own way gives us a glimpse of the meaning of that reign. Each shows that the domination of sin and death, the presence of which causes the profound emotion in Jesus, has come to an end, and that the power of God in Jesus is at hand with new hope and new life. However, this reign does not come without a price. There must be a decision to convert and to embrace the demands of this reign in order to be a disciple of Jesus. The parables address this dimension of the reign. Each in its own way depicts some facet of this new manner of living. Our concern here is Christian compassion modeled after the compassion of God. To be converted to such a disposition is indeed a sign of the reign of God.

Eleos, the word that denotes emotion roused by undeserved suffering in others, is employed most frequently in the New Testament for 'compassion' or 'mercy.' When referring to God, it is thought of in the Hebrew sense of 'steadfast love' (*hsd*), the covenantal faithfulness of God that can be traced throughout the history of salvation. It carries this meaning in both the Canticle of Mary, known as the Magnificat,[76] and in the Canticle of Zachariah.[77] However, it is also used to describe God's disposition toward sinners. As with *raḥᵃmim*, the contexts of this word yield the notion of new life or rebirth through the mercy of God.[78] It seldom appears without either a direct or an indirect reference to the divine/human relationship.

This mercy is implored of Jesus when someone begs him for a cure. In each biblical account, Jesus is addressed with a messianic title that once again alerts us to the presence of the reign of

---

74. Lk 10:37. The word used here is *eleos*.
75. Mt 18:33. Forms of *eleein* are used.
76. Lk 1:50; 54.
77. Lk 1:72; 78.
78. Eph 2:4; Ti 3:5; 1 Pt 1:3.

God.[79] This same mercy becomes part of an early Christian formula for greeting and blessing.[80] It takes on an eschatological meaning when it is promised to those who show compassion to others.[81] Thus compassion in Jesus, as well as in the followers of Jesus, is a harbinger of the reign of God.

The Compassion of the Christian
Children of our Father

The exhortation to compassion is found in the Sermon on the Plain, Luke's version of the revolutionary new way of living preached by Jesus.[82] It follows Jesus' teaching on love of enemies. There he insists that it is not enough to love those who love us, or to give to those from whom we can expect some return. Such love and such giving is found even in the wicked. Christian love goes beyond this kind of attachment and loyalty. It is much more than merely an attitude of mind. It is an active love, a love that is willing to do good regardless of the cost. The disciples of Jesus are called to be "children of the Most High" who "is kind to the ungrateful and the wicked."[83] The compassion of God, as described here, is open to all; it does not discriminate between those who love God and those who do not. So must Christian compassion be open to all. In fact, this passage from Luke suggests that the recipients of our compassion should be precisely those from whom we feel alienated, those with whom we have been in conflict, those who might take advantage of us or from whom we can expect no return favor.

The reign of God proclaimed by Jesus, requires more of us than merely that we be well disposed toward enemies. The followers of Jesus must be compassionate toward them just as their heavenly Father is compassionate. In particular they should reveal this spir-

---

79. Son of David - Mt 9:27; Mk 10:47f; Lord - Mt 17:15; Lord, Son of David - Mt 15:22; 20, 30f; Lk 18:38f. In Lk 17:13 he is called *epistata*, a Lukan word for 'Master.'

80. Gal 6:16; 1 Tm 1:2; 2 Tm 1:2; 16; 18; Ti 1:4; 2 Jn 3; Jude 2.

81. Mt 5:7.

82. Lk 6:27-36.

83. A Matthean parallel is found in the Sermon on the Mount, Mt 5:43-48. There they are exhorted to be perfect (*teleioi*) so that they might be children of the "heavenly Father" who makes the "sun rise on the bad and the good and causes rain to fall on the just and the unjust." In both instances the allusion is to an injunction from Lv 11:44; 19, 2: Be holy for I am holy." In this priestly tradition, holiness (*kadosh*) has cultic connotations. The worshiping community is there admonished

it of compassion in the matter of judging others.[84] It may be that the other has wronged us, but only God knows the circumstances and conditions of each life, and only God has the right to judge as to the guilt or innocence of another. As we saw in our examination of the ancient Hebrew understanding of this theme, God is indeed just and will demand repentance and conversion of life. We need not fear that the seriousness of a transgression perpetrated against us will be minimized should we hand over to God any right we may claim to exact strict justice in our dealings with others.

The compassion of God provides both a pattern for Christians to follow and a standard against which they can measure their lives. This kind of behavior calls disciples to a way of living that goes far beyond the ordinary dictates of social order. It is a style of living that will identify them as children of God, children who love and forgive as their Father loves and forgives. In addition to this, those who act as God acts will themselves be the recipients of God's good pleasure. Those who are compassionate because God is compassionate will, in turn, experience God's compassion towards themselves. They will be forgiven rather than judged or condemned.

Words like 'Father' and 'children' bring us once again into the language of familial intimacy, the language of covenant.[85] We saw that in the First Testament covenant was a voluntary alliance. The people who entered into such an arrangement may indeed have been related to each other by blood, but their attachment to God was by design. Blood ties became secondary; covenantal partners became as close as kinsfolk. The same usage is found in the New Testament.

---

to set itself apart from what might make it ritually unclean. Matthew may be challenging Christians to live lives of ethical holiness, lives appropriate to the reign of God, that will indeed set Christians apart from the rest of the world. Luke is more specific as to the character of this ethical holiness.

84. The teaching about love of enemies is followed immediately by the twofold injunction to refrain from judging others and to be liberal and unconditional in giving to others, Lk 6:37-42.

85. Of the eleven places in the First Testament where God is designated as 'Father,' i.e., Dt 32:5; 2 Sm 7:14; 1 Chr 17:13; 22:10; 28:6; Ps 89:26; Jer 3:4f; 31:9; Is 63:16; 64:8; Mal 1:6, only in Is 64:8 does the context suggest the theme of original generation. However, the contextual meaning of the word in the New Testament is twofold. In the first place, the relationship between Jesus and the Father is clearly one of generation. On the other hand, the one between Christians and God is more often one of re-generation or covenant.

The true brother, sister, or mother of Jesus is not a blood kinsperson, but the one who does the will of the heavenly Father,[86] the one through whom is born the reign of God.

The Reign of God

The reign of God can be understood as an alternate way of living in the world. We must never forget that this world has played a very active role in forming us into the people we have become. We possess many of the features of that world (e.g., our political and economic values) and we carry the effects of its history (e.g., our inherited prejudices). We are not separate from the world. In many ways, we *are* the world. The reign of God challenges our preconceived judgments, our unexamined values, and our uncritical perception of reality. It seeks to transform our world by opening us to new and better possibilities, to a more Christian way of perceiving the world and of living within it. The question that perplexes us here is not the degree to which believers willingly stand open before the reign of God, but their ability to recognize the demands of this reign. Just what constitutes this alternative way of living in today's world?

The implications of the reign of God are quite radical when we look at this alternative way of living from the perspective of compassion. We have seen that the compassion of God is unconditional and inclusive. What can be said of ours? Have we either explicitly or implicitly laid down conditions for granting compassion? Do we perhaps rank people who suffer in a manner similar to the way we sometimes categorized the poor, as those who are 'deserving' and those who are not?

At times those most in need of our compassion are people whose misfortune appears to be warranted. Such people are not unlike the needy depicted in the gospels, people who were relegated to marginality or invisibility within that society, people whose circumstances moved Jesus to compassion. According to the standards of that time, these people were not deserving of Jesus' concern. Their misfortune was considered just recompense for their sin. He was, in fact, constantly criticized by the respectable for his association with these outcasts, to which he replied:

---

86. Mt 12:46-50; Mk 3:31-35.

"Those who are healthy do not need a physician,
but the sick do. I have not come to call the
righteous to repentance but sinners."

Luke 5:31f

Is our compassion ethnocentric? denominational? nationalistic? in any way chauvinistic? Is it merely an emotional response to the plight of those we love or of those who suffer some misfortune that we can understand or with which we can empathize or sympathize? Does it reach out to our political rivals? to our opponents in armed conflict? to criminals who have seriously wronged us? to people who do not particularly like us? Can we show compassion to people whom our society has dismissed as beyond help or unworthy of our concern? It is precisely in such situations that the inbreaking of the reign of God can transform our own minds and hearts and offer us an alternative way of perceiving reality and living in the world.

God's compassion is also constant and always forgiving. It stands ready to welcome all people at all times. To be compassionate like God means that we too must be willing to forgive, seventy times seven times if necessary.[87] This does not suggest that we be naive about human malevolence, nor irresolute in the face of injustice. It means, instead, that we never resign ourselves to the irrevocability of human infidelity as if there is no hope for a change of mind and heart.

The parable of the compassionate Samaritan depicts a startling alternative way of living. This man was not merely moved by the plight of another human being, even one of another ethnic group. The injured man belonged to the society that had ostracized the Samaritans. He was an adversary. This is the kind of compassion that is set before us as a model. Such an attitude of openness is quite difficult to maintain in a society that is quick to condemn and slow to forgive, a society that not only justifies but actually glorifies revenge, a society that regards every stranger as a potential adversary.

Finally, like the compassion of God, our own compassion can become pregnant with creative potential. Its forgiving love can repair bonds that have been severed by human indifference or mal-

---

87. Mt 18:22.

ice. It can create an atmosphere where the fragile spark of reconciliation can burst forth into the blazing fire of love and commitment. It can make walls of suspicion, isolation, and segregation crumble. Compassion is the unifying dynamic of God's love that reminds us that initially we all came forth from the same divine womb and now, more particularly, we are all invited into the renewed family of God. Wherever there is alienation, wherever there is estrangement, wherever there is selfishness and disregard for others, there the reign of God must be brought to birth. The challenge before us is a comprehensive one. However, every person can incarnate some aspect of the compassionate reign of God. The future of our world and of the human race depends on our willingness to do this. We can and we must work for peace and reconciliation, for the fullness of life that the Bible calls shalom, for the personal, social, and ecological harmony and balance that alone will enable us to live lives of well-being and purpose. We can and we must be compassionate as our loving God is compassionate.

2

Compassion in Theology

WAYNE WHITSON FLOYD JR.

This chapter has three goals. First, it traces the origins of a theological interpretation of religious compassion in the Jewish and Christian traditions. Second, it presents one, constructive, theological interpretation of the meaning of compassion, developed in dialogue with Christian thought in particular. Third, the chapter concludes by evaluating the implications of such a theology of compassion for a variety of forms of ministry.[1]

Roots of a Thology of Compassion

Origins of Religious Compassion in Judaism

We may do well to begin with an overview of the understanding of compassion which is evidenced in both the Hebrew Bible and in Jewish theology.[2] In Judaism, from the writing of the Bible to the pre-

---

1. I wish to thank Mara E. Donaldson and Joel W. Huffstetler for their editorial assistance in preparing this manuscript.
2. Cf. Roland E. Murphy, "Biblical Insights into Suffering: Pathos and Compassion," in *Whither Creativity, Freedom, Suffering?: Humanity, Cosmos, God*, ed. Francis A. Eigo (Villanova: The Villanova University Press, 1981); from a Jewish perspective see S.Y. Agnon, *Days of Awe* (New York: Schocken Books, 1965); from a Christian viewpoint, see Terence E. Fretheim, *The Suffering of God: An Old Testament Perspective* (Philadelphia: Fortress, 1984).

sent, compassion has played a key role in humanity's search to understand the nature of both divinity and human beings. The Hebrew biblical noun compassion, *rachamim* (e.g., Dt 13:17: "that the Lord may . . . have compassion on you"), and the verb *racham* (e.g., Mi 7:19: God "will again have compassion upon us"), along with the adjective *rachum* (e.g., Ps 103:8: "the Lord is full of compassion and mercy")[3] all are used to describe God's being and God's activity—and by analogy, the being and activity of humanity as well.[4]

According to twentieth-century scholar Abraham Joshua Heschel, the prophets, especially, understood the inability of the Hebrew mind to conceive of a God indifferent to suffering.[5] This was the case particularly in the face of Israel's experiences both of the divine distaste for injustice[6] and of a corollary, God's compassionate demand for justice.[7] Thus, for Heschel, "the Tetragrammaton, the great Name, we do not know how to pronounce, but we are taught to know what it stands for: 'compassion'."[8]

Despite Heschel's own attempt to distinguish humanity's practice of prophetic compassion from the notion of *imitatio dei*, or imitation of God,[9] there is a long tradition in Judaism which makes just that connection. For example, in the *Babylonian Talmud*, redacted about 500 C.E., compassion is referred to as one of the ten agencies through which the world was created.[10] "Compassion is a Divine attribute, and God is often referred to as 'the compassion-

---

3. See Robert Young, *Young's Analytical Concordance to the Bible* (Nashville, Tenn.: Thomas Nelson, 1982). The root of all these terms in Hebrew is rechem, womb; thus there is a nurturing, life-giving connotation to the Jewish concept of compassion that is not evident in translation.

4. Biblical quotations are from the Revised Standard Version of the Bible, copyrighted 1946, 1952, 1971, 1973 by the Division of Christian Education of the National Council of the Churches of Christ in the U.S.A., except for Psalm 103 which is Miles Coverdale's translation from *The Book of Common Prayer* (New York: The Church Hymnal Corporation, 1979).

5. Abraham Joshua Heschel, *The Prophets*, 2 vols. (New York: Harper Torchbooks, 1975), 2, p. 64ff.

6. Heschel, *The Prophets*, vol. 2, p. 73ff.

7. Heschel, *The Prophets*, vol. 1, pp. 195-220.

8. Abraham Joshua Heschel, *Man is Not Alone. A Philosophy of Religion* (New York: Farrar, Straus & Giroux, 1951), p. 148.

9. Heschel, *The Prophets*, vol. 2, pp. 101-103.

10. *Hagigah*, 12a, part of the 4th volume of *Seder Mo'ed*, the 2nd section of *The Babylonian Talmud*, trans. Rabbi Dr. E. Epstein (London: Soncino Press, 1952).

ate One (ha-Rachaman),' even when angry [Pesahim, 87b]; thus, man's practice of compassion is one of the main examples of *Imitatio Dei.*"[11] As Lou Silberman has noted, "the rabbis conceived of the practice of compassion as an *imitatio dei*, . . . the way of God in which man was commanded to walk (Dt 8:6)."[12] Thus, in the words of *Midrash Rabbah* from the sixth century C.E., "as God is compassionate, be thou compassionate" [*Siphrei, Ekev* 89].[13]

Maimonides, the twelfth-century Jewish scholar, even "declared that arrogant, cruel, misanthropic, and unloving persons were to be suspected of not being true Jews."[14] And thirteenth-century Jewish kabbalistic mysticism drew on this tradition in its notion of the Shekinah, sometimes understood as the female aspect of the divine, in which "God himself separates himself from himself, he gives himself away to his people, he shares in their sufferings, sets forth with them into the agony of exile, joins their wanderings."[15] In a like manner the eighteenth-century Hasidic master, Rabbi Moses Leib of Sassov, could say that "to know the needs of men and to bear the burden of their sorrow—that is the true love of man."[16] Even Heschel clarified his position later in life, distinguishing between *imitatio dei* (the idea of human imitation of God) and *imago dei* (the idea of humanity created in the image of God) when in an interview he said: "God created a reminder, an image.

----

11. R.J.Z. Werblowsky and G. Wigoder, ed., *The Encyclopedia of the Jewish Religion* (New York: Holt, Rinehart and Winston, 1966) p. 95. *Pesahim* is part of volume 2 of *Seder Mo'ed*. Cf. *Yevamot* 79a, the first volume of *Seder Nashim* in the Talmud, which speaks of mercy as a necessary characteristics of all Jewish people, and *Bezah* 32b, part of the third volume of *Seder Mo'ed*: "Whosoever shows compassion to God's creatures is surely of the seed of Abraham, and he who fails to show compassion is certainly not of such descent."

12. Lou H. Silberman, "Compassion," in *Encyclopedia Judaica* (Jerusalem: Keter Publishing House, 1972), p. 855. Cf. S.H. Dresner, *Prayer, Humility and Compassion* (Philadelphia: Jewish Publication Society of America, 1957), p. 193.

13. A section within *Siphrei Deuteronomy*; see *Midrash Rabbah*, 3rd ed., trans. Rabbi Dr. H. Freedman (London: Soncino Press, 1983). Also see S. Schechter, *Some Aspects of Rabbinic Theology* (New York: Macmillan, 1909), pp. 200-201.

14. *Mishne Torah, Yad, Issurei Bi'ah*, 19:17, quoted in Silberman, "Compassion," p. 855.

15. Franz Rosenzweig, *The Star of Redemption*, trans. William W. Hallo (Notre Dame: Notre Dame Press, 1985), p. 409; cf. Gershom G. Scholem, *Major Trends in Jewish Mysticism* (New York: Schocken Books, 1954), p. 230, on the suffering of the Shekinah in the *Zohar*; and Dorothee Sölle, *Suffering* (Philadelphia: Fortress, 1973), pp. 145ff.

16. Quoted in Silberman, "Compassion," p. 856.

Humanity is a reminder of God. As God is compassionate, let humanity be compassionate."[17]

Origins of Religious Compassion in Christianity

In light of this heritage from Judaism, the Christian theologian might well suppose that a proper and sufficient understanding of religious compassion in Christianity would be grounded primarily in the church's understanding of God as Creator, the one who made humanity in the divine image.[18] Or one might attempt to found religious compassion on theological anthropology, the inquiry into the nature of that human being created in the image and likeness of God.[19]

However, the place where the Christian theological understanding of religious compassion long has been centered and out of which it continues to find vitality in the present, is Christology: the theological understanding of the person and work of Jesus Christ. Both the compassion of God and the possibility of genuine human compassion are exemplified in the Christian community's affirmations concerning who Jesus was—divinity incarnate, God made flesh.[20] And both divine and human compassion are given their proper interpretation through Jesus' life, teachings, actions, death, and the community's proclamation of this One as the conqueror of all suffering, even death—and thus as Christus-Messiah: the Christ.

Among twentieth-century Protestant theologians, Karl Barth has been perhaps the most trenchant about this. In Barth's terms, the *imago dei*, the image of God in human beings, is the reflection of God's way of being-in-compassionate-relationship with humanity. "God is in relationship, and so too is the man created by him. This is his divine likeness."[21] As Jesus is interpreted as God-in-relationship

---

17. Abraham Joshua Heschel, "Abraham Joshua Heschel Last Words: An Interview by Carl Stern," *Intellectual Digest* (June, 1973), p. 78.

18. See Jung Young Lee, *God Suffers for Us: A Systematic Inquiry into a Concept of Divine Passibility* (The Hague: Martinus Nijhoff, 1974), pp. 46-52 on compassion and creation.

19. E.g., see John Macquarrie, *Principles of Christian Theology*, Second Edition (New York: Scribner's, 1977) or his essay, "Love," in *In Search of Humanity. A Theological and Philosophical Approach* (New York: Crossroad, 1985), pp. 172-186.

20. See Lee, *God Suffers*, pp. 52-57 on compassion and incarnation: cf. Rosemary Haughton, *The Passionate God* (New York: Paulist, 1981).

21. Karl Barth, *Church Dogmatics*, Vol. III/2, trans. G.W. Bromiley et al. (Edinburgh: T&T Clark, 1960), p. 324.

to human beings, so human beings similarly are interpreted as made in the *imago dei* through their relationships to God and to one another. God's image in humanity is seen in the similarity between God's relationships and human relationships. "Between these two relationships as such—and it is in this sense that the second is the image of the first—there is correspondence and similarity. There is an *analogia relationis*"[22]—an analogy of relationships.

As Edward Schillebeeckx, the contemporary Dutch Roman Catholic theologian has put it, "God's concern for man becomes the criterion, the standard, and at the same time the boundless measure of our concern for the needy."[23] This is exemplified in Jesus' teachings, such as the story of the Good Samaritan in the Gospel of Luke 10:29-37. What is it to be a neighbor, Jesus is asked? It is to be like the Samaritan, who found a stranger beaten and half dead; and "when he saw him, he had compassion" (Luke 10:33).[24] The Greek word translated compassion here is *splangchnizomai*: to have the bowels yearning, to be wrenched in one's gut.[25] Barth is correct to say that "the expression is a strong one which defies adequate translation."[26] It is the word used of the parent of the Prodigal Son in Luke 10:33, who upon seeing the lost child return, "had compassion." But, Barth notes, *splangchnizomai* is especially "ascribed to Jesus Himself."[27]

In each case it is crucial that Jesus depicts compassion as involv-

22. Barth, ibid., p. 220; cf. Dietrich Bonhoeffer, *Creation and Fall. A Theological Interpretation of Genesis 1-3* (New York: Macmillan, 1976), p. 38f., which used the concept of *analogia relationis* almost two decades before Barth.

23. Edward Schillebeeckx, *The Schillebeeckx Reader*, ed. Robert J. Schreiter (New York: Crossroad, 1987), p. 283.

24. See Thomas Merton's insightful interpretation of this parable, "The Good Samaritan," in *A Thomas Merton Reader* (Garden City, N.Y.: Image Books, 1974), pp. 348-356.

25. See Helmut Köster, "Splanchnon," *Theological Dictionary of the New Testament*, vol. 7, ed. Gerhard Friedrich (Grand Rapids, Mich.: Eerdmans, 1971), pp. 548-549.

26. Karl Barth, *Church Dogmatics, Vol. IV/2, The Doctrine of Reconciliation* (Edinburgh: T&T Clark, 1958), p. 184.

27. Barth, *Church Dogmatics*, Vol. III/2, p. 211, which continues: "in the face of the leper (Mk 1:41), the two blind men at Jericho (Mt 20:34), the dead man at Nain and his mother (Lk 7:13), the hungry crowd in the wilderness, (Mk 9:36 and parallels), and especially the spiritual need of the Galilean masses: 'because they fainted, and were scattered abroad, as sheep having no shepherd' (Mt 9:36)."

ing not merely a responsive disposition of *solidarity* with a stranger, one with whom someone is estranged, or those in suffering and need.[28] Jesus "does not merely help. . . . from without, standing alongside." Rather, compassion involves the radical risk of the involvement of one's very self into the context of the distress of the sufferers. In the face of the suffering of others, Jesus "interposes Himself for them. . . . He gives Himself to them. . . . He puts Himself in their place. . . . He makes their state and fate his own cause."[29] Compassion involves heeding the call to *redemptive commitment*—or discipleship—whose quintessence among Jesus' teachings is the charge at the end of the story of the Good Samaritan: "Go and do likewise" (Lk 10:37).[30]

Jesus' life is an even more compelling exemplar of compassion than his teachings. In the sufferings of the passion story, and centrally in the crucifixion on the cross, Jesus makes clear that *compassio*, suffering with the neighbor, "was not merely a matter of [Jesus'] turning to them with some great gift, but of [Jesus'] giving Himself, His life, for them. It was a matter of dying for them."[31] "This is my commandment," Jesus is said to have told his disciples, "that you love one another as I have loved you. Greater love has no man than this, that he lay down his life for his friends" (Jn 15:12-13). This is the meaning of compassion.

Thus, the Christian meaning of salvation, seen through the lens of compassion, would of necessity be beyond any merely inward transaction on a purely spiritual level. If this One who suffers with humanity is the God-human, Immanuel, God with us, then as the German Reformed theologian Jürgen Moltmann has concluded, God's own self "is involved in the history of Christ's passion. If this

---

28. Other words in the New Testament for compassion are *eleeo*, to show mildness, kindness (Jude 22); *sumpatheo*, to suffer with another (Heb 10:34); *sumpathes*, suffering with another (1 Pt 3:8); *oikteiro*, to have pity or mercy.

29. Barth, *Church Dogmatics*, Vol. III/2, p. 212.

30. See Lucien J. Richard, *A Kenotic Christology: In the Humanity of Jesus the Christ, the Compassion of our God* (Washington, D.C.: University Press of America, 1982), pp. 222; cf. G.S. Hendry, *The Gospel of the Incarnation* (Philadelphia: Westminster, 1958), pp. 100-107.

31. Barth, *Church Dogmatics*, Vol. III/2, p. 212. See Lee, *God Suffers*, pp. 57-63; Monika K. Hellwig, *Jesus: The Compassion of God: New Perspectives on the Tradition of Christianity* (Wilmington, Del.: Michael Glazier, 1983), pp. 109-123; and Douglas John Hall, *God and Human Suffering. An Exercise in the Theology of the Cross* (Minneapolis: Augsburg, 1986), pp. 93-121.

were not so, no redeeming activity could radiate from Christ's death."[32] Jesus' com-passionate death reveals the divine com-passion in relationship to humanity.

The *imago dei*, the image of God in humanity, therefore, is an *analogia relationis*, an analogy of relation: "the voluntary laying oneself open to another and allowing oneself to be intimately affected by him; that is to say, the suffering of passionate love."[33] As James Cone, the American black theologian, has summarized, "the cross of Jesus reveals the extent of God's involvement in the suffering of the weak. He is not merely sympathetic with the social plan of the poor but becomes totally identified with them in their agony and pain."[34] To be created in the image of the com-passionate God means: "Go and do likewise."

Constructive Position: A Theology of Compassion

The theological foundations of compassion stated here are themselves one particular way in which compassion is intelligible in the context of Christianity. They are the basis upon which one possible theology of compassion might be developed that would speak to a variety of the tasks of the practice of ministry.

For Lack of a Definition: Compassion

Given its particular Jewish and Christian theological origins, what does this word, compassion, then mean?[35] Is it most properly a

32. Jürgen Moltmann, *The Trinity and the Kingdom: The Doctrine of God,* trans. Margaret Kohl (New York: Harper & Row, 1981), p. 21; cf. his *The Crucified God: The Cross of Christ as the Foundation and Criticism of Christian Theology,* trans. R.A. Wilson and John Bowden (New York: Harper & Row, 1974), p. 243. Dorothee Sölle's *Suffering* (n.b. pp. 26-27) argues directly against Moltmann's position, especially as he stated it in *The Crucified God.*

33. Moltmann, *Trinity,* p. 23.

34. James Cone, *God of the Oppressed* (New York: Seabury, 1975), p. 175; see also Vishal Mangalwadi, "Compassion and Social Reform: Jesus the Troublemaker," in *The Church in Response to Human Need,* ed. Vinay Samuel and Christopher Sugden (Grand Rapids, Mich.: Eerdmans, 1987), pp. 193-205.

35. Lawrence Blum, "Compassion," in *Explaining Emotions,* ed. Amálie Rarty (Berkeley: University of California Press, 1980), p. 516, n. 1: "Compassion has a particular cultural history: its sources are Christian, it was further developed by Romanticism, especially by the German Romantics." This, however, completely ignores the Jewish roots of religious compassion! Also see William Eckhardt, *Compassion: Toward a Science of Value* (Toronto: CPRI Press, 1973).

noun, primarily an emotion one feels? Or is it a verb, an action one takes? The roots of the word lie in the Latin *compassus*, the past participle of *compati*, which means to suffer, bear [*pati*] with [*com*]. The participial form itself, having the function both of an adjective and a verb, displays the ambivalence usually experienced with the word com-passion. Is compassion a quality of *persons* ("a person of deep compassion") or *experiences* ("they were moved by the compassion they felt") or *deeds* ("that was a compassionate response")?

There are, besides compassion, a number of other-directed affects and ethical postures.[36] Among these are empathy, sympathy, pity, and love, to name only a few of the more prominent, and problematic, competitors. A Christian theology of compassion obviously draws upon, and yet wishes to distinguish itself in significant ways, from each of these.[37]

First, compassion has a strong connection with what is usually called *empathy*, "the capacity to apprehend directly the state of mind and feelings of another person."[38] One cannot be open to the suffering of another person without at least some minimal empathetic ability to enter "into another person's frame of reference . . . in such a way that one can understand from the inside, so to speak, what that other is feeling."[39]

Yet compassion in the Christian theological sense need not depend entirely on empathy. In many instances one can tell very well

---

36. E.g., see Andrew Purves, *The Search for Compassion. Spirituality and Ministry* (Louisville: Westminster/John Knox Press, 1989), pp. 56-59, and William J. Prior, "Compassion: A Critique of Moral Rationalism," *Philosophy and Theology*, vol. 2 (Winter, 1987), pp. 173-191.

37. Cf. Heinz Brunotte and Otto Weber, ed., "Mitleid," in *Evangelisches Kirchenlexikon*, vol. 2 (Göttingen: Vandenhoeck & Ruprecht, 1962): pp. 1392-1393. The German theological vocabulary distinguishes among *das Mitleid* (compassion), *Mitgefühl* (fellow-feeling, sympathy), *Erbarmen* (pity), *Barmherzigkeit* (mercy, kind-heartedness), and *Einfühlung* (empathy). Cf. Josef Hoefer and Karl Rahner, ed., *Lexikon für Theologie und Kirche* (Freiburg: Herder Verlag, 1959).

38. Warren Reich, "Speaking of Suffering: A Moral Account of Compassion," *Soundings* 72:1 (Spring, 1989), p. 106, n. 7. Also see Robert L. Katz, *Empathy: Its Nature and Uses* (New York: Free Press, 1963) and Don S. Browning, ed., *Pastoral Care and the Jewish Tradition. Empathetic Process and Religious Counseling*, (Philadelphia: Fortress, 1985), pp. 50-60. In theological German, empathy translates *Einfühlung*, literally "feeling into" the experience of another.

39. Purves, *The Search for Compassion*, p. 57.

that another is suffering, whether or not one is particularly good at "putting oneself in the place of the other, understanding and sharing the other's emotional experience, and seeing the world as he or she sees it."[40] Empathy may be most important not as the entrée into the dynamic of compassion, but in the subsequent process of fitting one's response appropriately to the specific need of the neighbor. Moreover, empathy more often than not is a passive rather than an active emotion, whereas a commitment to activity is itself true of even the affective side of compassion.

Closer to the Jewish and Christian traditions' meaning of compassion is the word sympathy: *sympátheia*, "the human ability to understand and to share the feelings of other human beings."[41] Etymologically, the roots of sympathy are the Greek equivalent of the Latin *com* [with] + *pati* [suffer]: *syn* [with, together] + *páthos* [suffer].[42] Yet the modern usage and connotations of sympathy have taken a decidedly different route.

For example, in the Scottish tradition sympathy came to have a strictly utilitarian meaning, such as in the philosophy of social-contracts of David Hume.[43] In the French Enlightenment, in such thinkers as Jean-Jacques Rousseau, compassion itself came to share a similarly utilitarian meaning: "a natural feeling which, by moderating the violence of love of self in each individual, contributes to the preservation of the whole species."[44]

Yet sympathy was to be given its primary modern meanings by nineteenth century German romantics such as Arthur Schopenhauer, themselves heirs of Rousseau's definition of com-

---

40. Graeme M. Griffin, "Compassion," in *Westminister Dictionary of Christian Ethics*, ed. James F. Childress and John Macquarrie (Philadelphia: Westminister, 1986), pp. 190-191.

41. Griffin, "Compassion," *Westminister Dictionary*, p. 612; also see Reich, "Speaking of Suffering," p. 106, n. 7: "*Sympathy* refers to the ability to understand and share the feelings of other human beings." Cf. Philip Mercer, *Sympathy and Ethics* (Oxford: Clarendon Press, 1972).

42. See F.E. Peters, *Greek Philosophical Terms. A Historical Lexicon* (New York: New York University Press, 1967), pp. 152-155.

43. See David Hume, *A Treatise of Human Nature*, ed. with an analytical index by L.A. Selby-Bigge (Oxford: At the Clarendon Press, 1975): pp. 499-500.

44. Jean-Jacques Rousseau, *Discourse on the Origins of Inequality*, quoted in Frederick Copleston, *A History of Philosophy*, vol. 6, part I (Garden City, N.Y.: Image Books, 1960), pp. 92-93; also see Jean-Jacques Rousseau, *Emile, or on Education* (New York: Basic Books, 1979): pp. 221-227.

passion as a feeling. The Romantics saw compassion as an emotional or affective foundation for an approach to ethics that would counter the supposed overemphasis on rationality and duty in such eighteenth century Enlightenment thinkers as Immanuel Kant.[45]

However, once the affective, or emotional, aspect of compassion was cut off from its active, or decisional, aspect—as in the evolution of the concept of sympathy—it became increasingly easy to trivialize compassion entirely, such as in the notion of pity. In pity,

> one holds oneself apart from the afflicted person and from their suffering, thinking of it as something that defines that person as fundamentally different from oneself. . . . That is why pity (unlike compassion) involves a kind of condescension .[46]

This led Romantics such as Friedrich Nietzsche to despise pity and compassion as of one cloth. For Nietzsche, compassion [*Mitleid*] is merely "a glorification of weaknesses which then becomes institutionalized and thus give dominance to sick instead of healthy people."[47] Yet even Nietzsche himself realized that such a pity-ful view of compassion comes about only when the emotion of pity "occurs apart from efforts to alleviate the suffering that has brought it into being."[48] Compassion turns to mere pity only when the empathetic and sympathetic responses to need are not followed by the action of the person so moved.

Yet this is precisely what has happened in Christianity as compassion has become subsumed under the general category of love, particularly love defined as *agape*. All too often, love has declined to a sort of feeling reminiscent of Aristotle's *eunoia*, or goodwill. And

---

45. Arthur Schopenhauer, *The World as Will and Idea*, vol.I, trans. R.B. Haldane and J. Kemp (London: Kegan Paul, Trench, Trubner, 1906) p. 485. "All true and pure love is sympathy (*Mitleid*), and all love which is not sympathy is selfishness (*Selbstsucht*)." Cf. Schopenhauer, *On the Basis of Morality*, trans. E.F.J. Payne (New York: Library of Liberal Arts, 1965), pp. 49-115, for his attack on the Kantian ethics of duty. Also see Max Scheler, *The Nature of Sympathy*, trans. Peter Heath (London: Routledge & Kegan Paul, 1965), particularly pp. 39-40, 135-137 on *Mitleid* or compassion.

46. Blum, "Compassion," p. 512.

47. Irving Singer, *The Nature of Love*, vol. 3 (Chicago: University of Chicago Press, 1987), pp. 73-74.

48. Singer, *The Nature of Love*, vol. 1, p. 74.

as Aristotle himself was aware, "those who feel goodwill . . . only *wish* well to those for whom they feel goodwill, and would not do anything with them nor take trouble for them."[49]

Love, especially as it has come to be understood in terms of *agape*, as opposed to *eros*, has lost much of the inherent movement from emotion to action that is essential to compassion. *Agape*, the distinctive bestowal of the divine compassion, has become so estranged from other Christian forms of love that the actions characteristic of human love lose all sense of their theological justification or foundation.[50] Ironically, this represents a reversion to the meanings of love "in prebiblical Greek," in which "*eros* is a passion, . . . while the verb *agapan* and the noun *agapesis* . . . denote the cooler and calmer love of rational preference."[51]

In the influential work of Anders Nygren, *Eros and Agape*,[52] for example, the portrayal of *agape* as "spontaneous and 'unmotivated'" and "indifferent to value,"[53] serves to sever *agape*, as the height of Christian love, from its obvious motive to redeem the sufferer from suffering. In speaking of Jesus' death on the cross as 'unmotivated', for example, Nygren seems to forget this motive of redemption, which includes the motive of overcoming injustice, and thereby severs the connection between love and justice that is essential to compassion.[54]

The result of such a lack of discrimination between *compassion*, on the one hand, and empathy, sympathy, pity, and love, on the other hand, is that most contemporary treatments of compassion understand it primarily from a psychological perspective, as "one among a number of attitudes, emotions, or virtues which can be called

---

49. Aristotle, *Nicomachean Ethics, The Basic Works of Aristotle*, ed. Richard McKeon (New York: Random House, 1941), p. 1167a.

50. Singer, *The Nature of Love*, vol. 1, distinguishes four main types of love in Christianity: "Eros: The Mystical Ascent" [pp. 162-197]; "Philia: Fellowship and Union" [pp. 198-232]; "Nomos: Submission to God's Will" [pp. 233-267]; and "Agape: The Divine Bestowal" [pp. 268-311].

51. John Burnaby, "Love," "I. Historical Perspectives," in *Westminister Dictionary*, p. 354.

52. Anders Nygren, *Agape and Eros*, trans. Philip S. Watson (Chicago: University of Chicago Press, 1982). "Nomos and philia tend to be neglected" in Nygren's work, according to Singer, *The Nature of Love*, vol. 1, p. 161.

53. Nygren, *Eros and Agape*, pp. 75, 77.

54. Nygren, *Eros and Agape*, pp. 86, 118-19; cf. Gene Outka, "Love," vol. 2, "Contemporary Discussion," in *Westminister Dictionary*, p. 77ff.

'altruistic' in that they involve a regard for the good of other persons."[55] Yet even Lawrence Blum, one such articulate defender of an
affective approach to compassion, admits that in genuine compassion "it is not enough that we imaginatively reconstruct someone's
suffering; . . . In addition we must care about that suffering and
desire its alleviation."[56]

There is a long Christian theological tradition that has emphasized precisely this verbal aspect of compassion, stressing not merely the desire of compassionate persons to allay suffering, but their
active participation in its alleviation. Tertullian, the second-third
century Roman Christian theologian, and Jerome, the fourth-fifth
century Christian scholar, both used the term *compas-sion-em*: to
suffer together with another.[57] Compassion has been used in the
English language with this meaning since at least 1340. Indeed, at
least as early as William Shakespeare (1588), and as late as the
philosopher David Hume (1761), *compassion* was used as a transitive
verb,[58] although as Samuel Johnson tellingly remarked, it was "a
word scarcely used."[59]

Compassion for the Christian retains marks of both its emotional, affective, adjectival forms and its active, participatory, verbal
forms as well. Thus compassion means, first, a radical openness to
the sufferings, the *páthos*, of others.[60] To suffer *with* another, one
first must *suffer* with another. This means, to 'suffer' the other, to listen, to hear the cry of the other, as God has done in Christ.

Second, this means not merely to experience the sentiment of
'compassion,' but to enter into the place, the context, of the other,
including the other's suffering. As Moltmann has written, "love
makes the suffering of the other unbearable for the one who

---

55. Blum, "Compassion," p. 507.
56. Ibid., p. 511.
57. James A.H. Murray, *A New English Dictionary on Historical Principles*, vol. 2,
(Oxford: Clarendon Press, 1893), p. 714.
58. *The Oxford English Dictionary* (Oxford: Oxford University Press, 1971), p. 714.
It lingered on into the nineteenth century as the verb, "compassionate." See
William Shakespeare, *Titus Andronicus*, iv.i. p. 124: "Can you heare a good man
grone And not relent, or not compassion him?" [quoted in *The Oxford English
Dictionary*, p. 714].
59. Samuel Johnson, *A Dictionary of the English Language* (Philadelphia: Moses
Thomas, p. 1818).
60. See F.E. Peters, "páthos," *Greek Philosophical Terms*, pp. 152-155.

loves."[61] The loving practice of grace, *charis*, is never cheap; it is costly, for it is the gift of oneself. "God suffers because of us, for He wants to suffer us. . . . Can we suffer those who are different from us? May the others suffer us? Can we suffer ourselves? Whom can we 'not endure'?"[62]

Even so, compassion is not thereby to be confused with *masochism*. For, third, as Leonardo Boff, the Brazilian liberation theologian, has noted, according to Christianity's understanding of compassion, "suffering cannot be sought for itself. . . . Suffering worthy of human beings . . . is the suffering that comes from a commitment to the arduous, victorious struggle with the suffering caused by the bad will of human beings ."[63] That is to say, compassion is redemptive, it desires not merely to share but to overcome the suffering of the other. This is not to say that some pain is not instructive, indeed humanizing: the pain that teaches the hand to stay clear of the fire, the suffering from one's misdeeds that inclines one not to repeat them. Compassion, however, recognizes that not all suffering is beneficial, that there is that dehumanizing suffering that refuses to be rationalized.[64] Compassion includes the resistance to such suffering, as heard in the words of W.E.B. DuBois, spoken in the face of violence against blacks in Atlanta in 1906, and which still speak against the violence in Soweto in 1990:

Mad with madness of a mobbed and mocked and murdered people.
. . . we raise our shackled hands and charge Thee, God, by the bones of

---

61. Jürgen Moltmann, *The Passion for Life* (Philadelphia: Fortress, 1978), pp. 42-43.

62. Ibid., p. 31. Also see Wayne Whitson Floyd Jr., *Theology and the Dialectics of Otherness: On Reading Bonhoeffer and Adorno* (Lanham, Md.: University Press of America, 1988).

63. Leonardo Boff, *Passion of Christ, Passion of the World*, trans. Robert R. Barr (Maryknoll, N.Y.: Orbis Books, 1987), p. 121. This is the problem of Katzoh Kitamori's *Theology of the Pain of God* (Richmond, Va.: John Knox Press, 1946), pp. 89-93; it leaves itself open to the charge of masochism. For a helpful distinction between pain and suffering, see Reich, "Speaking of Suffering," pp. 85-86.

64. Failure to see this leads to theological views which open to gross abuse, such as that expressed by Emil Brunner, *Christian Doctrine of Creation and Redemption*, trans. Olive Wyon (Philadelphia: Westminster, 1952), pp. 182-183: "In the presence of the Cross we cease to talk about 'unjust' suffering. On the contrary, as we look at the Crucified all suffering gains a positive significance." Cf. Hall, *God and Human Suffering*, pp. 38-40 on "first world apathy"; cf. Dorothee Sölle, *Suffering*, Ch. 2, "A Critique of Post-Christian Apathy."

our stolen fathers, by the tears of our dead mothers, by the blood of Thy crucified Christ: What meaneth this? Tell us the Plan; give us the Sign![65]

Compassion refuses to make sense of that suffering for which there is no sense.

The Dynamic Process of Compassion

Compassion thus includes (a) a disposition of solidarity toward the neighbor's sufferings plus (b) the action of entering into the context of that suffering as one's own, with (c) a commitment to overcoming the cause of the suffering itself. Indeed, compassion might best be described as a dynamic process which includes both affective and active dimensions.[66] This dynamic process has these three aspects, each of which deserves further exploration.

First, as Warren Reich has noted, "the meaning of compassion requires an openness both to [such a] process and to the singular event happening to the sufferer."[67] Clearly, compassion begins with one's availability to be encountered by the actual sufferings of a particular other. Often, in the name of compassion, we altruistically "throw ourselves zealously into the large, vague causes that

---

65. W.E.B. DuBois, "A Litany in Atlanta," *Black Voices*, ed. Abraham Chapman (New York: New American Library, 1968), pp. 372-373.

66. My understanding of the dynamic process of compassion is especially indebted to Henri Nouwen's analysis in his audiotape presentation *Compassion* (Chicago: Thomas More Association, 1970) [cf. McNeill et al., *Compassion*], in which he describes the three moments of compassion as Solidarity, Voluntary Displacement, and Discipleship. Others also have noted the dynamic, processive nature of compassion. See Arthur H. Becker, "Compassion: A Foundation for Pastoral Care," *Religion in Life*, 48:2 (Summer, 1979), pp. 143-152, who defines the process of compassion as involving Identification, Submissive Resonance, and Advocacy for the Other (including a Realistic Assessment of Resources to Fulfill that Advocacy). Reich, in "Speaking of Suffering," distinguishes three phases of suffering: (1) Mute Suffering [pp. 86-88], (2) Expressive Suffering [pp. 88-91], and (3) New Identity in Suffering [pp. 91-92]. He then proposes three forms of response: (A) Empathy, Silent Compassion [pp. 93-94], (B) Expressive Compassion (diagnosis, story, translation statement, interpretative statement) [pp. 94-97], which is for the sake of (C) Having a Compassionate Voice of One's Own: A New Identity [pp. 97-99]. Also see H.R. Niebuhr, *The Responsible Self: An Essay in Christian Moral Philosophy* (New York: Harper & Row, 1978), pp. 61-68, on three comparable elements in a theory of responsibility. What has been lacking for the most part, however, is a clear statement of the theological foundations for this sort of threefold understanding of compassion. Such is my purpose in this section of the present chapter.

67. Reich, "Speaking of Suffering," pp. 84-85.

bear the clear label of magnanimity but never bring us too objectionably close to the hurt that is starkly written in one man's eyes."[68] This, however, is not even the beginning of what Christianity wishes to label compassion.

Compassion, even initially, manifests itself in *responsive solidarity* with the real sufferings of the real, concrete neighbor. Such solidarity is the beginning of compassionate love. This is manifested in a Zen tale:

> Soyen Shaku walked past a house where he heard much crying because the master of the house lay dead. He entered, being well known in the locality, sat down, and cried with them. Said one of those present, 'Master, how can you cry? Surely you are beyond such things?' Soyen Shaku answered gently, 'It is this which puts me beyond such things.'[69]

It is what the Hebrew word *hesed* tries to convey: *steadfast, obligated love* in the concrete.[70] Helmut Thielecke had this in mind when he wrote: "Tell me how much you know of the sufferings of your fellowman and I will tell you how much you love them."[71]

But "solidarity requires that one enter into the situation of those with whom one is solidary: it is a radical posture."[72] It demands, second, a *radical contextualization* of concern. Nouwen has called this a "voluntary displacement" from one's ordinary, proper places,[73] a dislocation out of the safety of apathy into the risk and costliness of responsible compassion: the *practice of mercy*. Mercy, St. Thomas Aquinas wrote, "takes its name *misericordia* from denoting a man's

---

68. Ruth E. Durr, *A Shelter from Compassion* (Wallingford, Pa.: Pendle Hill, 1956), p. 16.

69. Hall, *God and Human Suffering*, frontispiece. This connection is retained in the English word, "Care," which itself comes from *kara*, to lament.

70. See Nelson Glueck, in *Hesed in the Bible*, ed. Elias L. Epstein, trans. Alfred Gottschalk (Cincinnati: Hebrew Union College Press, 1967). Also see Daniel R. Bechtel, "Hermeneutical Wanderings from Hosea to a Hymn," *Prism: A Theological Forum for the United Church of Christ* 3:2 (Fall, 1988) pp. 85-92.

71. Helmut Thielecke, *Our Heavenly Father* (New York: Harper & Row, 1960), p. 93.

72. Paulo Freire, *Pedagogy of the Oppressed* (New York: Seabury, 1973), p. 34.

73. See Donald P. McNeill, Douglas A. Morrison, and Henri J.M. Nouwen, *Compassion: A Reflection on the Christian Life* (Garden City, N.Y.: Doubleday, 1982), pp. 62-64. Cf. Wayne Whitson Floyd Jr., "Proclaiming the Divine Hospitality," *The St. Luke's Journal of Theology* 32:4 (September, 1989), pp. 265-268.

compassionate heart (*miserum cor*) for another's unhappiness."[74]
Mercy, according to Augustine of Hippo, is "heartfelt sympathy for
another's distress, impelling us to succor him if we can."[75]

In Kierkegaard's compelling words, "Only when the compassionate person is so related by his compassion to the sufferer that in
the strictest sense he comprehends that it is his own cause which is
here in question, does compassion acquire significance, and only
then does it perhaps find a meaning."[76] Compassion means to place
one's entire self at risk for the sake of the other, not because the one
in need next time might be oneself, but solely for the sake of the
other. "Greater love has no man than this, that a man lay down his
life for his friends" (Jn 15:13).

The radical contextualization of compassion, the willingness to
place oneself at genuine risk for the sake of a concrete, particular
another, is not a matter of like-for-like. Beyond one's own claims to
justice, or the merit of the other's claim on oneself,[77] genuine compassion means to place one's whole self at the disposal of the other,
simply on the basis of the need of the other, rather than on the
basis of what the other deserves or what is shared in common
between one's own life and the other.

Blum, for example, inquires into the extent to which compassion
depends upon "a sense of shared humanity, of regarding the other as
a fellow human being."[78] For him "compassion does not require even
that its subject have experienced the sort of suffering that occasions
it. . . . A detailed and rich understanding of another person's outlook and consciousness . . . is not required for compassion."[79]

"Love your *enemies*" (Mt 5:44), was Jesus' extravagant demand.
Compassion in this sense is not a self-regarding emotion, one "in

---

74. Thomas Aquinas, *Summa Theologiae*, II-II. 30, quoted in James Childress,
"Mercy," in *Westminster Dictionary*, p. 381.

75. Augustine, *City of God*, 9.5, quoted in Childress, "Mercy," in *Westminster
Dictionary*, p. 381.

76. Søren Kierkegaard, *The Concept of Dread*, translated by W. Lowrie (Princeton:
Princeton University Press, 1944), p. 107.

77. See Childress, "Mercy," in *Westminster Dictionary*, p. 381.

78. Blum, "Compassion," p. 511. This demand for "likeness," for example,
would make more difficult a case for claiming compassion for an animal, or for the
earth, human responsibility to both of which are intrinsic to religious definitions
of compassion.

79. Blum, "Compassion," p. 510.

which the person's plight is regarded as a symbol of what could happen to oneself. It is not actually necessary that one believe that the afflicting condition could happen to oneself."[80]

This is because compassion, third, demands not messianic aspirations, but the human vocation of active justice. Compassion is always an *imitatio*—or better, it is the *imago dei* in us. "We are compassionate" must be understood by Christians as the a*nalogia relationis*—by analogy with God's compassionate justice in Jesus Christ. As McNeill et al. state, "we cannot profess our solidarity with those who are oppressed when we are unwilling to confront the oppressor. Compassion without confrontation fades quickly into fruitless sentimental commiseration."[81] This is a particularly uncomfortable aspect of compassion when one's own life is itself caught up in the complicity of the oppressor. As Leo Tolstoy once quipped: "I sit on a man's back, choking him and making him carry me, and yet assure myself and others that I am very sorry for him and wish to ease his lot by all possible means—except by getting off his back."[82]

Compassionate justice means humanity's participation in the *missio dei,* the work of God in the world. It means *redemptive commitment,* costly discipleship, the conversion to justice. Such commitment cannot be private; it demands public involvement, the dislocation out of being hostage to one's inwardness into the world which God has hallowed as the place of the divine habitation. Not only does it demand what the German language calls a *Nächstenethik,* an ethic of the neighbor, an ethic of human beings in their co-relationships as individuals. Redemptive commitment demands a *Sozialethik,* a social ethic, an ethic of human communities in their relationships among/between each other, as well. "Being a neighbor implies action. Compassion or neighborliness is not simply a matter of sentiment or good intentions. It involves action that seeks

---

80. Blum, "Compassion," p. 517, n. 7. "Nevertheless," Blum argues, "the limits of a person's capacities for imaginative reconstruction set limits on her capacity for compassion. . . . Persons who are in general quite poor at imagining the experiences of others who are different from themselves, may well be less likely to have compassion for them" (p. 510).

81. McNeill, Morrison, and Nouwen, *Compassion,* p. 124.

82. Leo Tolstoy, *What Then Must We Do?* (Oxford: Oxford University Press, 1975); see Singer, *The Nature of Love,* vol. 3, pp. 49-65 on Tolstoy.

to effectively alter the situation of those who are in need."[83]

The compassionate vocation of justice is thus commitment to the service of hope. It must be *redemptive* com-passion, satisfied with no less than redeeming even the suffering of the past, which has no less claim on people today because they have passed it by.[84] Thus, as Lawrence Blum has noted, "because being compassionate involves actively giving thought to the relief of the sufferer's condition . . . compassion often involves resisting regarding situations as absolutely irremediable." For this very reason, "the compassionate person may . . . fail to see and hence to face up to the hopelessness of the sufferer's situation."[85] This is not because of the naivete of true compassion, but because it is a form of living out the Gospel that is grounded in the very promise that God triumphs even in the face of utter hopelessness. In Johann Baptist Metz's words, "the hope of Christians in a God of the living and the dead and in the power of that God to raise men from the dead is a hope in a revolution for all men, including those who suffer and have suffered unjustly, those who have long been forgotten and even the dead."[86] God is the God of the living and the dead, the hopeful and those "beyond hope," whose suffering is beyond remembering.

Compassion and the Páthos of God

For Christianity the theological foundation of religious compassion is humanity's *imitatio* of the *páthos* of God-in-Christ, the affirmation of humanity created in the image of incarnate-and-crucified-divinity. A Christian theology of compassion depends upon whether or not one can conceive of God's suffering, the passion of God's own self for the sake of God's creation. But is God capable of suffering, *páthos*, passion? Or is God incapable of suffering, a-pathetic, im-passible?

---

83. Jack Nelson-Pallmeyer, *The Politics of Compassion* (Maryknoll, N.Y.: Orbis Books, 1986), p. 12. For an argument to the contrary, see Diogenes Allen, *The Traces of God in a Frequently Hostile World* (Cowley, 1981), Ch. 7, "Human Need and Christian Action," pp. 87-97.

84. See Hall, *God and Human Suffering*, pp. 142-147; Nelson Pallmeyer, *Politics*, pp. 102-117.

85. Blum, "Compassion," p. 515.

86. Johann B. Metz, *Faith in History and Society* (New York: Crossroad, 1980), p. 76. Cf. Soren Kierkegaard, "The Work of Love in Remembering One Dead," in *Works of Love*, trans. Howard and Edna Hong (New York: Harper & Row, 1962), pp. 317-329.

Such questions have troubled theologians at least since the time of Origen, who spoke about God's suffering in terms of "the suffering of love, the compassion which is at the heart of mercy and pity."[87] Anselm of Canterbury in the eleventh century gave a now classic summary of the paradox concerning the divine impassibility or passibility:

> But how are thou compassionate, and, at the same time, passionless? For if thou art passionless, thou dost not feel sympathy; and if thou dost not feel sympathy, thy heart is not wretched from sympathy for the wretched; but this it is to be compassionate. But if thou art not compassionate, whence cometh so great consolation to the wretched? How then, art thou compassionate and not compassionate, O Lord, unless because thou art compassionate in terms of our experience, and not compassionate in terms of thy being.[88]

On the one hand, Christians have proclaimed belief in an "immortal, invisible, God only wise, in light inaccessible hid from our eyes,"[89] a God who in the words of the Anglican Articles of Religion, is "without body, parts or passions."[90] On the other hand, Christians have trusted their lives to One whose very heart is, in Anselm's words, "wretched from sympathy for the wretched," who is the author of "so great consolation . . . in terms of our experience." And most Christians have for the past millennium followed in the footsteps of Anselm's resolution of the problem of God's passibility by trying to deny that God's own self suffers. But thereby Christian thinkers have lost a close theological, as opposed to psychological, connection between divine and human compassion.

One striking exception to this, chronicled in J.K. Mozley's *The*

---

87. See Moltmann, *Trinity*, p. 24, concerning Origen's *Commentary on Romans* (VII.9; Migne, *Patrologia Graeca*, 14.1129A), *Selecta in Ezechielem* (Migne, *Patrologia Graeca*, 13.812A), and *Homilia VI in Ezechielem* (Migne, *Patrologia Graeca*, XIII, pp. 714f.).

88. Anselm of Canterbury, *Proslogium*, in *Basic Writings*, trans. S.N. Deane (LaSalle, Ill.: Open Court, 1974), Ch. VIII, 13; Anselm concluded that God remains impassible.

89. Words by Walter Chalmers Smith, *The Hymnal 1982* (New York: The Church Hymnal Corporation, 1982), p. 423.

90. See the "Articles of Religion," in *The Book of Common Prayer* (New York: The Church Hymnal Corporation, 1979), p. 867; also see K. Woollcombe, "The Pain of God," *Scottish Journal of Theology* 20 (1967), p. 129.

Impassibility of God. A Survey of Christian Thought,[91] was the late nineteenth- and early twentieth-century Anglican theology of the eucharistic sacrifice. Here a branch of the Christian tradition took seriously, in its practice as well as its theology, the possibility that "the cross on Golgotha has revealed the eternal heart of the Trinity."[92]

Some examples from this little-known English theological tradition are revealing in their use of language about the passion of God. In 1906 C.A. Dinsmore put in typical English pastorale prose what was on the mind of many, when he wrote:

> There was a cross in the heart of God before there was one planted on the green hill outside of Jerusalem. And now that the cross of wood has been taken down, the one in the heart of God abides, and it will remain so long as there is one sinful soul for whom to suffer.[93]

In 1913 C.E. Rolt surmised that since "man is a noble and a godlike being only so far as he, in patient love, has suffered. . . . Therefore God is God only in the fact that He, in perfect patience, has undergone all that the word suffering can possibly mean."[94] B.H. Streeter argued that the "capacity to feel, and if need be to suffer, is surely involved in the very conception of God as love."[95] And Canon V. F. Storr in 1924 asserted that "the Cross of Christ was no afterthought on the part of God, but was the expression at a definite historical period of something which represents an eternal actuality in the divine life."[96]

---

91. J.K. Mozley, *The Impassibility of God: A Survey of Christian Thought* (Cambridge: At the University Press, 1926), pp. 140-166.

92. In the words of Moltmann, *Trinity*, p. 31; Moltmann goes on to trace this theme of the compassionate God in Miguel de Unamuno's *The Tragic Sense of Life,* trans. J.E. Crawford Flitch (New York: Dover Publications, 1954), pp. 207-215, and Nicolas Berdyaev's *The Meaning of History,* trans. George Reavey (New York: Scribner's, 1936), p. 44ff.

93. C.A. Dinsmore, *Atonement in Literature and Life* (Boston: Houghton, Mifflin, 1906), pp. 232-233.

94. C.E. Rolt, *The World's Redemption* (London: Longmans, Green, 1913), p. 228.

95. B.H. Streeter, "The Suffering of God," *The Hibbert Journal* 47 (April, 1914), p. 605.

96. Canon V.F. Storr, *The Problem of the Cross* (London: SCM, 1924), p. 124. Cf. G.A. Studdert Kennedy, *The Hardest Part* (London: Hodder and Stoughton, 1918), p. 43: "For the foolishness of God is wiser than man, and His weakness is stronger than our strength. If the Christian religion means anything, it means that God is Suffering Love, and that all real progress is caused by the working of Suffering Love in the world."

Perhaps Maldwyn Hughes in the same year summed up a quarter-century of like-minded Anglican thought when he said: "Our contention is not simply that Christ reveals a suffering God, but that the sufferings of Christ were the sufferings of God."[97] If so, then when Christians view humanity as created in the image of God, the *imago* is not just of a relationship—*imago relationis*—but of a *particular* relationship. God's solidarity with creation extends to God's radical involvement with that creation's very brokenness itself, a voluntary displacement of the divine self onto the cross, that the world might be redeemed from its own brokenness for its vocation as God's creature.[98]

Compassion and the Practice of Ministry

A theologically defensible statement of the páthos of God, therefore, can be argued to be necessary for any adequate theological interpretation of compassion. And if the *theologia crucis*, the theology

97. Maldwyn Hughes, *What Is the Atonement? A Study in the Passion of God in Christ* (Cambridge: Cambridge University Press, 1924), p. 102. This English tradition is continued in the present in the work of such theologians as Paul S. Fiddes, *The Creative Suffering of God*, n.b. "The Central Place of the Cross," pp. 25-31.

98. Besides this largely neglected English eucharistic theology, the only other modern emphasis on the com-passion of God was the nineteenth century *kenotic* movement (from kenosis, or selfemptying) which focused theological attention on the notion of God having 'emptied' the divine self of divinity in becoming a human being. And it is only in the past thirty years that renewed discussion has once more taken place concerning the significance of such a theological affirmation of God's passion, the divine capacity to suffer for and with God's creation. See Karl Barth, *The Humanity of God* (Richmond: John Knox, 1960); Paul Tillich, *Systematic Theology*, vol. 3 (Chicago: University of Chicago Press, 1963), pp. 404-405; Woollcombe, "The Pain of God"; Jung Young Lee, *God Suffers for Us*, pp. 23-45 on traditional views of the divine impassibility; Geddes MacGregor, *He who Lets Us Be: A Theology of Love* (New York: Seabury, 1975), pp. 23-42; Richard E. Creel, *Divine Impassibility: An Essay in Philosophical Theology* (Cambridge: Cambridge University Press, 1986) who distinguishes four often-obscured, but distinct, aspects of the claims for and against divine impassibility: impassibility of the divine nature, will, knowledge, and feeling; S. Paul Schilling, *God and Human Anguish* (Nashville: Abingdon, 1977), pp. 235-260; Moltmann, *Trinity*, pp. 21-60; Moltmann, *Crucified God*, pp. 270-274; Warren McWilliams, "Divine Suffering in Contemporary Theology," *Scottish Journal of Theology* 33:1 (February, 1980), pp. 35-53, and *The Passion of God. Divine Suffering in Contemporary Protestant Theology* (Macon, Ga.: Mercer University Press, 1985), pp. 3-24; Andrew Purves, *The Search for Compassion*, pp. 60-81; Paul S. Fiddes, *The Creative Suffering of God* (Oxford: Clarendon Press, 1988); and Kazoh Kitamori, *The Theology of Change: A Christian Concept of God in Eastern Perspective* (Maryknoll, N.Y.: Orbis Books, 1979).

of the cross, is the theological foundation of Christian religious compassion, then it is the theological key to that ministry which would be
a student and practitioner of compassion among humanity.

Compassion in Practice

At least three forms of contemporary theological reflection are
distinctive contributors to theology's deepening understanding of
religious compassion, particularly as they influence Christianity's
practice of ministry. These are (a) third-world Christian liberation theologies, (b) feminist and black Christian liberation theologies, and (c)
the 'theology' of compassion in non-Christian religious traditions.

Third-world liberation theologians have made the most dramatic
contributions to contemporary understandings of compassion as
responsive solidarity.[99] The emergence of liberation theologies challenges the seriousness with which ministry is interpreted primarily
not as ministry to others, but as ministry for and *among* others.[100]
Liberation perspectives on compassion urge first-world Christians
toward a form of steadfast love that embraces the world as the only
place in which to find the neighbor's need in its concreteness. And
a liberated and liberating compassion is capable of the 'longer
view' of the vagaries of history outside the present and understands
the responsibilities entailed in the theologian's critical insight into
the evolution of oppression.

Liberation approaches chasten any self-congratulatory attempts
at *contextualization,* reminding us that voluntary poverty and involuntary, dehumanizing impoverishment are quite different matters.
Liberation theologies not only criticize the first-world's comfort-
able, middle-class expectation of a cheap and easy solidarity with the
sufferings of the world, but also they provide first-world theology with
an opportunity to be liberated from its own bondage to a life of
self-interest.[101] Liberation theologies are a reminder that authen-

---

99. See Matthew L. Lamb, *Solidarity With Victims: Toward a Theology of Social
Transformation* (New York: Crossroad, 1982). From a third-world woman's per-
spective see Marianne Katoppo, *Compassionate and Free. An Asian Woman's Theology*
(Geneva: The World Council of Churches, 1979).

100. See Norbert Greinacher and Norbert Mette, *Diakonia: Church for the Others*
(Edinburgh: T&T Clark Ltd, 1988), n.b. part II, 'I see the Distress of my People':
Divine Compassion as a Christian Commission."

101. See Johann B. Metz, ed., *Christianity and the Bourgeoisie* (New York: Seabury,
1979); cf. Freire, *Pedagogy of the Oppressed.*

tic entry into the sufferings of the vast majority of human beings, who are not as privileged either in possessions or power as are the citizens of the first world, may indeed mean not just the recognition of north-Atlantic culture's own role in causing that suffering, but its renunciation as well.

Finally, liberation theologies require one to ask once more about the motivation for compassion: the liberation of all God's creation from those inner and outer "principalities and powers" that keep creation prisoner to that which does not deserve its allegiance. Theology is confronted with the need for lives of this-worldly commitment, to borrow a concept from Dietrich Bonhoeffer.[102] Liberation theologies offer the chance to remember that a compassionate life is not merely individual, but demands a compassionate *polis*, or society, as well. Compassion is thus always *political*, concerned not just with individual interiority, but with the redemption of all of creation, social and natural, as well.[103]

In a similar fashion, black and feminist liberation theologies refuse to allow religious compassion to become an emotion that precedes ministry. They recognize compassion, instead, as the central form which ministry takes. As James Cone has written, "Christians are called to suffer with God in the fight against evil in the present age. . . . This vocation is not a passive endurance of injustice but, rather, a political and social praxis of liberation in the world."[104] And as feminist theologians have reminded even the black male tradition, this means that men must listen more often

---

102. Dietrich Bonhoeffer, *Letters and Papers from Prison, The Enlarged Edition*, ed. Eberhard Bethge (New York: Macmillan, 1978), p. 370 [21 July, 1944]: "By this-worldliness I mean living unreservedly in life's duties, problems, successes and failures, experiences and perplexities. In so doing, we throw ourselves completely into the arms of God, taking seriously, not our own sufferings, but those of God in the world."

103. See Moltmann, *Crucified God*, Ch. 8, "Ways Towards the Political Liberation of Mankind," pp. 317-340; Nelson-Pallmeyer. *The Politics of Compassion*; and Enrique Dussel, *Ethics and the Theology of Liberation*, trans. Bernard F. McWilliams (Maryknoll, N.Y.: Orbis Books, 1978). From a Christian Evangelical liberation perspective see Jim Wallis, "The Powerful and the Powerless" and the repudiation of his position by Lloyd Billingsley, "Radical Evangelicals and the Politics of Compassion," in *Piety and Politics: Evangelicals and Fundamentalists Confront the World*, ed. Richard John Neuhaus and Michael Cromartie (Washington, D.C.: Ethics and Public Policy Center, 1987), pp. 189-202, 205-216.

104. Cone, *God of the Oppressed*, p. 177.

than men speak, open to voices that redescribe the parameters of compassion itself.[105]

Feminist theologians have drawn attention back to the close connection between *rachamim*, the Hebrew word for compassion, and the root word to which it is most intimately connected, *rechem*, or womb. For example, Phyllis Trible has pointed out that *rachamim*, compassion, "connotes simultaneously both a mode of being and the locus of that mode," *rechem*, or womb. This singular noun *rechem*, or uterus, "in the plural, *rachamim* . . . expands to the abstractions of compassion, mercy, and love."[106] This maternal quality of compassion is seen in Hebrew stories such as that of the two harlots facing King Solomon with a single child to divide between them (1 Kgs 3:16-28). And this maternal compassion is then attributed also to brothers,[107] then to fathers,[108] and finally to God's own self,[109] unfolding "new dimensions of the image of god male and female."[110]

Even so, other feminist theologians rightly have warned against viewing compassion in stereotypically 'female' terms, as most properly akin to emotive, "soft," and sentimental styles of mothering which value self-denial, self-sacrifice, and self-abnegation for the sake of one's children. Rather, the movement from *responsive solidarity*, to the risk of radical *contextualization*, to the costliness of *redemptive commitment* requires a strong sense of self. Certainly compassion means something radically different from egoistic self-absorption and self-preoccupation. Yet in order to understand the dynamics of compassion, the theologian must be able "to distinguish justifiable self-sacrifice from faithless self-abnegation . . . . Women writers contend that the ideal of self-sacrifice has been

---

105. E.g., see Katie Geneva Cannon, "Moral Wisdom in the Black Women's Literary Tradition," in *Weaving the Visions: New Patterns in Feminist Spirituality*, ed. Judith Plaskow and Carol P. Christ (San Francisco: Harper & Row, 1989), pp. 281-292.

106. Phyllis Trible, *God and the Rhetoric of Sexuality* (Philadelphia: Fortress, 1978), p. 33.

107. The story of Joseph's meeting for the first time his brother Benjamin (n.b. Genesis 43:30).

108. Psalm 103:13: "As a father shows compassion [*rachamim*] upon his children . . . " See Trible, *God and the Rhetoric of Sexuality*, pp. 34-56.

109. Psalm 103:13, which continues " . . . so Yahweh shows compassion [*richam*] upon those who fear him."

110. Trible, *God and the Rhetoric of Sexuality*, p. 56.

applied one-sidedly in the Christian tradition."[111] Self-denial may address the 'male' sin of Promethean pride, but it leaves unattended the 'female' sin of slothful loss of human dignity.[112] From feminist theology Christianity learns anew that compassion is not to lose one's self; it is to give of one's self for the service of God's mission in the world. Solidarity in love is born of the doing of justice, and that dynamic process is what is called compassion.[113]

Finally, Christian theologians and other practitioners of ministry would do well to remember that the Jewish and Christian traditions are not the only religious resources for understanding compassion. Asian Christian theologians, such as C.S. Song, remind us that "for too long Christian theology has been busy hearing the groanings of its own churches. It has developed systems and traditions that enable Christians to hear only the voices of their own popes, bishops, and theologians."[114] Compassion may be just the sort of theological topic that can encourage both ecumenical perspectives within the larger Christian community[115] and comparative religious interchange between Christian theology and other religious traditions.

For example, among the three Western monotheisms, Islam as well as Christianity and Judaism has a strong concept of compassion. The Koran frequently describes Allah with the noun *marhamah* (mercy or compassion), the adjective *rahim* (merciful or compassionate) or with the verb *rahima* (to be compassionate).[116]

But perhaps nowhere else is compassion more central to the great religious traditions of the world than in Mahayana Buddhism,

---

111. See Gene Outka, "Love," "II. Contemporary Discussion," in *Westminster Dictionary*, p. 358.

112. See Ana Maria Tepedino, "Feminist Theology as the Fruit of Passion and Compassion," in *With Passion and Compassion: Third World Women Doing Theology*, ed. Virginia Fabella and Cercy Amba Oduyoye (Maryknoll, N.Y.: Orbis Books, 1988), pp. 165-172.

113. See Lynn N. Rhodes, *Co-Creating: A Feminist Vision of Ministry* (Philadelphia: Westminster, 1987), n.b. Ch. 4, "Mission: Justice and Solidarity."

114. C.S. Song, *The Compassionate God* (Maryknoll, N.Y.: Orbis Books, 1982), p. 168.

115. See Thomas Ryan, "Ecumenism and Compassion," *Midstream: An Ecumenical Journal* 25:2 (April, 1986), pp. 184-189.

116. See Hanna E. Kassis, *A Concordance of the Qur'an* (Berkeley: University of California Press, 1983), pp. 1002-1006.

where it is one of the four universal virtues.[117] This is especially significant in the figure of the *bodhisattva*, who "by virtue of his decision to decline the rewards of *nirvana*, 'until the last blade of grass has been liberated,' is revered as an infinite and inexhaustible reservoir of compassion (*karuna*)."[118] Christianity will not have come to a complete understanding of the distinctiveness of its own view of compassion, rooted in the figure of Jesus Christ, until it has more fully understood the role of compassion in other forms of human religious self-understanding.

Compassion: Concluding Implications for Ministry

A fully developed Christian theology of compassion would require a fundamental rethinking of many assumptions concerning the practice of ministry.[119] It would mean a re-visioning of (a) the nature of ministry in general, particularly, that of the laity, as distinct from the ordained ministries of designated clergy; (b) the nature of the community called the Church; (c) the shape of ordained ministry in particular; and (d) the Church's posture toward the natural world.

First, a theology of compassion would encourage a rethinking of the meaning of "ministry" itself. Compassionate *diakonia*, the service of "the whole people of God" to the *missio dei*, the divine redemptive mission in the midst of the world, would become the hallmark of Christian identity. If ministry centers on compassion, then the dynamic process of *solidarity* with the needs of others, the *contextualization* of ministry within the risk and costliness of concrete, worldly responsibilities, and the active justice that flows from *commitment* to the crucified God together "become the core and

---

117. See "Compassion," in *A Dictionary of Comparative Religion*, ed. S.G.F. Brandon (New York: Scribner's, 1970). Also see David Brandon, "Compassion," in *Zen in the Art of Helping* (London: Routledge & Kegan Paul, 1976), pp. 47-61.

118. C. Bruce Long, "Love," in *The Encyclopedia of Religion*, vol. 9, ed. Mircea Eliade (New York: Macmillan, 1987), p. 35, who continues: "The *bodhisattva* . . . actively shares others' sufferings and takes their pains upon himself in order to relieve them of the burdens that are beyond their capacity to manage." Also see Clarence H. Hamilton, ed., *Buddhism: A Religion of Infinite Compassion* (New York: Liberal Arts Press, 1952).

119. A highly eccentric, and often flawed if not entirely misleading, previous attempt to address this topic, was Matthew Fox, *A Spirituality Named Compassion and the Healing of the Global Village, Humpty Dumpty and Us* (Minneapolis: Winston, 1979).

even the nature of authority."[120] Such is a ministry primarily of the laity, centered in baptism rather than ordination, oriented to the least of God's creatures and their need, a community of compassion, "standing together with them under the cross."[121]

Therefore, second, a theology of compassion would form the basis of a new theology of the church, or ecclesiology. Douglas John Hall, a Canadian theologian, has argued that a diaconal church would have to rethink its identity as "a *koinonia* of compassion to which the hurting world may turn,"[122] an *ecclesia crucis*—what Leonard Allen has called *The Cruciform Church*.[123]

However, such a church would be shaped not only by God's suffering in the cross of Jesus, but also by the theology of the resurrection of the body. A compassionate ecclesiology would nurture a vision of a resurrection church community in the shadow of the cross. Christianity proclaims the divine involvement in suffering not for the sake of suffering, but for the sake of God's creative purposes among those for whom suffering stands in the way.[124] Christian compassion involves *redemptive* suffering, the offering of one's self for the sake of the other, not merely to share in the other's suffering, but in order to announce God's desire for the triumph of life over death, even to the point of the resurrection of the dead themselves. For the compassionate minister, lay or ordained, "until the time when the communion of love is firmly established in the world of strife and conflict, of pain and suffering, God moves on in compassion. We have no alternative but to move on with God."[125]

Thus, in Henri Nouwen's words, "perhaps the main task of the [ordained] minister is to prevent people from suffering for the

---

120. Henri J.M. Nouwen, *The Wounded Healer: Ministry in Contemporary Society* (Garden City, N.Y.: Doubleday, 1972), p. 40.

121. Willem A. Visser 't Hooft, quoted in Geiko Mueller-Fahrenholz, "No Communion Without Compassion: Visser 't Hooft. An Interview," *Christian Century* 101:5 (February 15, 1984), p. 170.

122. Hall, *God and Human Suffering*, pp. 123-147; also pp. 90-91.

123. Douglas John Hall, *Lighten Our Darkness: Toward an Indigenous Theology of the Cross* (Philadelphia: Westminster, 1976), p. 220ff.; C. Leonard Allen, *The Cruciform Church: Becoming a Cross-Shaped People in a Secular World* (Abilene, Tex.: Abilene Christian University Press, 1990), n.b. chap. 7, "The Ordeal of Compassion," pp. 173-184.

124. Fiddes, *Creative Suffering*, p. 109.

125. Song, *The Compassionate God*, p. 260.

wrong reasons."[126] The compassionate ordained minister would not only engage differently in pastoral counseling, ministering in solidarity with the suffering of one's parishioners,[127] but also would enable the community of faith to engage in its own acts of radical contextualization and redemptive commitment. Compassion is not only something that a person needs to receive in order to be healthy. It is something one needs to do among others as well. Ordained clergy therefore have a dual responsibility both to minister to the needs of others—those who are suffering for the wrong reasons— and to empower the laity for their own ministries of compassion— to embolden them to suffer for the right reasons.

Finally, compassion leads ministry into an ethic of responsible commitment to the whole of creation, not just to human beings. Heschel put it magnificently when he wrote that "dark is the world to me, for all of its cities and stars, if not for the breath of compassion that God blew in me when [God] formed me of dust and clay."[128] A theology of compassion would renew the centrality of a redemptive commitment to stewardship. For example, process theologies, under the influence of Alfred North Whitehead, Charles Hartshorne, and others, have argued for a Christian understanding of love as compassionate action, not as an affection, along with a vision of a God who is "lovingly and ceaselessly active in the created order,"[129] com-

---

126. Nouwen, *The Wounded Healer*, p. 95.

127. Purves, *The Search for Compassion*; also see Becker, "Compassion: A Foundation for Pastoral Care."

128. Heschel, *Man Is Not Alone*, p. 147. The vast majority of theological literature is unable to speak directly of global compassion—for the earth, for all of creation. Conspicuous examples to the contrary are Douglas John Hall's two books, *God and Human Suffering*, pp. 49-71, and *The Steward: A Biblical Symbol Come of Age*, rev. ed. (Grand Rapids, Mich.: Eerdmans, 1990); Sallie McFague, *Models of God: Theology for an Ecological, Nuclear Age* (Philadelphia: Fortress, 1987); and Jürgen Moltmann, Creating a Just Future (New York: Trinity Press, 1989).

129. David A. Pailin, "Process Theology," in *Westminster Dictionary of Christian Theology*, p. 470. See Charles Hartshorne, *The Divine Relativity: A Social Conception of God* (New Haven: Yale University Press, 1948), p. 133. This would in many ways simply be in continuity with the tradition of St. Francis, who "could express a loving kinship with all other animate beings because they too were the offspring of a perfect God whose goodness appeared in whatever he chose to make. Everything was to be loved as a way of loving God. Only with nineteenth-century philosophers such as Schopenhauer does one find, in a fully developed form, the idea that nonhumans should be loved as fellow sufferers within a world that has no perfection to it" [Singer, *The Nature of Love*, vol. 3, p. 18].

passionately at work in natural as well as social reality.[130]

A theology of compassion must move beyond solidarity with suffering to those active commitments whose goal is God's redemptive purpose amongst creation. This will always demand the faith and courage voluntarily to displace oneself from any secure, privileged context, to meddle dangerously in adversity, to interfere at personal risk in wrongdoing, to be unpopular due to one's intolerance with any suffering for the wrong reasons. It will never be easy. But is rests on the divine promise, wrought from God's very being, that "Everything," perhaps especially the suffering of genuine compassion, "is grace."[131]

---

130. See John B. Cobb Jr. and David Ray Griffin, *Process Theology* (Philadelphia: Westminster, 1976), p. 44; John B. Cobb Jr., *Process Theology as Political Theology* (Philadelphia: Westminster, 1982).

131. "Tout est grace," Georges Bernanos, *The Diary of a Country Priest*, trans. Pamela Morris (New York: Macmillan, 1970), p. 255 [translation altered].

3

The Psychology of
Religious Compassion

GARY L. SAPP

Explaining why people behave in benevolent or unselfish ways has
never been an easy task for Western psychology. This is particularly true when psychologists offer empirical explanations for behaviors described as compassionate, caring, loving, and/or sympathetic. Contemporary psychological theories of motivation based on
empirical explanations of behavior have consistently provided egoistic accounts of helping behavior that reject the role of altruism.
These egoistic accounts suggest that those caring behaviors which
seem most central to our humanity are, in actuality, deceptive,
sometimes hypocritical devices for disguising our true self-serving
motives. Definitions inspired by this viewpoint include "love" (two
mutually reinforcing organisms), "joy" (the anticipation of reinforcement),[1] and a characterization of the helping behavior of missionaries as "a manifestation of healthy doses of a reaction formation."[2]

While many psychologists reject the motivational role of altruism,

---

1. B.F. Skinner, *Science and Human Behavior* (New York: Free Press, 1953).
2. Rudolf Eckstein, "Psychoanalysis, Sympathy, and Altruism," in *Altruism,
Sympathy, and Helping,* ed. Lauren Wispé (New York: Academic Press, 1978), p.
168.

certain philosophers have attacked Western notions of compassion as pandering to sentimentality and weakness. Nietzsche[3] found nothing honorable or virtuous in one's manifestations of compassion. He stated, "my experience gives me a right to feel suspicious in regard to all so-called "selfless" tendencies, in regard to the whole "love of one's neighbor" which is ever ready and waiting with deeds and advice . . . they are signs of weakness. . . . The overcoming of pity I reckon among noble virtues."[4] Nietzsche also attacked Arthur Schopenhauer, a strong proponent of compassion, charging him with a maudlin preoccupation with suffering.[5]

As I explicate the psychological foundations of religious compassion, this chapter is predicated upon three assumptions. First, performing religious compassionate acts is a "good," because the sharing of compassion reflects the essence of God (see chapters by Bergant and Floyd). Hence, these acts are not only desirable; they are also the sacred duty of a religious person. Religious compassionate acts may require great courage for aiding and assisting another person may be foolish, ill-advised, and illogical when judged by contemporary societal standards. Second, there is a body of empirical support for the assumption that acts of religious compassion may be motivated by altruism.[6] The implication is that religious compassionate acts are not masochistic, neurotic spasms of guilt, attempts to achieve need reduction, or actions of an overly harsh superego. Rather, compassion is shared with another because the sharer has initially received compassion from his/her God through loving experiences with others. The context of religious compassion, then, is a community sharing in a spirit of love.[7] Finally, religious compassion has a behavioral component. It is not just high-minded verbalizations but is ultimately realized in caring action toward others. Compassion is manifested on the road from

---

3. Friedrich Nietzsche, *Beyond Good and Evil*, trans. Walter Kaufmann (New York: Random House, 1966).

4. Friedrich Nietzsche, *Ecce Homo*, in *The Philosophy of Nietzsche*, trans. C.P. Fadiman (New York: Modern Library, 1954), pp. 824–825.

5. Nietzsche, *Beyond Good and Evil*.

6. C. Daniel Batson, *The Altruism Question: Toward a Social Psychological Answer* (Hillsdale, N.J.: Lawrence Erlbaum, 1991).

7. Wendy Farley, "Tragic Vision and Divine Compassion: A Paradigm of God's Relationship to Ruptured Existence" (Ph.D. dissertation, Vanderbilt University, 1988).

"Jerusalem to Jericho" when the compassionate one crosses over to help the stranger.

Conceptualizations of Compassion

A major difficulty posed by the concept of compassion is formulating an acceptable definition for it. *Webster's Third New International Dictionary*, 1981, defines compassion as "deep feeling for and understanding of misery or suffering and the concomitant desire to promote its alleviation: spiritual consciousness of the personal tragedy of another or others and selfless tenderness directed toward it." Other sources[8] define compassion as deep sympathy; sympathy coming from the Greek "*sympatheia*" or the Latin "*sympathia*" meaning with (syn) feeling (pathos). Sympathy has generally referred to the propensity of individuals to perceive and respond to the suffering of another; a capability often identified as the basis for social bonding.

A definition of compassion which emphasized its emotional parameters was offered by Arnold Jersild: "Compassion is the ultimate and most meaningful embodiment of emotional maturity. It is through compassion that a person achieves the highest peak and deepest reach in his search for self-fulfillment. . . . Compassion means to partake in passion, to participate in feeling rather than viewing it as a spectator might. . . . A central and essential feature of compassion can perhaps best be expressed by the idea of acceptance. . . . The ability to pierce the disguises of feelings, to detect a vein of anxiety or grief beneath what seems to be angry or fresh and impudent behavior, and to feel moved by the hurt that is concealed is one of the most hard won properties of compassion. . . . There are elements of compassion one can possess only at the price of pain. There are other elements that one can possess through having known the meaning of joy. But the full tide of compassion comes from all the streams of feeling that flow through human existence."[9]

Compassion in the Promotion of Peace

William Eckhardt, a psychologist who emphasizes the role of compassion in the promotion of peace, defines compassion as a

8. Lauren Wispé, "Toward an Integration," in *Altruism, Sympathy and Helping*, ed. Lauren Wispé (New York: Academic Press, 1978), p. 319.

9. Arnold Jersild, *The Psychology of Adolescence* (New York: Macmillan, 1963), pp. 405-406.

multifaceted construct. It is composed of "a radical faith in human nature, altruistic values, cognitive creativity, justice defined as equality, behavior aimed at actualizing all of these values, and a social structure compatible with and congenial to their actualization."[10] He also includes a counter example, compulsion, which is the opposite of compassion. Compulsion is a neurotic state arising out of unconscious, unresolved conflicts which drive individuals in ways that run counter to the achievement of a vital spirituality. It is a mindless out-of-control propensity by peoples and governments to do evil.

In an attempt to articulate ultimate values, Eckhardt suggests that while physical facts are useful for determining the truth or falsity of theories based upon physical phenomenon, social facts are not analogously useful for testing outcomes of social theories. He suggests that all facts are contaminated by human theories and human values. Facts are evaluated on affective, ideological, and moral grounds and thus are never value-free. Theories of human behavior are also determined more by values than facts. Hence, a value-based theory of truth which will incorporate not only the facts but their value orientations is needed.

Eckhardt's candidate as the ultimate value which can serve to determine truth is compassion. Compassion is the norm by which all other values, theories, and facts in the social sciences should be evaluated. The standard of reference is the authenticity and utility of these concepts in contributing to human development. In this context Eckhardt perceives compassion as a dominating, loving passion which has hung on a cross (Mt 27:35), brought back the demon-possessed from the tomb (Lk 8:26-29), cared for a wounded stranger on the road from Jerusalem to Jericho (Lk 10:30-37), magnanimously accepted the return of a wayward son (Lk 8:26-39), and grieved over the fate of the common people (Mt 9:36-38). It is an irrepressible force which while scorned and punished many times in history, continues to reappear in the minds and hearts of people. In this context compassion is an authentic value, the ultimate criterion for testing the truth of theories in social science. A theory is "true" to the degree that it promotes the devel-

---

10. William Eckhardt, *Compassion: Toward a Science of Value* (Oakville, Ontario: CPRI Press, 1972). p. 268

opment of compassion in human affairs. Further, the theory should promote altruistic practices whose effects satisfy the value of compassion.[11]

Eckhardt defines the concepts that constitute his value theory of truth from the standpoint of compassion versus compulsion. The relationship of compassion to terms such as freedom, justice, love, and truth, etc., situates compassion as a core construct of personality that gives focus and meaning to one's life.

An empirical analysis of compassion was reported in a series of studies by Eckhardt.[12,13,14] In the first study 122 Canadian university students and adults responded to a 466-item questionnaire containing 67 affective, cognitive, and ideological scales. A factor analysis yielded a general factor of compassion which incorporated three primary factors: (1) an ideological factor: pacifism, religious nonconformity, socialism, political idealism, (2) a cognitive factor: knowledge of foreign affairs, and (3) an affective factor: mental health, introversion, faith in human nature, permissive and rational childhood disciplines, social responsibility, and empathy.

A reduction of the questionnaire incorporating items based on Lawrence Kohlberg's moral dilemmas (stage 4 choices versus stage 6 choices) was administered to 236 American students and faculty.[15] The general factor of compassion versus compulsion again emerged and the added dimension of morality suggested that compassion was characterized by principles of universality and consistency. Eckhardt suggests that if one compares compassion and compulsion, compassion is analogous to Sigmund Freud's ego, Immanuel Kant's categorical imperative, The Golden Rule, and Jean Piaget's notion of reciprocity. Compulsion relates to the Freudian id and to Piaget's concept of egocentricity.

---

11. Eckhardt, *Compassion: Toward a Science of Value.*

12. William Eckhardt and Theodore Lentz, "Factors of War/Peace Attitudes," *Peace Research Reviews* 1:5 (1967).

13. William Eckhardt, "Ideology and Personality in Social Attitudes," *Peace Research Reviews* 3:2 (1969).

14. William Eckhardt and Norman Alcock, "Ideology and Personality in War/Peace Attitudes," *Journal of Social Psychology* 81 (June, 1970), pp. 105-116.

15. William Eckhardt, Thomas Sloan, and Edward Azar, "Measurement of Compassion," *Peace Research Reviews* 4 (1972), pp. 29-31.

Compassion as the Power of Love

Employing a phenomenological orientation, Wendy Farley[16] conceptualizes compassion as comprising four areas: (1) sympathetic knowledge as a precondition of compassion, (2) compassion as an enduring disposition, (3) compassion as an articulation of love, and (4) compassion portrayed as a form of power.

If the compassionate person is to be responsive to the suffering of others, s/he must have an access to the growing power of sympathy. A major distinction between sympathy and compassion is that sympathy is a cognitive or perceptual phenomenon directed toward discrete events in awareness. Compassion transcends single events as it is a continuing and enduring involvement with the world. Also, human experience and human relationships are not simply juxtaposed fragments of knowledge, rather they occur in a complexity of diverse elements that are interwoven.

Compassion as an enduring disposition serves as a determinant of an individual's cognitive structure and elements of consciousness. As such, compassion becomes a central guiding focus such that it is "immersed in the world as a kind of love which is sensitive to suffering, and which sorrows for and responds to suffering." One's interaction with the world is sensitized to such a degree that "cognition, perception, feeling, acting, and valuing will be directed toward suffering and its alleviation."[17] Compassion then is a master motive of continuing concern such that the suffering of the world continually impinges upon one's consciousness.

Farley believes that "compassion is open to the pain of the world because it loves the world. It is love which gives to compassion eyes to see the suffering it encounters, love which fires compassion with desire to alleviate suffering, and it is love which constitutes the enduring disposition through which compassionate consciousness engages the world."[18]

Compassion shares the general features of love and all love includes a component of compassion. The uniqueness of compassion is that it "combines knowledge of the dignity and value of crea-

---

16. Farley, "Tragic Vision and Divine Compassion."
17. Ibid., p. 181.
18. Ibid., pp. 182-183.

tures present in every form of love with sympathetic knowledge of suffering."[19] One of the most salient features of compassion is that it is a power providing a vehicle through which one enters into another's suffering in order to ameliorate the suffering with the power of love.

Compassion is a form of love which does not insult the sufferer with gratuitous pity, rather it respects the integrity of the one in need. Farley suggests that the compassionate one clearly perceives the "interior self" of the sufferer, recognizes the personhood of the sufferer, and thereby is truly sympathetic.[20] As Max Scheler (quoting Thomas Aquinas) pointed out "those who are in pain are consoled when their friends sympathize with them, first, because sympathy shares the burden of pain and so lightens it, and second, because one sees that one is loved and the pleasure of being loved mitigates sorrow."[21]

Viewing compassion as a kind of power suggests that it works both internally and externally to grant power to individuals to overcome their dependence and despair. Farley suggests that effective resistance to the debilitating effects of suffering requires a courage to resist the "destruction of the spirit as well as the situation generating the suffering."[22] This concept of empowerment not only relates to provision for the homeless, the hungry, and the disenfranchised, but it reaches to the marginal people of society enabling them to "resist injustice and to fight despair and guilt themselves."[23]

Compassion as the Basis for Morality

Schopenhauer conducted a thorough, multifaceted analysis of compassion identifying it as the sole basis of morality.[24] David Cartwright[25] evaluated Schopenhauer's claim that (1) compassion is the basis of and incentive for actions having moral worth, and

---

19. Ibid., p. 191.

20. Ibid., p. 193.

21. Max Scheler, *The Nature of Sympathy*, trans. Peter Heath (Great Britain: Archon Books, Shoe String Press, 1954).

22. Farley, "Tragic Vision and Divine Compassion," p. 200.

23. Ibid., p. 203.

24. Arthur Schopenhauer, *On the Basis of Morality*, trans. E.F.J. Payne (Indianapolis/New York: Bobbs, Merrill, 1965).

25. David Cartwright, "Studien zum Stand der Schopenhauer-Forschung," in *Zeit der Ernte*, ed. Wolfgang Shirmacher (Stuttgart: Frommann-holzboog, 1982), pp. 60-61.

(2) all actions displaying moral worth arise from compassion. Cartwright suggests that Schopenhauer establishes this claim by maintaining that ethical value is conferred by the motive of an action rather than its consequences, and that there are three basic motives which underlie human functioning: egoism, malice, and compassion. Egoism is "the desire for one's well-being, malice is the desire for another's misfortune, and compassion is the desire for another's well-being."[26]

Cartwright rejected Schopenhauer's contention that examining actions judged as morally worthy and oriented to voluntary justice and loving kindness could preclude egoism and malice as their motives. Egoism cannot confer moral worth to actions because it is a motive that is primarily egocentric in orientation, Cartwright believes. The ethical significance of actions is found only "in reference to others."[27] Egoistic actions are neither good nor bad, but malicious actions are morally reprehensible because their goal is to promote another's suffering. The criterion of an action of moral worth is the absence of egoistic motivations coupled with the lack of a desire to do harm to another. Since compassion is not egoistic and malicious, it satisfies this negative criterion "only insofar as an action has sprung from compassion does it have moral value; and every action resulting from any other motive has none."[28]

Cartwright also points out that Schopenhauer proscribes hurting others. The fundamental principle of justice is defined as, `"hurt no one. . . . The first degree of the effect of compassion is that it opposes and impedes the sufferings I intend to cause others by my inherent antimoral forces."[29] To explain the basis of philanthropy, Cartwright indicates that Schopenhauer conceptualizes compassion as moving from a posture of restraining one from injuring another toward assisting another. This basic principle of philanthropy, help everyone as much as you can, undoubtedly arises from compassion which is the only motive that leads to acts of pure, loving-kindness.[30]

---

26. Ibid.

27. Ibid.

28. David Cartwright, "The Ethical Significance of Sympathy, Compassion, and Pity" (Ph.D. dissertation, University of Wisconsin, Madison, 1981), p. 144.

29. Schopenhauer, *On the Basis of Morality*, pp. 148-149.

30. Cartwright, "Studien zum Stand der Schopenhauer-Forschung," pp. 60-61.

After enunciating the virtues attributed to compassion, Cartwright clarifies the conception of compassion and delineates the framework in which compassion is said to occur.[31] He indicates that to Schopenhauer compassion is broadly defined as "a relationship between two sentient beings, one who is, or will be suffering, and one who apprehends the suffering."[32] Understanding one's suffering motivates the moral agent to either refrain from causing hurt to the suffering one, (justice) or, attempt to reduce or remove the source of the other's suffering (philanthropy). Schopenhauer defines compassion then, as "the immediate participation . . ., independent of all ulterior considerations, primarily in the suffering of another, and thus in the prevention or elimination of it. . . . As soon as the compassion is aroused, the weal and woe of another are to my heart in exactly the same way, although not always in the same degree, as otherwise my own are. Hence the difference between him and me is now no longer absolute."[33]

Cartwright considers Schopenhauer's analysis of the ethical significance of compassion to be flawed as there is insufficient proof to accept compassion as both the criterion of actions having moral worth and the source of justice and philanthropy. Further, Schopenhauer attempts to tie his model of compassion to metaphysics contending that what contemporary psychologists would call empathic responding cannot be explained psychologically or empirically and hence is "the great mystery of ethics."[34] Cartwright finds this position to be strained and suggests that compassion requires rational and empirical explanations as opposed to metaphysical ones. This, of course, is also my contention.

Schopenhauer's model is valuable because it offers a multifaceted analysis of compassion and provides a rich description of the phenomenon of compassion. However, what is most important in Schopenhauer's analysis is his recognition that compassion is a motive that confers moral worth to actions. Cartwright clearly illustrates this point stating that "compassion is unconditionally morally valuable because it is always good to desire to help someone who needs help. Further, compassionate agents display a morally appro-

---

31. Ibid., p. 70.
32. Schopenhauer, *On the Basis of Morality*, p. 148.
33. Ibid., p. 144.
34. Ibid.

priate attitude toward another's pain and misery—a desire to relieve
or eliminate them. Compassion is connected to philanthropy and
benevolence . . . because it leads to helping others and acts of lov-
ing-kindness. Insofar as it includes the adoption and pursuit of
another's well-being, compassion may also play an integral role in
justice. If we are to treat others equally or fairly, we must realize
that their interests and welfare are important—worthy of our consideration. By participating in the other's situation via compassion,
we begin to transcend egocentric positions."[35]

Cartwright also offers an extended analysis of compassion comparing it with sympathy and pity. He describes these three emotions as "fellow-feelings" which refer to individuals who, by virtue of
their existence are sharing certain general experiences, e.g., leisure,
pain, joy, sorrow, contentment, misery, happiness, unhappiness,
members in the "fellowship of humanity.[36]
Compassion differs from both sympathy and pity in that it is more
limited in scope and is used in a limited number of ways. A common German word for compassion (Mitleid) which means to
"suffer with" was often used by philosophers as a primary definition. For example, Benedict Spinoza described compassion as
"the imitation of emotions; when it is referred to pain, it is called
compassion."[37]

Cartwright views compassion as the sharing of the negativity of
"negative emotional sympathy" and "status suffering," or "pain of
other sentient beings." It also involves a disposition to assuage or
remove the suffering of the recipient. Compassion contains an
emotional element in that the compassionate person imagines how
the sufferer feels. Assuming emotions appropriate to the sufferer's
emotional state, the compassionate one "participates in the recipient's misery"[38] and attempts to foster the well-being of the sufferer.
Cartwright maintains that "compassion *always* intends to promote
the recipient's welfare . . . and the compassionate agent always

---

35. Ibid., p. 147 ff.
36. Cartwright, "The Ethical Significance of Sympathy, Compassion, and Pity,"
p. 74 ff.
37. Benedict Spinoza, *The Chief Works of Benedict de Spinoza*, trans. R.H.M. Elwes,
2 vols. (New York: Dover Publications, 1959).
38. Cartwright, "The Ethical Significance of Sympathy, Compassion, and Pity,"
p. 74.

adopts the recipient's interests."[39] This intention suggests that compassion will always be altruistic in its motives. While there may be payoffs for the agent such as pleasure or relief from perceiving a decrease in the recipient's suffering, these payoffs are maintained not to be the immediate ends of compassion. Compassion, then, is other directed as the recipient is valued as an end in him or herself.

Other important characteristics are that the compassionate agent does not feel pity for the recipient and, hence, does not feel a sense of superiority. "The reason for the recipient's suffering is not used as a basis for judgments of superiority."[40] Nor is the agent contemptuous of the recipient as moralistic agents often are. Rather the agent demonstrates respect for the recipient. Since compassion involves consolation, the agent translates this respect, care, and concern into action. Compassion leads to help, help that is offered only for the recipients' well-being.

Finally, Cartwright suggests that the recipients of compassion will respond very differently from those who are objects of pity. Being pitied somehow diminishes the self-esteem and pride of the recipient. However, compassion implies no condescension or negative assessment of the recipient. It manifests no lack of respect for the recipient as respect for the other is displayed by an altruistic concern for his/her well-being.

Compassion As Other Regard

Jeffrey Singleton[41] conducted an analysis of compassion that would be functional for the religious educator. Beginning with the term "other regard," he searched relevant philosophical, psychological, and theological sources that discussed related terms such as "friendship," "benevolence," "social interest," "harmony," "agape," and "compassion." From these accounts he identified seven characteristics of "other regard." (1) Other regard is altruistic—it values other individuals as ends, not means. Concern for the welfare of others is expressed both interpersonally and societally "through a striv-

---

39. Ibid., p. 75.
40. Ibid., p. 76.
41. Jeffrey Singleton, "Implications of the Theories of Lawrence Kohlberg and Carol Gilligan for Teaching Compassion in the Church" (Ph.D. dissertation, Temple University, 1987).

ing for the attainment of social goals and an ideal human community."[42] (2) Other regard is based on sympathy and empathy and "a sense of harmony in the universe and an awareness of the interdependence of all things."[43] (3) Other regard is "action as well as sentiment."[44] (4) Other regard satisfies but exceeds the demands of justice. (5) Other regard is a natural tendency requiring development. (6) Other regard as a quality is inherently pleasant and is essential to physical and psychological health. (7) Other regard includes appropriate self-love.

Singleton concluded that compassion is the most appropriate term that incorporates, and/or conveys the meaning of these seven criteria, and he defined it as "deep feeling for and understanding of the misery of suffering and the concomitant desire to promote its alleviation. . . . A spiritual consciousness of the personal tragedy of others and selfless tenderness directed toward it."[45]

Uniqueness of Religious Compassion

A significant question concerns whether conceptions of compassion in religious contexts are unique and differentiated from the models of compassion I have just examined. Compassion is a central tenet of many religions who proclaim that caring, compassion, and helpfulness are sacred duties of the believer. Western religions particularly contend that the source of compassion is the love of God ("Every good and perfect gift is from above" [Jas 1:17]), and that this love is manifested in the compassionate behavior of believers. "Shouldest not thou also have had compassion on thy fellow servant, even as I had pity on thee" (Mt 18:33). The power of love is seen to be so compelling that the believer *must* be compassionate. In truth she/he could not do otherwise. As Farley points out, "What thrusts compassion into the world so that beings' beauty and sorrow are evident to it is not an accidental exposure to suffering through sympathetic knowledge, but loves' self-transcending delight and care for being. Compassion is open to the pain of the world because it loves the world. It is love which gives to com-

---

42. Ibid., p. 32.
43. Ibid., p. 34.
44. Ibid., p. 32.
45. Ibid., p. 35.

passion eyes to see the suffering it encounters, love which fires compassion with desire to alleviate suffering, and it is love which constitutes the enduring disposition through which compassionate consciousness engages that world."[46] Compassion as conceptualized in Western religions assumes that God's love (*agape*) is the ultimate source of motivation, not egoism or some "fellow feeling."

For others combining the term "religious" with compassion may restrict the manifestation of compassion to a select group of individuals. One major function of religion is to serve as a source for extending the range of kinship.[47] However, most religions are also inclusive, having an ordained, a priesthood, and an elite. These elected ones may be in the "Body of Christ" or the "Family of God," but unbelievers may be the "infidel," "the degenerate," or the one who has committed the unpardonable sin. Thus while religions may encourage compassion and care, treatment of those on the outside may be punitive, judgmental, rejecting, and callous. From this perspective, religious compassion could be a more restricted, parochial concept than philosophical conceptions of compassion which should be applied and experienced universally.

Given the claims of major Western religions, linking the concept of compassion with the term "religious" has three significant implications. First, the behavior of being compassionate toward others should be more commonly manifested in religious settings than in other organizational settings. Second, the motivation of compassion should be altruistic, selfless, and other-directed. This motivation is inexorable as it derives from God's love for man and is manifested person to person. Third, compassion is manifested in behavior designed to assist the needy. These implications are discussed later in the chapter.

A Model of Religious Compassion

The descriptions of compassion by Eckhardt, Nietzsche, Schopenhauer, Jersild, Cartwright, Farley, and Singleton indicate its diverse connotations. Depending on one's frame of reference, com-

---

46. Farley, "Tragic Vision and Divine Compassion."

47. C. Daniel Batson, "Sociobiology and the Role of Religion in Promoting Prosocial Behavior: An Alternative View," *Journal of Personality and Social Psychology* 45 (1983), pp. 1380-1385.

passion is a virtue, a character flaw, the basis for personal morality, a lifestyle, pity, sympathy, or the core construct in a value-based theory of truth. Perhaps the most crucial aspect in formulating a model of religious compassion is to establish that its source of motivation is altruistic. Failing to do so denies the moral significance and spiritual validity of religious compassion. It is thereby reduced to one of those "virtues" condemned by Kohlberg in his criticisms of character education as a "bag of virtues."[48]

Considering these difficulties, I offer a conceptualization of religious compassion which eventuates in helping behavior. The model drawn from Schopenhauer,[49] Cartwright,[50] and C. Daniel Batson,[51] begins with a summary definition of compassion as a person's sympathetic disposition to respond altruistically to the suffering of another. This disposition culminates in actions designed to (1) remove or alleviate the suffering of the recipient, (2) increase the welfare of the recipient, and (3) promote or heighten a positive emotional state of the recipient. The formal statement of the model which is adapted rather literally from Cartwright[52] is that a person manifests compassion toward others when:

a) The two individuals are sentient beings in psychological contact.

b) The compassionate person perceives that the recipient is in need and in distress (a negative valued mental state).

c) The compassionate person imaginatively realizes the recipient's need and distress.

d) The compassionate person both sympathizes and empathizes with the recipient (feels a negative valued emotion).

e) Realizing the recipient's distress, the compassionate person desires the recipient's well-being (without egoistic satisfaction for him/herself) and, hence, is altruistically concerned for the recipient's welfare.

---

48. Lawrence Kohlberg, "The Cognitive-Developmental Approach to Moral Development," *Phi Delta Kappan* 56:10 (1975), p. 671.

49. Schopenhauer, *On the Basis of Morality*.

50. Cartwright, "The Ethical Significance of Sympathy, Compassion, and Pity."

51. Batson, "Prosocial Motivation: Is It Ever Truly Altruistic?" in *Advances in Experimental Social Psychology*, vol. 20, ed. Leonard Berkowitz (New York: Academic Press, 1987), pp. 65-122.

52. Cartwright, "The Ethical Significance of Sympathy, Compassion, and Pity," p. 87.

f) The compassionate person is disposed to help the recipient.
g) The compassionate person engages in altruistically motivated helping.[53]

A Model for Religious Compassionate Behavior

Affect	Motivation	Behavior
Sympathy/empathy	Altruism	Prosocial behavior which
	Religious prosocial motivation (love)	a) Alleviates suffering
		b) promotes welfare
		c) heightens positive emotional state

While incorporating the thinking of philosophers, this conceptualization is informed by an empirical social psychological research
base. This is not to say that relevant research in personality, developmental psychology, or the "genetics of altruism,"[54] is ignored.

---

53. It must be acknowledged that altruistically motivated helping behavior will
not always occur even though it might appear disingenuous to suggest that the
compassionate person may not necessarily aid the recipient. After all, is this not
what the issue is all about, that many of us talk a good game but often fail to
come through in moments of crises. However, I would be remiss if I failed to indicate that there is "none righteous—no not one." The religious and psychological literature is replete with numerous examples of failure to help from individuals that one might otherwise describe as compassionate. Certainly this is
one of the great, riveting questions in ethics, theology, and psychology. At this
stage of the analysis I propose that the compassionate person, much like the
fable of Frankie and Johnnie, will render assistance nearly all of the time. My definition of compassion is displayed "on the Jericho road" and not necessarily in
the pulpit or the psychological laboratory. (See John Darley and C. Daniel
Batson, "From Jerusalem to Jericho: A Study of Situational and Dispositional
Variables in Helping Behavior," *Journal of Personality and Social Psychology* 27:1
[1973], pp. 100-108.)

54. Batson, "Religion as Prosocial: Agent or Double Agent?" *Journal for the
Scientific Study of Religion* 15 (1976), pp. 29-45.

However, using empirical behavorial science studies as a basis for accounting for human behavior precludes some of the speculation that has characterized similar attempts in the past.

The Role of Sympathy and Empathy

Empathy has been identified by many writers as the key motivator for compassion.[55] Lauren Wispé[56] supports this notion but found considerable disagreement regarding the definition of empathy. In an attempt to resolve this difficulty, he offered definitions for both sympathy and empathy: "Sympathy refers to the heightened awareness of the suffering of another person as something to be alleviated. . . . Sympathy intensifies both the representation and the internal reaction to the others dilemma."[57] Also, the other's suffering is experienced immediately as something to be alleviated. From this perspective sympathy is defined in terms of negative emotions; it is the painful awareness of another's suffering and the necessity of ameliorating that suffering.

Empathy is "the attempt by a self-aware self to comprehend unjudgmentally the positive and negative experiences of another self."[58] Since the emotions are difficult to apprehend and interpret, empathic responding requires a great deal of effort to maximize accuracy of perception. Other processes that underlie empathy are one's imaginal and mimetic capabilities. From a phenomenological perspective, the act is one of apprehending another's perceptual self.[59] In comparing and contrasting sympathy and empathy, Wispé indicates that "in empathy the self is the vehicle for understanding, and it never loses its own identity."[60] Since sympathetic responding is more concerned with communion than accuracy, self-awareness is reduced rather than augmented. The lowering of awareness can reduce the accuracy of one's perception; consequently, the highly sympathetic person may emotionally distort the situation.

---

55. Batson, *The Altruism Question*, pp. 86-87.
56. Lauren Wispé, "The Distinction Between Sympathy and Empathy: To Call Forth a Concept, a Word in Needed," *Journal of Personality and Social Psychology* 50:2 (1986), pp. 314-321.
57. Ibid., p. 318.
58. Ibid.
59. Ibid.
60. Ibid., p. 310.

This can be particularly deleterious in counseling or therapeutic situations in which the therapist either overidentifies with the client, romanticizes the client's appropriate responses as only logical in a bizarre world, or attempts to remove the client from the "evil environment."

Wispé also suggests that empathy is the substitution of ourselves for others, whereas in sympathy we substitute others for ourselves. In empathy the empathizer "reaches out" for the other person. In sympathy, the sympathizer is "moved by" the other person.[61] "To know what it would be like if I were the other person is empathy. To know what it would be like to be that other person is sympathy."[62] Wispé indicates that in empathy I act *as if* I were the other person,[63] but in sympathy I *am* the other person.[64] The objects of empathy and sympathy are different, since in empathy the point is to understand the other person. In sympathy the object is the other person's well-being. Empathy is a way of knowing and sympathy is a way of relating.

The development of empathy and sympathy as core constructs in altruistic motives is emphasized by Martin Hoffman[65 66 67] who defines empathy as "an involuntary . . . experiencing of another's emotional state."[68] Hoffman believes that the tendency to respond empathetically is innate, but its development begins with "empathic distress." This emotional state is "a conditioned affective response based on the similarity between distress cues from someone else in the immediate situation and elements of one's own actual distress experienced in the past."[69] From six to twelve months of age, the

61. Ibid., p. 318.

62. Ibid., p. 310.

63. Carl Rogers, "Empathy: An Unappreciated Way of Being," *Counseling Psychologist* 2 (1975), pp. 2-10.

64. Alison Macfie, "Adam Smith's Moral Sentiments as a Foundation for His *Wealth of Nations*," *Oxford Economic Papers*, vol. 11 (1959), pp. 209-228.

65. Martin Hoffman, "Empathy, Role-Taking, Guilt, and Development of Altruistic Motives," in *Moral Development and Behavior: Theory, Research, and Social Issues*, ed. Thomas Lickona (New York: Holt, Rinehart and Winston, 1976), pp. 124-143.

66. Martin Hoffman, "Is Altruism Part of Human Nature?" *Journal of Personality and Social Psychology* 40 (1981), pp. 121-137.

67. Martin Hoffman, "The Development of Empathy," in *Altruism and Helping Behavior*, ed. J.P. Rushton and R.M. Sorrentino (Hillsdale, N.J.: Erlbaum, 1981).

68. Ibid., p. 126.

69. Hoffman, "Is Altruism Part of Human Nature?" pp. 121-137.

child develops a sense of "person permanence" which is a sense of another's existence as a separate entity from one's self. Concurrently, the child may engage in role taking in familiar, highly motivating natural settings. A third capability, awareness that other individuals have their own personal identities, replete with inner states and unique life circumstances, develops by about age six. These three capabilities interact in a developmental sequence with the child's emerging cognitive capabilities to produce sympathetic distress. The role of sympathetic distress as the central motive that evokes altruistic action is described by Hoffman as:

> Once people are aware of the other as distinct from the self, their own empathic distress, which is a parallel response—a more or less exact replication of the victims presumed feelings of distress—may be transformed at least in part into a more reciprocal feeling of concern for the victim. That is, they continue to respond in a pure empathic, quasi-egoistic manner—to feel uncomfortable and highly distressed themselves—but they also experience a feeling of compassion, or what I call sympathetic distress for the victim, along with a conscious desire to help because they feel sorry for him or her and not just to relieve their own empathic distress.[70]

Discussing why empathic distress should lead to helping, Hoffman suggests that empathic distress is unpleasant and helping the victim to reduce his distress is usually the best way to reduce one's personal distress. Evidence for this view is found in research which indicates that when adults are exposed to someone in distress, "the time between observation of the distress and helping decreases with both the intensity of empathic arousal and the magnitude of the pain experienced by the victim."[71]

The Motivation of Compassionate Behavior

While many philosophers contend that altruism is manifest in many areas of human functioning, behavioral scientists writing

---

70. Martin Hoffman, "Development of Prosocial Motivation: Empathy and Guilt," in *The Development of Prosocial Behavior*, ed. Nancy Eisenberg (New York: Academic Press, 1982), p. 290.

71. Hoffman, *Moral Development and Behavior*, p. 136.

from psychoanalytic and learning theory perspectives are not as sanguine. Rudolf Eckstein forcefully articulates the psychoanalytic position when he points out "much of the past psychoanalytic literature looked at certain excesses of altruism, generosity, and love as symptoms of inner struggle. Although apparently socially valuable, expressions of positive behaviors were actually expressions of illness that in the long run would prove dysgenic. . . . Anna Freud claimed that much generosity could frequently be understood as an offering of treats in order to avoid tricks, so that much altruism could be considered as avoidance of, or masking of, aggression . . . . Even on a large social scale many areas of charity . . . turn out to be condescending pity, secret hostility, tragic guilt or self-advertisement."[72]

Learning theorists, arguing for the primacy of reinforcement, cannot escape from the view that all prosocial behavior is motivated by some form of self-benefit. However, their attempts at defining reinforcement are quite ingenious. One can receive either public acclaim and esteem for virtuous and selfless behavior (as in the case of the pharisee and the publican), or one can experience "self rewards, congratulations for being kind and caring, and [one] can avoid self-censure, thereby escaping guilt and shame."[73] Even the behavior of heroes and martyrs is ultimately reduced to egoism, for they may have acted to gain heavenly rewards or to avoid the censure of those that remain. Even more ignobly, they were silly, foolish, or simply guilty of poor judgment.

Ronald Cohen states that "altruism is not a strong position either logically or empirically."[74] He cites the hedonistic paradox which is the reiteration of the belief that "even the most unselfish act may produce a psychological reward for the actor."[75] His position rests upon the lack of evidence for a constancy of affect-intensity across all cultures. If one views affect as a socially developed construct, cultures will manifest different amounts of it. This is true because

---

72. Eckstein, *Altruism, Sympathy, and Helping*, pp. 167-168.
73. Albert Bandura, *Social Learning Theory* (Englewood Cliffs, N.J.: Prentice-Hall, 1977).
74. Ronald Cohen, "Altruism: Human, Cultural, or What?" in *Altruism, Sympathy, and Helping*, ed. Lauren Wispé (New York: Academic Press, 1978), p. 82.
75. Ibid., pp. 82-83.

some groups will simply not value a significant degree of emotional investment in another person. Specifically, Cohen believes that Western notions of sympathy and empathy don't make much sense in cultures that are technologically underdeveloped and suggests that empathy is a feature of modernization.[76]

Altruistic Motivation of Religious Compassion

One of the primary advocates for the notion that motivation can be altruistic is C. Daniel Batson.[77][78] Batson now has a two-decade history of seminal, creative research efforts that have addressed the question of egoism versus altruism. In supporting the notion of altruistic motivation, Batson described a model that compares and contrasts egoistic and empathically induced altruistic motivation for helping. His conception of motivation assumes "that empathic emotion can evoke motivation directed toward the ultimate goal of reducing the others' need."[79]

The empathy-altruism hypothesis is based on the assumption that the magnitude of altruistic motivation is a direct function of the magnitude of empathic emotion. While reducing another's distress also brings intrinsic and extrinsic rewards, feeling empathy for the recipient motivates one to help as an end in itself. The decision to help someone in need is a deliberation involving relative-benefit analysis while the actor is simultaneously experiencing powerful conflicting motives. The actor experiences motives evoked by the perception of the one in need and hence shares the recipient's pain and suffering. Simultaneously, she/he also experiences motives to avoid the pain and suffering; to refrain from becoming involved or possibly risking one's personal safety. Batson indicates that "as a general principle, if more than one motive exists, and if a given behavior can reach the goal of one of these motives but not others, then failure to obtain the incompatible goals is the cost associated

---

76. Ibid., p. 83.

77. C. Daniel Batson and Rebecca Gray, "Religious Orientation and Helping Behavior: Responding to One's Own or to the Victim's Needs?" *Journal of Personality and Social Psychology* 40 (1981), pp. 511-520.

78. C. Daniel Batson, *The Altruism Question*, pp. 86-87.

79. C. Daniel Batson and Janine D. Flory, "Goal-Relevant Cognitions Associated with Helping by Individuals High on Intringic, End Religion," *Journal of Scientific Studies of Religion* 29:3 (September, 1990), pp. 346-360.

with this behavior. The magnitude of the cost will be a function of the magnitude of the motivational force to reach the unobtained goals."[80]

Helping will occur if (a) helping is possible, (b) the relative benefit of helping is perceived to be positive, and (c) the relative benefit of helping is perceived to be more positive than the relative benefit of having someone else help.[81] If the relative benefits of helping are perceived to be negative, then help will not be rendered. Consequently, the altruistic helper will experience a state of cognitive dissonance which may be resolved by denying that the other was really in need or by rationalizing that the person didn't merit the help. Since these behaviors preclude goal attainment the empathic/sympathetic bond will be broken and altruistic motivation for helping will attenuate.

Religious Compassion and Religiousness

As I suggested earlier, the proper sentiment and motivation should eventuate in helping behavior. However, religious persons don't always help those in need. This is the central issue that we must consider as I examine the role of religious sentiment and religious orientation in its relation to compassion.[82]

Compassion in any social context is laudable; however, religion has historically "owned" compassion as a core construct. Certainly many religions have long traditions that relate to helping the "weary and heavy-laden." There is also evidence from self-reports of religious individuals indicating that they are more responsive to the needs of

---

80. Batson, *Advances in Experimental Social Psychology*, p. 103.

81. Ibid., p. 95.

82. I use sentiment to mean one's outlook on life or a system of beliefs. Gordon Allport offered an excellent definition: "a disposition, built up through experience, to respond favorably, and in certain habitual ways, to conceptualize objects and principles that the individual regards as of ultimate importance in his own life, and as having to do with what he regards as permanent or central in the nature of things." Sentiment can be manifested at various developmental levels; it can be incipient or mature, and it may vary in its consistency. The exemplar of an absolutely consistent religious sentiment is the "religious genius," Christ. Religious orientation refers to how people are religious; the ways in which people most consistently express their religiousness. Religious orientation is considered to be indicative of one's religious sentiment. Gordon Allport, *The Individual and His Religion* (New York: Macmillan, 1956).

others than are the nonreligious. C. Daniel Batson and Rebecca Gray report the findings of a 1973 Gallup Poll in which 58.7 percent of the 526 respondents who reported having attended church in the previous seven days said that they almost always took concrete action on behalf of others whereas only 31.4 percent of the 862 nonattenders said that they did.[83]

Other writers have been somewhat more critical of the concept of "Christian compassion." Milton Rokeach indicated that while Christianity taught love and charity, his data from a national survey did not support the claim that Christians valued being loving or helpful more than did non-Christians.[84] Nor did he find evidence that being loving and helpful are distinctively Christian values. C. Daniel Batson and W. Larry Ventis reviewed thirteen studies that examined whether the faithful practice what they preach.[85] Eight of the studies employed either self-reports or other's ratings of the respondents' helping as outcome measures. These studies support Batson and Gray's contentions regarding Christian helping, although the relationship between religious involvement and helping was weak. "The more religious are seen both by themselves and others as valuing helpfulness more and as being somewhat more helpful."[86]

The last five studies controlled for social desirability (social desirability could affect self-reports of helpfulness since helpfulness is esteemed as a positive trait in our society) by using behavioral measures. The outcomes were quite different from those in the first group in that no evidence was found that the more religious would engage in more helping. An illustrative study measured religious involvement using self-reports of orthodoxy, frequency of prayer, frequency of church attendance, and the Religious Value score on the Allport, Vernon, and Lindzey Scale.[87] The willingness of uni-

---

83. Batson and Gray, "Religious Orientation and Helping Behavior," pp. 511-520.

84. Milton Rokeach, "Value Systems in Religion," in *Review of Religious Research* 11 (1969), pp. 24-39.

85. C. Daniel Batson and W. Larry Ventis, *The Religious Experience: A Social-Psychological Perspective* (New York: Oxford University Press, 1982).

86. Batson and Gray, "Religious Orientation and Helping Behavior," pp. 511-520.

87. Lawrence Annis, "Emerging Helping and Religious Behavior," *Psychological Reports* 37 (1976), pp. 717-718.

versity students to help a young woman, after hearing a ladder fall that could possibly have injured her, was examined. No reliable differences in the rate of helping as a result of any of the measures of religious involvement were obtained. The rate of helping, overall, was 48 percent.

To explain the compassionate behavior of religious individuals Batson,[88] following Gordon Allport, proposed a three-dimensional model of religiousness: religion as Means (extrinsic orientation), End (intrinsic orientation), and Quest (search for the meaning of life).[89] The extrinsically oriented person was characterized as one who adopts a pharisaical approach to religion and uses it in a strictly utilitarian way. Religion is "useful for the self in granting safety, social standing, solace, and endorsement for one's chosen way of life."[90]

In contrast, the intrinsically oriented person "lives his religion perceiving it as the master motive of life and an end in itself. . . . The intrinsic form of the religious sentiment regards faith as a supreme value in its own right. . . . A religious sentiment of this sort floods the whole life with motivation and meaning."[91] In Allport's later writings the positive description of the intrinsic believer, described as a "reflexive, critical, highly differentiated, sincere, humble person who thought for himself, who cared and who put his beliefs into action"[92] gave way to more negative formulations (quoted in Batson, "Religion as Prosocial: Agent or Double Agent?"). These included references to compulsive, conforming behavior and unquestioning acceptance of religious dogma. These conceptual changes left room for a new religious orientation (Quest) which Batson defined as "an endless process of probing and questioning by individuals generated by the tensions, contradictions, and tragedies in their own lives and in society. Not necessarily aligned with any formal religious institution or creed, they are continually raising ultimate

---

88. Batson, "Religion as Prosocial: Agent or Double Agent?" *Journal for the Scientific Study of Religion* 15 (1976), pp. 29-45.

89. Gordon Allport, "Religious Context of Prejudice," *Journal for the Scientific Study of Religion* 55 (1966), pp. 447-457.

90. Ibid., p. 447 f.

91. Ibid., p. 455.

92. Richard Hunt and Morton King, "The Intrinsic-Extrinsic Concept," *Journal for the Scientific Study of Religion* 10 (1971), pp. 339-356.

"whys" both about the existing social structure and about the structures of life itself."[93]

To operationalize the three religious orientation constructs, Batson adapted and/or developed six scales: (1) the Intrinsic Scale and (2) the Extrinsic Scale (both from Allport's Religious Orientation Scale), (3) the External Scale, (4) the Internal Scale, (5) the Interactional Scale (all from the Religious Life Inventory), and (6) the Doctrinal Orthodoxy Scale (a measure of one's agreement with traditional Christian Doctrines). He hypothesized that these scales would form a three-dimensional measure of religious orientation: Religion as Means to other ends (Extrinsic and External Scales), religion as an end in itself (Internal and Doctrinal Orthodoxy scales), and religion as Quest (Interactional scale). Batson conducted two, now classic, studies to determine the validity of his scale.

In the first study, euphemistically entitled "From Jerusalem to Jericho,"[94] sixty-seven seminary students completed the religious orientation measure. Subsequently, as they left the testing lab, forty of the seminarians were confronted with a shabbily dressed, coughing and groaning young man who appeared to need help. The outcome of the study was, would the seminarians help and, if so, what kind of help would be offered? Twenty-four of the students (60 percent) did not view the distressed young man as their "neighbor" as just sixteen offered to assist him. Nor was one's religious orientation relevant as it did not predict who would aid the victim. The only significant predictor was a situational variable, whether or not the seminarian was in a hurry.

A significant finding was that the helpers who scored high on the Quest dimension offered help more tentatively than those who scored high on the End (intrinsic) orientation. The latter individuals were persistent in their offers of help often ignoring the protestations of the "victim." John Darley and C. Daniel Batson suggested that this persistent style of helping was directed more to resolving the helper's internal need, while the Quest orientation was more responsive to the victim's statement of need and "more open to the victims definitions of his own needs."[95] The "Questors" were more truly compassionate.

---

93. Batson, "Religion as Prosocial: Agent or Double Agent?"
94. Darley and Batson, "From Jerusalem to Jericho," pp. 100-108.
95. Ibid., p. 107.

In another study Batson surveyed fifteen male university under-graduates involved in campus organizations with different religious orientations—the evangelicals (scoring high on the End dimension) and the social science group (scoring high on the Quest dimension). The goal of the study was to "assess the degree to which they were willing to accept the expressed need of a person seeking help as the person's true need."[96] Subjects adopted the role of a lay referral counselor in a volunteer referral agency. They read and heard information about their "clients" and subsequently completed referral recommendations. On the referral forms they indicated what they considered to be the locus of the client's problem, internal to the client or situational. The Quest dimension was found to relate more highly to a situational perception of the source of the client's problem and to the client's perception of the problem than did the End dimension.

Another study measured racial prejudice via a questionnaire and then in a situation where responses had clear behavioral consequences.[97] Findings suggested that the End dimension might be associated with a desire to be seen as concerned about the welfare of another, whereas the Quest dimension was associated with a rejection of prejudice, and, hence, reflects a genuine sense of respect, tolerance, and compassion for others.

Batson and Gray further examined whether being religious leads a person to be more responsive to another's needs.[98] They tested two hypotheses: (1) helping associated with the End dimension is motivated by an internal need to help, and (2) helping associated with the Quest dimension is motivated by the desire to relieve the expressed needs of the victim. Somewhat similar to the "Good Samaritan" paradigm, sixty female undergraduates were confronted by a lonely young woman who stated that she either did or did not desire help. Also the young woman's degree of social appropriateness was varied. In one condition she stated that she dealt with her problems by praying (high social appropriateness), in the other

---

96. Batson, "Sociobiology and the Role of Religion," pp. 1380-1385.

97. C. Daniel Batson, Stephen Naifeh, and Suzanne Pate, "Social Desirability, Religious Orientation, and Racial Prejudice," *Journal for the Scientific Study of Religion* 17:1 (1978), pp. 31-41.

98. Batson and Gray, "Religious Orientation and Helping Behavior," pp. 511-520.

condition, by drinking (low social appropriateness). This study was somewhat unique in that the young woman and the subjects never saw each other. All communication and, hence, offers to help or a failure to offer help, was written. Consistent with the first hypothesis, the End dimension was related to offers of help whether or not the "victim" desired it. The Quest dimension related positively to offers of help when desired but related negatively when it was not desired.

To examine whether religious prosocial motivation is altruistic or egoistic, Batson and Janine Flory identified possible egoistic goals of motivation: social and self rewards for living up to one's high prosocial standards, and avoiding shame and guilt for failing to live up to these standards.[99] In order to distinguish between altruistic and egoistic motivation, two techniques were employed. In the first study, university students learned of the plight of a seven-year-old boy (Billy) who had a rare genetic disease. Treatment for the disease was described as costly and the family was indigent. The subjects were then told of an opportunity to participate in a walkathon to help raise money for Billy. The only qualification was that they must pass a physical fitness screening task which was described as either "moderately stringent" or "extremely stringent." Subjects then decided whether or not to volunteer for the walkathon, chose the number of miles they would walk (five to twenty miles), performed the qualifying task, and completed Batson's three-dimensional measure of religious orientation. The effort the potential helper expended on the qualifying task provided the basis for inferring whether she/he was altruistically motivated to reduce the recipient's suffering or egoistically motivated to avoid guilt and enhance self-esteem. (Batson and Flory indicated that the qualifying standard must be difficult enough so failure could be attributed to the task and not to lack of effort.)

Results of this study were congruent with the studies just reviewed in that the Means (extrinsic) orientation was associated with decreased prosocial motivation. For these subjects Billy might be ill, but they had better things to do. Those manifesting the End (intrinsic) orientation agreed to help *only* when their likelihood of having to help was slight. This outcome suggests that their true motiva-

---

99. Batson and Flory, "Goal-Relevant Cognitions," pp. 346-360.

tion was a desire to "reap the self benefits of appearing helpful without having to follow through."[100] For all subjects the Quest orientation was unrelated to helping, suggesting no change in the level of prosocial motivation. Yet, when the responses of those in the easy versus difficult helping standard were separated, the Quest orientation was positively related to performance on the qualifying task. These subjects were willing to help Billy even if the cost to themselves was high. This behavior suggests an altruistic versus an egocentric goal.

Synthesis and Final Thoughts

The studies previously reviewed suggest that there is a moderate, but significant relationship between compassion and religious belief. However, the way in which one is religious is the *key* to understanding how religious belief might motivate compassionate behavior. The implication is that the End (intrinsic orientation) may present a facade of the "true believer," a belief in brotherhood, and a high moral image. However, this image may not reflect a selfless concern for others, nor does it appear to increase altruistic motivation to help. The essential motivation appears to be "a self-centered desire to obtain social or self-reward for being a good person."[101] In contrast, the Quest orientation seems to be the source of altruistic motivation for care and compassion as it is associated with increased brotherly love. As Batson and Ventis indicate, "A Quest orientation to religion is related to reduced intolerance and increased sensitivity to the needs of others."[102]

The outcomes of these studies also confirm that there is a sociocultural component in religion that has a powerful psychological and social impact on its adherents. Most religions embrace the virtues of compassion, care, and concern and institutionalize these values in a variety of ways: support for missions, church charities, social outreach projects, and sponsoring homes for abandoned children and abused mothers. These acts are obviously meritorious and (arguably) whether individuals contributing to these efforts do so out of compassion or out of desire for social or self-rewards is irrelevant. Good

---

100. Ibid., p. 358.
101. Batson and Gray, pp. 518-519.
102. Batson and Ventis, p. 297.

deeds *are* done and the mission of the religious body is carried forward.

I have previously suggested that accounting for compassionate behavior is an enigma for the behavioral sciences. Similarly, behaving in compassionate ways also may be perplexing to many who view themselves as religious. This is so since many biblical teachings are "outrageous." In the New Testament Christ enjoined his followers to "love your enemies, bless them that curse you, do good to them that hate you and pray for them which despitefully use you and persecute you. That ye may be the children of your father which is in heaven" (Mt 5:44-45). This is an audacious request, for it articulates a moral and ethical standard that is lofty and challenging. If one is ultimately self-seeking, behaving compassionately makes little sense interpersonally, socially, or legally. Sharing compassion, then, might not always be perceived as rational and exemplary, for these actions often transcend ordinary social bonds of personal obligation and reciprocity.

Another significant issue concerns the role of religion in promoting compassionate behavior. Donald Campbell suggested that there is little evidence for innate altruistic impulses in humans. In his experience the primary causal variable that accounts for human prosocial behavior is social evolution. "Social evolution has had to counter individual selfish tendencies which biological evolution has continued to select as a result of the genetic competition among the cooperators."[103] To Campbell the role of religion in society is both necessary and constructive. He felt that religion and religious functions, particularly religious preaching, indoctrination, and moralizing are powerful forces to shift personal egocentric goals toward the "prosocial goals that are necessary to perpetuate society."[104]

Batson[105] also found a key role for religious variables but in a way that was quite different from Campbell. Batson is primarily interested in the kinship images of religion, not in religious declarations and preachments. Batson suggests that "there is a genetic pre-

---

103. Donald Campbell, "On the Conflicts Between Biological and Social Evolution and Between Psychology and Moral Tradition," *American Psychologist,* 30 (1975), pp. 1103-1126.
104. Ibid.
105. Batson, "Sociobiology and the Role of Religion," pp. 1380-1385.

disposition to respond to the distress of others, especially close kin, with empathic emotion (feelings of sympathy, compassion, soft-heartedness, warmth, etc.) . . . [and] . . . empathic emotion can evoke altruistic motivation, motivation directed toward the end state goal of seeing the other's distress reduced."[106] If humans do possess a kin-specific altruistic impulse mediated by empathic emotion, then parents should empathize with children, children with siblings, etc. However, once the limits of this immediate empathy which is based on kin-specific relationships are exceeded, no larger social bond is felt. There is, then, no reason to respond altruistically to others. However, the role of religion becomes paramount in answering the question "who is my brother?" For, religion can broadly extend the range of applications to transcend the narrow kin-specific impulse. This broadening could take place in the form of "kinship imagery." The teaching of the brotherhood of man and God as the Father of us all may function to build "cognitive bridges, encouraging an . . . altruistic response to people not included among those close kin to whom we are innately predisposed to respond altruistically."[107]

A related issue concerns distinguishing between institutional versus individual religious compassion (see following chapter). It is a paradox that of the three religious orientations, the End (intrinsic) orientation is the most closely associated with high involvement in institutional religion[108] and in helping others by contributing to these institutions.[109] However, these intrinsically motivated individuals do not individually portray truly compassionate attitudes in that oftentimes their motives are self-serving. They seek to enhance social status and the appearance of doing good, while simultaneously attempting to reduce guilt. In contrast those high on the Quest dimension would appear to be idealistic exemplars of Christ's admonitions to the faithful. They are truly "seekers of the truth," but they also tend to be less involved in organized religion.

---

106. Ibid, p. 1383.

107. Ibid., p. 1384.

108. Richard Gorsuch and Sam McFarland, "Single vs. Multiple-Item Scales," *Journal for the Scientific Study of Religion* 11:1 (March, 1972), pp. 53-64.

109. Larry Nelson and Russell Dynes, "The Impact of Devotionalism and Attendance on Ordinary and Emergency Helping Behavior," *Journal for the Scientific Study of Religion* 15:1 (March, 1976), pp. 47-59.

Indeed, many do not affiliate with organized religion at all.[110]

Although the motivation of the intrinsically religious does not appear to be truly compassionate, there is no doubt that the needs of society are often dealt with at an institutional level. Thus the intrinsically religious, even though their ultimate concern might be to appear virtuous in society, are able to participate in the compassionate activities of the institution. Those individuals high on the Quest orientation while being more "pure" in motives might refrain from institutional involvement and thus fail to participate in compassionate behavior on a broader level. However, on a personal level their motivation and behavior more nearly meet our criteria for compassionate behavior.

It is not feasible to effectively evaluate the claims of the individuals manifesting the respective religious orientations, since the extent of the ultimate good promulgated by those high on the Quest orientation versus those manifesting the End orientation cannot be precisely determined. One might argue that the behavior of the "Questors" is more responsive to the message of the New Testament. Perhaps these individuals are also more intrapsychically congruent, experience a greater degree of personality integration, and, hence, might be in a better state of mental health.

A final point concerns the efficacy of altruistic motivation in promoting and maintaining compassionate behavior. From the studies reviewed in this chapter, it is clear that even in laboratory settings altruistic-based motivation seems to be quite fragile. Both the rate of helping behavior and the nature of the motivation are rather easily decreased or modified by simple strategies such as (1) reflecting on the reasons for helping,[111] (2) suggesting that the actor may experience some significant discomfort,[112] (3) whether the potential helper is in a hurry,[113] or (4) whether the potential helper is suffi-

---

110. Batson and Ventis, *A Social-Psychological Perspective*, pp. 293-294.

111. C. Daniel Batson, James Fultz, Patricia Schoenrade, and Anthony Paduano, "Critical Self-Reflection and Self-Perceived Altruism: When Self-Reward Fails," *Journal of Personality and Social Psychology* 53 (1987), pp. 594-602.

112. C. Daniel Batson, Karen O'Quin, James Fultz, Mary Vanderplas, and Alice Isen, "Self-Reported Distress and Empathy and Egoistic Versus Altruistic Motivation for Helping," *Journal of Personality and Social Psychology* 45 (1983), pp. 706-718.

113. Darley and Batson, "From Jerusalem to Jericho," pp. 100-108.

ciently aroused by the need state of the one in distress.[114] From a social psychological perspective, compassion is not the passionate, powerful disposition described by Wendy Farley earlier in this chapter. Rather it is a tentative, incipient, perhaps universal, behavioral tendency that requires a great deal of nurturance to come to fruition. Certainly the writings of Carl Rogers and Robert Coles suggest that there is an innate empathic sensitivity in all people which will manifest itself if appropriate nurturing conditions are provided. Compassionate behavior is more likely to occur in settings in which compassion is articulated, modeled, reinforced, and cherished; hence, the importance of institutional religion and its positive stance toward helping others. One powerful function of institutional religion is to articulate the plight of those in need so that the religiously committed are first of all aware of these needs and, second, responsive to the organizational attempts to assist those in need.

Considering the tenuous nature of the motivation for helping others, perhaps religious compassion *is* somewhat of a miracle. Certainly in contemporary life, "true" compassion is a statistical improbability. For the recipients of this compassionate sharing, it is a bit of the Godlike being injected into a world that is dying for the lack of compassion. If this is so, perhaps a bit of humility is in order. Perhaps each of us should recommit ourselves to the personal, and institutional, sharing of compassion with the strangers among us.

---

114. Batson, *The Altruism Question*, p. 216.

4

The Sociology of Religious
Compassion

DONALD RATCLIFF

When one considers the matter of religious compassion, particularly from within a Judeo-Christian reference, it is not the presence of compassion that should cause surprise. Indeed, the Bible is
filled with examples of what should be the norm: self sacrifice for
others, particularly those in need. What should surprise and concern
us most is the *absence* of religious compassion, both individually
and corporately.

For example, one missionary agency I am familiar with gives its
missionaries a salary of about $6000 a year, but those impoverished
missionaries must raise more than twice that amount. The balance
pays for administrative costs. One of the administrative costs is support of the director and his wife, which totals over $50,000 each
year (plus free housing and use of an automobile), yet the director
and his wife are not required to raise their own support. Clearly,
this indicates a lack of compassion for the missionaries in the organization, and even less for the nationals associated with the organization, who are fortunate if they make half the missionary's salary.

While this extreme is hopefully rare among Christians, recent
revelations of exorbitant incomes for certain television evangelists
suggest that it may be more common than some may think. Funds

95

may be raised for compassionate causes, but if the cause is not carefully specified by the giver money may in fact go to pay for the lux-
urious lifestyle of the evangelist or his cohorts. How can people
prosper from money raised for compassionate causes? How can
people support TV evangelists, denominations, and parachurch
groups if only a fraction of the funds gets to the real need? How can
such organizations continue?

More common than these extremes, undoubtedly, would be a
general lack of compassionate efforts by individual religious people.
While religious giving is on the rise, less than half of all funds are
used for social programs.[1] Surveys of Christians by the American
Resource Bureau and the Gallup organization indicate that 70 percent are inclined toward hedonistic attitudes, 30 percent feel happiness and fun are the most important things in life, 20 percent
give nothing to the church, and only one in three tithe.[2] Yet 20 percent of church people believe there is too much emphasis upon
money in the church.[3] While a majority of religious individuals may
support certain compassionate efforts, it should concern us that a
significant minority do not, particularly when the compassionate
efforts involve federal programs (perhaps this implies a distrust of
government as much as a lack of compassion). For example, Gallup
polls[4] indicate that about 40 percent of Protestants (and 30 percent of Catholics) do not favor the government providing food and
shelter for the homeless and hungry. The polls also indicate that
about one-fourth of religious people do not feel the government has
a duty to help those who are not able to help themselves (there is no
significant difference between Catholics and Protestants on this
issue). Other Gallup polls[5] indicate that over 20 percent of the religious do not believe those suffering with AIDS should be treated with
compassion (there are no major differences between Catholics,
evangelicals, and non-evangelicals on this), a large majority do not

---

1. "Religious Giving on the Rise," *Christianity Today* 33 (September, 1989), p.
52.
2. George Barna and William McKay, *Vital Signs* (Westchester, Ill.: Crossway
Books, 1984), pp. 112, 141.
3. George Gallup and Jim Costelli, *The People's Religion* (New York: Macmillan,
1989), p. 255.
4. George Gallup and Sarah Jones, *100 Questions and Answers:* Religion in
America (Princeton, N.J.: Princeton Religion Research Center, 1989), 157.
5. Gallup & Costelli, *The People's Religion*, pp. 192-203.

favor increased aid for the unemployed or more programs for minorities, and about one-third do not favor increased funding to fight drug addiction. Thus there seems to be a definite lack of compassion among many Christians, both individually and corporately through governmental efforts.

From a sociological perspective, then, the concern is to isolate those social forces that work *against* compassion and hopefully minimize or eliminate them. Four sociological theories will help organize the search for the sociological foundations of religious compassion, theories that to a greater or lesser extent comprise the basis for nearly all sociological research and understanding at present. These four perspectives, functionalism, conflict theory, exchange theory, and symbolic interactionism, can be interfaced with religious concerns[6] and can significantly contribute to understanding why religious compassion does not occur more frequently. Following a survey of the theories and how they relate to religious compassion, particularly the lack of compassion, some specific sociological topics will be considered as they relate to religious compassion.

Functionalism

This first theory in sociology emphasizes that each system of society exists because it helps society *function* in a productive manner. Thus an educational system is functional when it adequately educates, an economic system is functional when it serves the economic needs of a society, and so on. When not functional a social system either changes or disappears, functionalism assumes.[7] Functionalist theory has much in common with biological adaptation theories, suggesting that systems emerge, change, or disappear to maintain equilibrium or balance in the body (biology), in nature (ecology) or in society (sociology). There is also correspondence between the equilibrium emphasized by Piagetian psychology and the present sociological theory.

While functionalism has received negative reviews from certain

---

6. Donald Ratcliff, "Creation, Redemption and Sociological Theory," *Creation Social Science and Humanities Quarterly* 10 (Summer, 1988), pp. 14-20.

7. Julian Bridges, "Origins, Development and Theories," *Sociology: A Pragmatic Approach*, 3rd ed. (Winston-Salem, N.C.: Hunter, 1986), pp. 21-22.

Christians,[8][9] the author of perhaps the finest source on the sociology of religious institutions[10] makes excellent use of this theory in explaining how organizations originate, mature, and deteriorate.

Drawing upon substantial sociological research, David Moberg[11] outlines the life cycle of a church, which can also account for the development of parachurch and denominational organizations as well. According to Moberg's schema, religious organizations generally evolve through five stages, ending in disintegration and death of the organization, repetitions of the cycle, or the birth of a new organization from the ruins of the old. (This outline has been expanded by making use of the work of Jerry Bergman,[12] Thomas Hoult,[13] and Derek Tidball.[14])

The first stage is that of *incipient organization*. This stage is generally accompanied by excitement and unrest. The social uneasiness may be due to a crisis and subsequent departure from an existing group, while the excitement often results in emotional expressions by participants. During the organization stage, people become aware of a specific need or needs (the *functional base*) that is/are not being satisfactorily met by other organizations. Thus the group forms and begins to meet.

Within a short time, leaders begin to emerge and the religious group becomes a *formal organization*. The group, now clearly separate from other groups, can be joined by those who formally commit themselves to it. It is at this point that a creed or "statement of faith" is most likely to be developed, and patterns, rules, and planning begin to predominate. This second stage is also marked by the beginning of *conservation*, which refers to efforts made to keep the organization going. People are interested not only in having

---

8. David Scaer, "Functionalism Fails the Test of Orthodoxy," *Christianity Today* 26 (February, 1982), p. 90.

9. Barry Hancock, "Christianity and Functionalism: The Paradox," *Journal of the American Scientific Affiliation* 35 (March, 1983), pp. 20-25.

10. David Moberg, *The Church as a Social Institution*, 2nd ed. (Grand Rapids, Mich.: Baker, 1984), p. 157.

11. Ibid., pp. 118-124.

12. Jerry Bergman, "The Sociology of Religious Organizations," *Journal of the American Scientific Affiliation* 39 (June, 1987), pp. 94-104.

13. Tom Hoult, *Sociology for a New Day*, 2nd ed. (New York: Random House, 1979), pp. 75-76..

14. Derek Tidball, *The Social Context of the New Testament* (Grand Rapids, Mich.: Academie, 1984), pp. 123-136.

their needs met (the functional base), but also give consideration to meeting the needs of the organization (conservation).

By the third stage, which emphasizes *maximum efficiency*, there is less emotional display and more dominance by leaders who emphasize rationality. Positive public opinion is cultivated and hostility toward other groups (if any) diminishes. There is a greater specialization of roles in the group, with boards, committees, and hierarchy becoming more prominent. The patterns of activity and communication become more rigid in the process, as the organization seeks maximal efficiency in how it deals with issues related to the functional base and conservation efforts. The latter significantly increases.

During the first three stages the organization is perhaps best conceptualized as growing, both in terms of vitality and usually numerically. The fourth stage, designated *institutionalization*, begins the process of decline. The leadership becomes more oriented toward its own concerns at this point, so that conservation is excessive. In other words, decisions made tend to be "for the sake of the organization" beyond what is really needed to survive. Even though members may talk about the functional base, actions are clearly more oriented toward self-perpetuation of the organization. The institution now becomes the master rather than the servant. Intimacy declines, with leaders increasingly becoming out of touch with the general membership.

Many, perhaps most, churches appear to be at this stage as indicated by the disproportionate funding of compassionate and self-serving measures. For example, churches spend less than 20 percent of the total church income for benevolences, an amount equal to that raised for new church buildings alone.[15]

The final stage, *disintegration*, is marked by corruption, obsolescence, red tape, and indifference. Members tend to only half-heartedly lend their support and many leave, while leaders and members who are emotionally attached to the organization do their best to preserve it. Perhaps the most important development at this stage is the birth of *dysfunction*, things done for the purpose of conservation that undercut the original functional base. For example,

---

15. Constant Jacquet, *Yearbook of American and Canadian Churches* (Nashville: Abingdon, 1989), pp. 258-260, 280.

a school at this stage might promote a good teacher to an administrative position so that she can raise funds (conservation), yet because of that promotion the overall quality of teaching (the functional base) deteriorates either because the replacement is inferior or because there is no replacement of the good teacher.

It is important to note that the fifth stage does not always spell an end to the organization. For example, there are governmental programs that are clearly at this stage of development but because of continued funding they are perpetuated. There is reportedly a church in the Atlanta area that no longer holds services or makes any other contribution to society but continues to exist because of a healthy endowment! Conservation may continue long after the functional base is lost.

Are the stages inevitable? Moberg states that it is possible to arrest an organization at one of the more productive stages, a sort of sociological "fixation."[16] The time period involved for the stages may involve hundreds of years or a much shorter timetable. I have seen religious groups that passed through all five stages inside a year, although Moberg believes that it usually takes at least a generation for the process to be completed. The process may also be reversed, or an organization may go through repeated cycles of different stages.

Implications for Religious Compassion

While Moberg's stages succinctly outline the development of many religious and other organizations, what specific implications can be drawn for religious compassion? Clearly compassion can be part of, or in some cases the entirety of, the functional base for a religious organization. Thus in the last two stages compassion becomes less and less likely, as concern for the organization is more predominant.

Concern for compassion can become lost in the bureaucracy of religious organizations. Here I am not only speaking of denominational structures but also tiny organizations and smaller local churches can become more structured than necessary. In many cases compassion becomes secondary to survival, even though many of the efforts for survival are clearly not required. The excessive

---

16. Moberg, *The Church as a Social Institution*, p. 123.

income for a bureaucrat becomes "necessary" so that he will not leave the organization (or because he is in control) to the exclusion of funds for compassionate causes for which the organization was founded.

What are the hopes for a sociological "fixation" or "regression" in a religious organization, so that the functional base of compassion is maximal? My experience suggests that this is often a difficult and painful process. Resisting the natural inclination toward surplus conservation and dysfunction is most likely if leaders realize the often debilitative results of bureaucratization, while regression may only occur if there is the likelihood of the organization being curtailed.

Some churches negatively react to the presence of parachurch organizations that function for the purposes of channeling funds for religious compassion. While such organizations certainly must not be naively accepted, as the Jim Bakker fiasco clearly indicates, the presence of such parachurch groups can also serve as a warning that the church organization may have progressed too far through the stages, or perhaps when religious compassion has not fully been incorporated into the organization's functional base. In some cases excessive bureaucratization may require that a program be dropped in favor of funding an outside agency that has that particular aspect of religious compassion as its functional base. Sometimes another branch of a church or denominational bureaucracy may be able to more efficiently deal with the specific area. On the other hand, rarely does the addition of more bureaucracy work to serve the functional base, at least in the long run.

Conflict Theory

This second major theory of sociology emphasizes conflict, disorder, and instability in society.[17] Conflict theory is the dominant perspective of most third-world sociologists and is popular among Western sociologists as well. These theorists disagree with the functionalist assumption that social systems are generally marked by being functional; the unity and functional aspects are illusory since

---

17. James M. Henslin, *Sociology: A Down to Earth Approach.* (Boston: Allyn & Bacon, 1993), pp. 23-24.

social systems make use of coercion by people with power and wealth. Those who have the power and wealth impose their will upon the impoverished and powerless, using the economic system, politics, education, religion, and other social structures to oppress the have-nots of society. Thus elite groups in society exploit and control the masses.[18]

While conflict theory obviously has its roots in the work of Karl Marx, many sociologists who hold to this theory are not considered Marxist; they are concerned about aspects of society other than just economics. For example, conflict theory sociologists often emphasize racial inequality, gender inequality, ageism, and many other issues. In each case conflict theories maintain that conflicts exist because a significant number of individuals are not given the rights due them by those in powerful positions or by society at large. (Sometimes conflict theorists are concerned with conflict in general, apart from rights and inequality.)

An assumption made by conflict theorists is that resources required by people are scarce, and thus when one person gains power and wealth, others must correspondingly lose in one of these areas.[19] In addition they assume that the stratification of people (e.g., classes in Western culture) works to the detriment for most (an assumption disputed by George Gilder). In sum, conflict theorists are concerned with power acquisition, how power is used to dominate certain groups of people, and the results of the unequal distribution of resources.[20]

While some writers[21] have emphasized how conflict theory is oppositional to functionalist theory, and the case made for that position is plausible, it is also possible to see them as complementary theories. Society's structures are marked not only by function, but also dysfunction; there is often a combination of stability and conflict in our social arrangements.

---

18. Richard Wallace and Wendy Wallace, *Sociology,* 2nd ed. (Boston: Allyn and Bacon, 1989), pp. 7-8, 10.

19. George Gilder, "The Dirge of Triumph," in *Taking Sides: Clashing Views on Controversial Social Issues,* ed. Kurt Finsterbusch and George McKenna (Guilford, Conn.: Dushkin, 1984).

20. Henslin, *Sociology: A Down to Earth Approach,* pp. 23-24.

21. Stan Gaede, "Functionalism and Conflict Theory in Christian Perspective," in *A Reader in Sociology: Christian Perspectives,* ed. Charles DeSanto (Scottdale, Pa.: Herald Press, 1980), pp. 184-186.

Implications for Religious Compassion

The conflict theory is clearly related to the topic of religious compassion. Conflict theorists, and their Marxist predecessors, observe how religion often has been noncompassionate. History includes many accounts of violence and oppression by leaders who espoused religious faith, sometimes using religion to force their will upon the masses.

Yet those accounts are clearly incomplete without acknowledging the many times that religion has fostered compassion personally and socially. One must be impressed with the compassion of a Mother Teresa and, from a very different tradition, the institutionalized compassion of the Salvation Army.

Indeed there may be considerable common ground for conflict theorists and those who hold to religious faith, as evidenced by liberation theology. A number of evangelical Christians also see value in the conflict theory perspective, including Lowell Noble[22] and well-known speaker/sociologist Anthony Campolo[23] (see his comments on Marxism and liberation theology in Campolo, *Partly Right*, for example).

The emphasis by conflict theorists upon the evils of oppression and inequality generally has the goal of rectifying such problems. This goal is compassionate by its very nature. That is not to conclude that every suggestion made by conflict theorists has ended in compassionate responses, but at least their desire to change things for the better is implicitly compassionate.

Conflict theory and the research it has engendered have provided ample documentation of what theologians term the "sin nature," the self-serving and basically selfish bent of humankind.[24] Psychologists such as O. Hobart Mowrer[25] and Karl Menninger[26] have emphasized in a productive manner both the personal and social aspects of sin from a nonreligious vantage point. Many of us lack compassion because we are not the way we are meant to be, a fundamental assumption in most religions. Conflict theory

---

22. Lowell Noble, *Sociotheology* (Jackson, Miss.: Voice of Calvary, 1987), pp. 21-28, 102.

23. Anthony Campolo, *Partly Right* (Dallas, Tex.: Jarrell, 1985), pp. 145-158.

24. Ratcliff, "Creation, Redemption and Sociological Theory," pp. 14-20.

25. O. Hobart Mowrer, *Abnormal Reactions or Actions?* (Dubuque, Iowa: William C. Brown, 1966).

26. Karl Menninger, *Whatever Became of Sin?* (New York: Hawthorn, 1973).

underscores the lack of compassion by many.

What is the solution to that lack of compassion? Here conflict theorists fall short; they suggest either reform or revolution, modifying present social structures or overturning them and starting fresh. Unfortunately neither of these options automatically results in compassion—the welfare state (an example of reform) may create servitude by fostering dependency, and a communist state (an example of revolution) may be very noncompassionate to those who dissent. Recent events in Eastern Europe and the former Soviet Union underscore the weakness of Marxian "solutions," as does the general worldwide trend away from socialism documented by John Naisbitt and Patricia Aburdene.[27]

In contrast, religion at its best can be most compassionate. The Old Testament emphasizes the need to take care of those who meet with misfortune, such as field owners leaving some grain for the needy to glean and the provision of no-interest loans for the poor. Some of the strongest statements in the Bible are the prophets condemning the wealthy that oppress the poor and Christ confronting religious leaders who cheated the masses by unfair money exchange. Likewise in the New Testament, James (1:27) states that true religion involves caring for the widows and orphans. One of the best historical examples of religion bringing an end to oppression is the influence of the Wesleyan revival in the late 1700s upon the end of slavery in the early 1800s.[28] Perhaps it is fair to suggest that conflict theory can help in understanding why compassion is needed and where, religious faith can give insight into how to apply compassion and provide the motivation to do so.

Exchange Theory

While the first two sociological theories emphasize the larger scope of social relationships, interrelationships at a more personal level are emphasized by exchange theory and symbolic interactionism. Exchange theory describes the importance of rewards and

---

27. John Naisbitt and Patricia Aburdene, *Megatrends 2000* (New York: Morrow, 1990), pp. 93-117.

28. Edward Coleson, "The Real Liberation Theology," *Creation, Social Science and Humanities Quarterly* 8 (1985), pp. 13-14.

costs in relationships, attracting people to rewarding relationships and producing dislike for those who are punishing. Similarities in values and other social traits between people result in a mutually rewarding relationship and a validation of one's own opinions,[29] while these must be weighed against costs such as fatigue, conflicts, and alternative interactions that must be foregone.

Perhaps the finest summary of the theory to date is Clifford Swenson's *Interpersonal Relationships*[30] in which he underscores a basic formula of PROFITS = REWARDS - COSTS. At this point this theory has much in common with classical economics as well as behavioral psychology. It departs from these, however, by the emphasis upon the sense of justice implicit in interactions: if one receives a lot more than one gives in a relationship, guilt tends to result, while if one gives more than one receives, the individual feels cheated and possibly bitter, making an end to the relationship more likely. A balance between rewards and costs tends to be the most satisfactory, and profits should also be approximately equal for the two or more individuals involved. However, even with the orientation toward balance, there is also the drive to maximize rewards and minimize costs in a relationship.[31]

Some have criticized exchange theory because of its emphasis upon self-interest and short-term rather than long-term consequences.[32] Many of these reactions have perhaps best been answered by psychologists defending behavioral psychology from similar criticisms (see Rodger Bufford[33] and Donald Ratcliff[34] for examples of such a defense from a Christian perspective). Whether we choose to ignore or attend to such factors, human nature is such that rewards and punishments do have a powerful effect upon behavior, a notion underscored repeatedly in the Bible. The biblical emphasis, in both the Old and New Testaments, is not merely rewards and punishments, but that we should cultivate behavior that leads to long-range rewards and eschew behavior that results in punish-

---

29. Wallace and Wallace, pp. 114-313.

30. Clifford Swenson, *Introduction to Interpersonal Relations* (Glenview, Ill.: Scott, Foresman, 1973), pp. 217-225.

31. Ibid.

32. Wallace and Wallace, *Sociology*, pp. 313.

33. Rodger Bufford, *The Human Reflex: Behavioral Psychology in Biblical Perspective* (San Francisco: Harper & Row, 1981), pp. 29-81.

34. Ratcliff, "Creation, Redemption, and Sociological Theory, pp. 21-25.

ment in the long run. Thus laws, such as the Ten Commandments, are a means of helping humans defer immediate gratification so as to gain long-term rewards such as stability and happiness as well as personal holiness.

Implications for Religious Compassion

Compassion of a religious or nonreligious nature would seem to fit into the costs category of exchange theory; compassion generally requires effort and often expense and/or time. Yet this is only part of the picture, as there are also rewards from compassion. Social psychologists such as David Myers often point to the relief from guilt resulting from compassion, which is a reward.[35]

Religious teaching has historically recognized that the gains from compassion are multiple in nature. First there is the concern with rewards in the next world from compassion in this one, such as Christ's statement in Matthew 10:42: "And whosoever shall give to drink unto one of these little ones a cup of cold water . . . shall in no wise lose his reward." Jesus clearly made compassion a matter of eternal destiny (Mt 25:31-46).

There are also rewards in this life from religious compassion. "Compassion," the child sponsorship program, encourages those being sponsored to pray for their supporters. Likewise the poor can teach the wealthy a great deal about the insufficiency of materialistic values. The latter was underscored to me while living in one of the poorest countries in the Western hemisphere some years ago. In the process of that experience, I learned that one can get by with a lot less than generally thought and be as happy and perhaps happier (perhaps I am a closet Franciscan!). While very few owned automobiles in my village, most everyone was in excellent physical condition from walking to and from, and working in the fields. Only two in the village of three thousand had a television, but the amateur dramatic enactments that were a regular part of church services were far more entertaining and beneficial.

Not only can the poor and unfortunate in this world teach us to reevaluate our values, but they can also help us reconsider the concept of profits. Clearly most people in the West are financially in bet-

---

35. David Myers, *Social Psychology*, 2nd ed. (New York: McGraw-Hill, 1987), pp. 467-468.

ter condition than the vast majority of the third world, but Westerners tend not to feel much guilt about this (exchange theory would predict guilt because of the inequality of profit) because the reference point for fairness is inadequate. Some television appeals may produce some guilt, but they are hardly equal to my experience of living in an impoverished country for a year. The reference point for most of us tends to be those with whom we circulate, while the level of aspiration tends to be those immediately above us on the social scale. We engage in "poortalk" in which we talk as if we are poor, when we are actually affluent in comparison with the rest of the world.[36] This poortalk causes us to be relatively insensitive to true poverty.

In essence what is needed is a new, more accurate reference point for individuals to be more motivated toward compassion. Rather than comparing ourselves with those around us and aspiring to the strata immediately above us, a world reference point is needed in which poverty is seen as the norm and our position perceived as privileged. This is perhaps more likely when one has spent time overseas, living shoulder to shoulder with those who are genuinely deprived. Consistent with exchange theory this is likely to produce a genuine guilt, hopefully encouraging sacrifice to equalize profits to a greater extent.

In specifically considering religious compassion, a transcendent reference point is appropriate. Traditional theology details the personal unworthiness of the individual, in contrast to the worthiness of the Divine. If unworthy, then a fair exchange would be to have nothing, a notion implicit in the New Testament Sermon on the Mount passage. God's forgiveness is thus a most extreme profit for us, motivating us to in turn give kindness and compassion toward others (to equalize our profits and theirs) so that their profit will likewise be positive.

Symbolic Interactionism

This fourth theory in sociology, more popular than exchange theory but less popular than either the functionalist or conflict theories, states that individuals make social constructions of reality.

---

36. Dawn Ward, "Social Stratification," in *Christian Perspectives on Sociology*, ed. Stephen Grunlan and Milton Reimer (Grand Rapids, Mich.: Zondervan, 1982), p. 120.

Interaction requires that people share definitions of themselves and their social situations, that individuals *confer* meaning to their experiences, and then that they act consistently with that interpretation of reality.[37] In this respect there is considerable overlap between this theory and both the philosophy of phenomenology and certain cognitive psychologies.

Symbolic interaction theory also emphasizes the importance of symbols in interpersonal relationships, and that symbolic meanings must be shared for communication to take place. Symbols may be either verbal or nonverbal (see James Lee for an excellent contrast between these kinds of content).[38]

Ratcliff[39] sees considerable merit in symbolic interactionism from a Christian perspective, particularly the variety espoused by David Karp and William Yoels.[40] Elsewhere he notes some reservations as well, such as the overemphasis upon human autonomy.[41] Yet this sociological theory correctly underscores the reality of human choice and the autonomy granted the human race by God, as well as the importance of constructing a worldview in synchrony with the world that genuinely exists.

Within the perspective of this theory, early sociologist George Herbert Mead described how people develop self-awareness. The symbolization process during interaction allows the individual to reflect upon himself and the social world within which he acts. This sometimes is developed through role-playing in childhood, thus symbolically representing the self in categories such as father, mother, or even princess or pest.[42]

Charles Cooley, another early sociologist, took this idea a step further by describing the now famous concept of the *looking-glass self*.[43] During the process of development, the child at first can imagine what one other person thinks of him, and thus he has the rudi-

37. David Karp and William Yoels, *Sociology and Everyday Life* (Itasca, Ill.: Peacock, 1986) pp. 9-24.

38. James Lee, *The Content of Religious Instruction* (Birmingham, Ala.: Religious Education Press, 1985).

39. Donald Ratcliff, "The Symbolic Interaction Theory of Karp and Yoels," *Newsletter of the Christian Sociological Society* 15 (1989), pp. 15-17.

40. Karp and Yoels, *Sociology and Everyday Life*, pp. 9-24.

41. Ratcliff, *Creation, Redemption, and Sociological Theory*," pp. 14-20.

42. Wallace and Wallace, *Sociology*, pp. 80-81.

43. Hoult, *Sociology for a New Day*, pp. 52-53.

ment of the self-concept. Eventually the child can imagine what a sibling or a friend thinks of him, and this broadens the self-concept a bit. Eventually the individual can imagine how several people and even society at large perceive him, which becomes more of a global concept of the self. What is most important, said Cooley, is that we take another person's perspective and then look back at ourselves from that perspective, and by doing this we develop a sense of self.

The result is that this self-construction occurs with the aid of others and their perceptions of us, but the construction is essentially self-made. This produces definite consequences. As the famous theorem of W.I. Thomas states, "If men *define* situations real, they *are* real in their consequences."[44] In other words, we react more to our created definitions of circumstances than we do to the actual circumstances.

Implications for Religious Compassion

Religious people generally define themselves as compassionate, in spite of behavior that others might not consider compassionate. How can this occur? Consistent with W.I. Thomas's theorem, it is because they define it as such. Thus a few coins in the offering plate or in the Salvation Army kettle confirms the self-created picture of a compassionate religious person. It is possible to be quite non-compassionate and simultaneously be convinced one is compassionate, as can be verified by even a cursory view of church history. According to the looking-glass self, the self-definition of being compassionate is most likely when others define you as compassionate.

How can one counteract that faulty self-definition? As noted earlier, experience overseas can help. In addition, examining models of genuine self-sacrifice can also provide a new perspective. Internalizing a new self-perception (what I am) and new values (what I should be) are fundamental to the religious enterprise and ideally should lead the person to reflection and reorientation. Religious groups should be involved in resocialization and the process of *re*creation of the self.[45]

---

44. Quoted in Rollo Tinkler, "Economic life," in *Sociology: A Pragmatic Approach,* ed. Julian Bridges, 3rd ed. (Winston-Salem, N.C.: Hunter, 1986), p. 201.

45. Robert McClusky, "Socialization," in *Christian Perspectives on Sociology,* ed. Stephen Grunlan and Milton Reimer (Grand Rapids, Mich.: Zondervan, 1982), p. 140.

Symbolic interaction theory emphasizes the importance of symbols during the interaction process. Symbols are referents; they refer to something other than themselves. The concepts in this chapter are referents and should not be confused with reality; for example social class, rewards and punishments, function and dysfunction, all of these are referents and thus constitute a pragmatic way of relating to reality; they are only a means to an end. Thus we use words such as "religious" and "compassion" and even "sociology" to refer to aspects of reality, and in the process these terms may very well modify our perception of reality. Acknowledging that these symbols are only referents implies that they can mean many things to many people (for example compassion may mean committing one's life to minister to the homeless for one person and picking up a hitchhiker to another) and only as people share those meanings can anything be communicated. Perhaps we can conclude from this that those in religious settings need to explicate their meaning of compassion precisely, in terms of lifestyle, for the concept of compassion to have any common meaning.

Symbolic interactionists sometimes speak of taking an "emic" position relative to others—the insider's view, the perspective of a member of a group, to better understand that group.[46] Taking an emic perspective is a close cousin to the psychological concept of empathy, feeling as the other person feels, in contrast to sympathy which is feeling sorry for another. Religious compassion involves more than sympathy, as sympathy can carry the connotation of condescension. Compassion may begin with sympathy, but in its richest form compassion moves to a sharing of the pain and difficulty, feeling as they do and carrying the load with them.

Sociological Contexts for Applying Religious Compassion

In this section several topics in the discipline of sociology will be briefly surveyed with an eye to applying religious compassion on a practical level. How, specifically, does religious compassion relate to the general topic areas considered by sociologists?

---

46. Barney Glaser, *Theoretical Sensitivity* (Mill Valley, Calif.: Sociology Press, 1978), p. 49.

Socialization

Socialization involves the question of how people learn to interact with others and become a part of society. To a considerable extent this area overlaps with child development; increasingly child developmentalists are including socialization as an important aspect of their subject matter (interestingly, sociologists have also begun including Piaget, Erikson, Freud, and other psychologically oriented theorists in sociology texts in recent years).

Thus the question confronting us is how can children be socialized to be compasssionate? Sociology at this point tends to describe the general influence of groups in the socialization process, including the family, school, church, and so on. In contrast psychology gives specific processes of learning, such as modeling, shaping, and so on. To socialize children to be compassionate requires a blending of sociology and psychology; there must be specific procedures used to be maximally effective in teaching compassion, but the social context must also be appropriate.

Sociologically there must be the potential for compassion. There are probably circumstances available for teaching compassion in most contexts, but the educator or parent may need to create specific opportunities to teach compassion. Since compassion involves a wide variety of behavior, specific acts of compassion will probably be the focus with small children, taught one at a time, and after a number of compassionate responses have been acquired, the individual will be more likely to understand, appreciate, and act upon the broader concept of compassion.

For example, a young child may be rather self-centered and unconcerned about the feelings of others. For her to use compassion may not immediately require her to become completely others-centered, but rather it might come in the form of hugging another child who is crying. This behavior might be encouraged by telling and enacting stories about giving affection to someone who is crying, discussing how someone feels when they are crying, drawing pictures of hugging a crying child, and encouraging children to watch for those who may feel sad or be crying and offer affection. Should this take place in a family context, the family would also need to model such behavior, hugging the child when *she* cries—modeling is one of the most important aspects of the socialization process. Affection for one crying is only one small skill taught which could be the first step toward empathy, to which other small skills would be added, and over the years the more generalized concept of compassion might be instilled. Such training could also occur in more standard educational contexts, such as religious day schools, Sunday schools, and released time instruction.

The family, the most important socialization agent, is indeed the place where children are likely to learn compassion. Thus it behooves Christians to protect the family and encourage legislation that encourages healthy family life. Governmental efforts that intrude upon family life or discourage families by inadequate tax credits for dependents should be confronted by religious groups. In addition religious organizations should help families by providing child care, services for "latch key" kids, and aid for those with handicapped children and other special needs.

Sociology underscores the importance of the "significant other" in the socialization process, the important people that significantly influence the person.[47] The most significant others for most small children are their parents. In middle childhood and early adolescence the peer group becomes more significant; then in adulthood the world in general tends to become the significant other, although the spouse and professional associates are also very influential.[48] A religious leader also can become a significant other, fostering religious compassion among the religiously committed through teaching and example.

Culture

Sociologists describe culture as the attitudes, beliefs and values within a society. The norms of a culture may encourage or discourage compassion; some societies encourage compassion generally, others encourage compassion primarily within families, and still others seem to encourage hostility rather than compassion. Are compassionate cultures more religious? To my knowledge this variable has not been broadly considered by anthropologists, but many religions do include important compassionate values. Unfortunately the gap between those values and behavior is often broad; too often intolerance and hostility supersede the more compassionate values (some extremist Islamic countries might be cited

47. Wallace and Wallace, *Sociology*, p. 81.
48. Campolo, *The Success Fantasy* (Wheaton, Ill.: Victor, 1980), pp. 20-22.

at this point). Certainly what religion is being followed is an important influence, some religions foster compassion more than others, but one must agree that even the most compassionate religious values may be overlooked because of concern of one's immediate purposes and segmented attention to a religious source of values (e.g., the Bible).

When compassion is to be given across cultural boundaries, the knowledge of cultural differences is crucial. Sociologists use the term "ethnocentrism" to designate the imposing of one's own cultural values upon others, seeing one's own culture as superior and others as innately inferior.[49] Ethnocentrism is opposite empathy; compassion cross-culturally requires an understanding of the other culture so that one's compassion will be consistent with societal norms if at all possible. This is important not only when attempting to be compassionate to an entirely different culture, but also when communicating and showing compassion to subcultures within one's own culture and in interethnic relations.

Perhaps an example will help at this point in understanding the general concept of ethnocentrism. A number of years ago, I spent six weeks on a tiny, backward island in the Caribbean. My assignment was to teach a general psychology class in a small Bible institute. I came prepared to give the same lectures I normally delivered in the United States. There was certainly interest in my teaching, but also an undercurrent of hostility in the class that I could not explain. After reflecting a bit, I decided to try a couple of simple examples from the local community in my next lecture. The result was that students began to enthusiastically discuss and debate the topic at hand; I had unknowingly been using American examples that were too detached from the students' experiences and thus had been teaching in an ethnocentric manner.

Religious compassion requires an understanding and appreciation of a cultural context that may be difficult and sometimes impossible to completely affirm for those trying to be compassionate. Many missionary groups are encouraging indigenization of efforts in recent years, encouraging nationals to implement programs of

---

49. Stephen Grunlan, "Biblical Authority and Cultural Relativism," in *Christian Perspectives on Sociology*, ed. Stephen Grunlan and Milton Reimer (Grand Rapids, Mich.: Zondervan, 1982), p. 150.

compassion because of their greater appreciation for their own local procedures and customs. Compassion that is maximally effective may require that Americans fund indigenous efforts.

Small Groups

The size of a group is related to its effectiveness. By far the most effective way to change behavior is through the dynamics of the small group, although different kinds of leadership and participation are needed depending upon the goals of the small group.[50] In each of the three types of small groups listed by Emory Griffin, compassion could play a part. First, in the task group compassion could be implicit in the task to be accomplished, such as raising funds for the poor or helping to build a house for a family that could not afford to hire it built. The second kind of group, the relationship group, emphasizes the development and growth of personal relationships. For someone who has been through a divorce this might indeed be the most compassionate response possible for the church. Sadly, the divorced are often overlooked by the church—one study found that in a broad sample of families, half of whom attended a church or synagog, not one was visited by a pastor, priest, or rabbi during divorce proceedings.[51] Wallerstein and Blakelee also document the intensity of pain felt by the children of divorce, lasting ten years and longer afterward, which underscores the need to help meet the needs of such people and many others that are hurting and lonely in the church. We need relationship groups. The third kind of group mentioned by Griffin is the influence group, a collection of people that want to change in some specific way (weight control, alcoholism, etc.). Clearly the church is being compassionate when it helps its members and others overcome such problems.

Sermons are notoriously ineffective in changing people's behavior and nearly all of a standard sermon is immediately forgotten.[52] In contrast, small groups can be formed that will activate people and aid compassion. Winston Johnson notes that this is not necessarily

50. Emory A. Griffin, *Getting Together* (Downers Grove, Ill.: InterVarsity, 1982), pp. 25-59.

51. Judith Wallerstein and Susan Blakelee, *Second Chance* (New York: Ticknor and Fields, 1988).

52. David Myers and Malcolm Jeeves, *Psychology Through Eyes of Faith* (San Francisco: Harper & Row, 1987), pp. 75-76.

an *immediate* consequence when small groups are implemented. He states that small groups generally progress through three steps: (1) personal and spiritual growth, in which the individual is ministered to and begins to minister, (2) the development of unity as the group begins to act as a community, and (3) mobilization in reaching out to others.[53] Religious compassion can exist at each of these stages, but at each stage of the small group it changes in context and orientation—from the individual, to the group, to those outside the group. Small, relationship-oriented groups should be a crucial ministry in any church that wants to be effective in this decade and into the next century;[54][55][56] given the choice between fellowship and good preaching, people will choose the former.

Collective Behavior

The term "collective behavior" is a designation that includes different kinds of crowds as well as fads and fashions. Can crowd behavior be compassionate? Crowds can be kind or cruel to a speaker, accepting or rejecting, and an individual within a crowd can be compassionate, but it is difficult to imagine an entire crowd being compassionate. Crowds by their very nature tend to not work very well as a unit, with their principal outcomes being clapping, laughing, booing, and similar behaviors. Sociologists generally describe acting crowds as causing damage and destruction.[57]

On the other hand crowds, including the specific variety called an audience, tend to be the dominant group formation in many churches. This kind of group is fairly efficient for providing entertainment (although one can argue that television is even more efficient), but personal interaction within a crowd generally occurs in spite of crowd behavior and is often disruptive of the crowd (or the crowd interferes with personal interaction, as in churches with

53. Winston Johnson, "Groups," in *Christian Perspectives on Sociology*, ed. Stephen A. Grunlan and Milton Reimer (Grand Rapids, Mich.: Zondervan, 1982), pp. 158-159.

54. Barna and McKay, *Vital Signs*, pp. 131-133.

55. George Barna, *America 2000* (Glendale, Calif.: Barna Research Group, 1989), p. 39.

56. Gallup and Costelli, *The People's Religion*, pp. 253-256.

57. Gene McBride, "Collective Behavior and Social Movements," in *Sociology: A Pragmatic Approach*, ed. Julian Bridges, 3rd ed. (Winston-Salem, N.C.: Hunter, 1986), pp. 359-375.

pews attached to the floor). The crowd context can be fairly effective in communicating if certain guidelines are followed, guidelines often ignored in sermons.[58] By following such guidelines there is some potential for changing opinions and possibly even motivating compassionate action in a crowd, religious or not, but as noted before, it tends to be much less effective than the small group. The guidelines suggested by David Myers and Malcolm Jeeves, and backed up by considerable research, include: (1) using concrete, vivid examples, (2) relating messages to what the people have already experienced or already know, (3) repeating information at spaced intervals, perhaps through music, in scriptures, in the sermon, in prayers, etc., (4) encouraging active rather than passive listening by encouraging parishioners to take notes and put things in their own words (perhaps through discussion after the service), and (5) having listeners act upon what they hear by being specific in what they should do in response to the message.

Collective behavior also includes fads and fashions. Some Christian sociologists have questioned whether these two kinds of collective behavior are appropriate for religious believers.[59] From a purely economic perspective, those who spend their cash excessively following fads and fashions are less able to spend those funds for compassionate causes. But it is unclear whether those who are current with fashions and fads are more or less compassionate. Some, such as the Franciscans, completely reject these by taking on the traditional garb of their predecessors, in stark contrast to Cliff Richard, multimillionaire rock and roll star in England, who has spent considerable time and effort working with compassionate projects. He has often been criticized for owning a Rolls Royce, yet he may have encouraged more compassionate giving to religious organizations by his fans than hundreds of other Christians who disparage fashion and fad.

The issue seems to be one of priorities. Compassion can have a major place in one's life, and yet that does not require the individual to be twenty years out of date in one's dress. Proper stewardship *should* cause a person to question the acquisition of cer-

---

58. Myers and Jeeves, *Psychology Through Eyes of Faith*, pp. 75-76.
59. Stanley Clark, "Collective Behavior and Social Movements," in *Christian Perspectives on Sociology*, ed. Stephen Grunlan and Milton Reimer (Grand Rapids, Mich.: Zondervan, 1982), pp. 320-321.

tain items only because the neighbors have them. Anthony Campolo often speaks of his children who, with a bit of encouragement from their father, chose to forego new bicycles and other toys so they could support an orphanage of children in Haiti. As teenagers, the children visited that orphanage and saw the children they had helped keep alive over the years. With tears streaming down their faces, they told their father of the tremendous joy that resulted, joy far greater than the toys would have provided.

Future Trends

What can be expected in the future regarding religious compassion? George Barna, director of the Barna Research Group, has evaluated recent trends in society and has projected the implications for the church of this decade and the next in his important report titled *America 2000*.[60] Among the many significant changes to be expected is that charitable giving to churches and other organizations is expected to increase in the future,[61] in spite of expected economic downturns and skepticism towards religious organizations. The number of charitable agencies should continue to slowly increase in number, increasing the competition for funds.[62] Parachurch organizations will suffer particularly from this crunch, as many of their older constituencies die. To continue to exist, such organizations will have to appeal to the Baby Boom generation, "who are notoriously less loyal, give smaller gifts, and are harder to reach with a message."[63]

Consistent with the recent book *Megatrends 2000*,[64] Barna sees a move away from parochialism to a broad, worldwide perspective of charitable work. Unlike Naisbitt and Aburdene, however, Barna sees this trend being prefaced with more interest in local efforts until the mid-1990s, which will be followed by the more global emphasis.[65] While Naisbitt and Aburdene forecast a move toward fundamentalist and New Age religious experience, Barna suggests

---

60. Barna, *America 2000*.
61. Ibid., p. 15.
62. Ibid., p. 54.
63. Ibid.
64. Naisbitt and Aburdene, *Megatrends 2000*, pp. 154-177.
65. Ibid., pp. 27-28.

that "We are most likely to be a nation of people more interested in having the church more integrally involved in issues of social justice and community action, than in matters related to religious content."[66]

What of personal involvement by Christians in individual compassionate efforts? Barna believes that there will be a crisis of leadership among the laity in the 1990s, with fewer individuals volunteering fewer hours of their time for compassionate efforts.[67] Yet the Baby Boomers may have increasing interest in short term missionary work if they can use their specific skills overseas to help those in need. However the emphasis of such personal service will be on the short time of commitment, in terms of one or two weeks slots, and on exciting and exotic locations rather than those marked by poverty.[68]

Barna states, "The Christian Church, in general, is in danger of losing its positive image. Many people feel that the Church has begun to place too much attention on unimportant matters (e.g., organizational structures) at the expense of caring for people and their needs."[69] This statement is consistent with my earlier analysis of the church development cycle. To summarize the coming era, Barna concludes, "Self-interest and self-indulgence . . . will be a cornerstone of the early twenty-first century philosophy. We will witness radical individualism, in which people display touches of social conscience (continued volunteerism, donations to charity, concern about poverty and environmental decay), but within the context of serving self first."[70]

Conclusion

After examining the sociological foundations for religious compassion, it is imperative that these not remain mentalistic. The ideas we have considered need to be activated in our churches, our religious organizations, our denominations. Behavior must change for this time to have been well spent. A danger implicit in writing about

---

66. Ibid., p. 29.
67. Ibid., p. 34.
68. Ibid., pp. 56-57.
69. Barna, *America 2000,* p. 27
70. Ibid., p. 17.

compassion is that the words mouthed can be taught so that others learn to mouth those same words, but nothing really changes as a result. Words without deeds are dead, the scripture reminds us. For the process to be complete, we must not forget that religious compassion requires information (cognition), sensitization (affect), and activation (behavior).

Anthony Campolo tells the story of leaving Haiti on a small airplane. Running after the plane was a woman holding a small sick child, dying of malnutrition. As the mother ran, she cried "take my child, save my child." Tony knew there were thousands of children in that country that needed help as much as that tiny one. He could do nothing; he had a schedule to meet and he was unable to take on such a child. The mother continued to scream and run after the plane as it took off, "take my child, please don't let my child die." Soon the plane was in the air and the sounds of the mother were drowned out by the airplane engines. Thinking of that event awhile later, Tony realized that the mother and child were a picture of much of the world today, crying to the rest of us that compassion is needed. He also realized who the child really was. As noted earlier, the Bible states that if we have compassion on the least, we are doing it to Christ. Jesus was the child who needed help, and most of us neglect that cry because of our self-concern. May we hear that cry for compassion and give what is needed!

PART II

RELIGIOUS COMPASSION IN
PASTORAL MINISTRY

5

Compassion in Religious Counseling

ANTHONY J. HEADLEY, JOE BOONE ABBOTT, GARY L. SAPP

"You may call God love
You may call God goodness
But the best name for God is compassion."

Matthew Fox,
Meditations with Meister Eckhart

Introduction

At some point in our lives, all of us undergo experiences that are characterized by anguish, pain, and suffering. These events are critical choice points of high personal drama and great significance which define the very shape of our existence. Our fateful response to these challenges may open the way to an enriched sense of self or lead to a retreat into cynicism, despair, and malaise. Perhaps the most significant factor in the positive resolution of these crises is an authentic encounter with a significant other, one who loves us enough to be compassionate toward us. Be it parent, relative, lover, friend, teacher, pastor, rabbi, or priest, the "other" becomes a powerful vehicle whereby we share compassion in a compelling life sustaining, healing event.

As the role of the compassionate other is central to our own personal development, so it is in the crucible of the counselor-client relationship. It is through this relationship that one of the major goals of counseling,[1] assisting clients to bring about critical life changes, is accomplished. We maintain that the compassionate encounter between counselor and client is a critical element in enhancing the efficacy of the counselor- client relationship. Specifically, we contend that in all counseling, and especially in religious counseling, the compassion shared by counselor and client constitutes a major variable facilitating the accomplishment of the goals of counseling.

It is not an overstatement to suggest that the counseling relationship demands from the counselor a level and intensity of compassion not only equal to but in all likelihood surpassing that required of physicians with their patients. Therefore, it is ironic that compassion is incorporated into medical standards[2] as a requirement for physicians, while the role of compassion is often taken for granted in religious counseling. In terms of the Bible, and especially the example set for Christians by Jesus, compassion surely should be a cornerstone for all Christian helping behavior, including that of religious counseling.

The major focus of this chapter is to examine the role of compassion in the ministry of religious counseling. In doing this, we hope that religious counselors will reexamine the nature and power of compassion and come to more fully appreciate what compassion is. Compassion has been a relatively neglected topic in the theological literature in the West, and also in various other key Christian ministries such as that of religious instruction. Only when religious counselors have a reasonably clear idea of the nature and scope of compassion will they be able to properly and effectively integrate the compassionate dimension into the counseling process. To further their understanding of compassion counselors are encouraged to read all the other chapters in this volume. Each

---

1. Throughout this chapter, the terms counseling and therapy and their cognates are used interchangeably.

2. Warren Thomas Reich, "Speaking of Suffering: A Moral Account of Compassion," *Soundings* 72 (Spring, 1989), p. 83.

chapter in its own way offers new insights from various key vantage points about the nature, thrust, and scope of compassion.

Correlative to the first focus of this chapter, we will add as a second major focus the significance of compassion as a central and yeasting ingredient in the counseling relationship. In so doing, we will encourage counselors and psychotherapists to reexamine the role which compassion plays in their own practices. But such a reexamination, important though it is, nonetheless must be complemented with some specific examples of the beneficial incorporation of compassion in the counseling encounter. Thus this chapter will endeavor to provide a few examples of how counselors can utilize compassion as they go about their all-important work of helping and healing those who are suffering.

In actualizing these two major foci, this chapter will define and lay bare the basic structure of compassion. In this way religious counselors may become more deeply aware of the various interlocking strands which form the cord of compassion. Additionally, the question will be raised—and this is a key question which might be a haunting one for the religious counselor—of whether compassion demands experiences of suffering similar to the person who comes to the facilator for help. We will also explore how compassion can be cultivated and fostered. An intriguing avenue will be the role of self compassion. Furthermore, we will examine the impact which a person's suffering has on the whole fabric of the counseling relationship itself and what a person's suffering does to the well-being of the counselor who attempts to be compassionate to the person in pain. Again, we will give a few examples so that religious counselors can gain a yet firmer purchase on how compassion can faciliate therapeutic change in the client.

The third section of this chapter will give a more concentrated treatment of specific examples than was presented in the previous two sections. The chapter concludes with a case for a more conscious, intentional, and systematic incorporation of compassion into the religious counseling field in general and into the religious counseling act in particular. Unless and until religious counselors become firmly convinced of the centrality of compassion both as a core construct in the field and as working axis for their actual practice, there is little likelihood that compassion will be conceptually or behaviorally integrated into the field of religious counseling.

The Nature of Compassion

In the Old Testament, the root word used for compassion is *rhm*. It often refers to the strong tie that God has with his children and his unconditioned choice, that is his grace.[3] While it yields many meanings, the term may refer to the deep love one has for another, usually the love of a superior for an inferior that is rooted in some natural bond. It can also mean womb and is frequently used to speak of a mother's love for her child. The word is less frequently used for men, but when it is, it can refer to a father's love. Additionally, the term is sometimes used to connote the feeling of mercy which persons have for each other because they are all human beings.[4]

The word *rehem* is translated tender mercy or compassion and refers to the seat of one's emotions or the expression of one's deep emotion. In reference to God, the word recalls that God's compassion is rooted in his love and his grace. Used in reference to persons, it describes the depths of feeling that a mother's love can reach.[5]

One finds similar meanings for compassion in other Jewish literature. Primarily, compassion is discussed as a divine attribute and as being extended to all God's creatures. Additionally, compassion is said to be one of the outstanding characteristics of the Jewish people, and its manifestation to God's other creatures is said to prove one's descent from Abraham. In contrast, the lack of compassion demonstrates that one is not a son of Abraham. By practicing compassion, one is in a very real sense imitating God.[6]

There are two themes which are emphasized in Jewish literature when one attempts to help another who suffers from an infectious disease. The first is the theme of self-protection, avoidance, and flight. The second is the theme of compassion. Compassion becomes a paramount demand when one has ensured that one has made adequate preparation for oneself in terms of self-protection.[7]

---

3. R. Laird Harris, Gleason Archer, and Bruce Waltke, eds., *Theological Wordbook of the Old Testament*, vol. 2 (Chicago: Moody, 1980), pp. 841-843.

4. Ibid, p. 841.

5. Ibid.

6. *Encyclopedia of the Jewish Religion*, ed. Raphael Werblowsky and Geoffrey Wigoder (New York: Holt, Rinehart and Winston, 1966), p. 95.

7. Ronald Green, "The Perspective of Jewish Teachings, *Religious Education* 83:2 (1988), pp. 221-232.

Compassion is similarly emphasized in the New Testament, especially in the ministry of Jesus. Its definition suggests a strong identification and feeling with another. Concerning compassion, Andrew
Purves wrote, "Compassion in the New Testament literally means to
have one's bowels turned over. The word refers to what we would call
a `gut-wrenching' experience. *Splanchnizomai,* compassion, this
rather unusual New Testament verb, refers to a feeling of solidarity with another that is virtually physical in its effect. There is nothing genteel or comely about compassion."[8] The noun for compassion also shares an organic basis with the Old Testament meaning
in which compassion shares a link with the word, "womb." In the
New Testament the noun "*splagchna*" refers to the nobler viscera, that
is the heart, lungs, liver, and kidneys. According to Arthur Becker,
"Compassion in the biblical sense is perception of another's pain,
hurt, sorrow, longing that is so intense and vivid and organismic
that 'you feel it in your guts'."[9]

Warren Reich suggested that a similar emphasis on compassion
can be found in Augustine's, *City of God.* However, Augustine uses the
term mercy as an equivalent term for compassion. Here, Augustine
may well be drawing from the Old Testament synonym for compassion. However, Reich noted that mercy was inappropriate for
contemporary use given its overtones of condescension.[10]

This short overview reveals certain facts about compassion. First,
compassion is very much an attribute of God as he interacts with his
creation, and it is related to his love for and his grace towards his creation. As the compassionate one, God is constantly attuned to and
actively intervenes in the suffering of his creatures. Second, compassion is expected of persons who are part of God's created order.
From this perspective, human compassion is derived and is indeed
an "*imitatio dei.*" Such imitation of God must demonstrate itself in
efforts of active compassion that seeks to alleviate the suffering of
others. Third, because we are all part of God's created order, we are
all inextricably linked to each other and must therefore try to
address the sufferings of all of God's creatures. According to Becker,

---

8. Andrew Purves, *The Search for Compassion* (Louisville: Westminster/John
Knox, 1989), p. 18.

9. Arthur Becker, "Compassion: The Foundation of Care of the Sick," *Trinity
Seminary Review* 5:1 (1983), pp. 14-21.

10. Reich, "Speaking of Suffering," p. 106.

compassion, defined as care for brothers and sisters is a part of our heritage from creation.[11] Finally, compassion is a "gut-level" feeling that brings us in touch with the pain and anguish of our fellow humans.[12]

Compassion is also a central tenet in Buddhism. In this tradition, compassion, "*karuna*," shares many of the themes already highlighted in the Judeo-Christian literature. Here compassion refers to, "the love for all beings as exemplified by a mother's love for a child."[13] Similar to the idea that compassion is something that is owed to other members of creation, Buddhism speaks about compassion as the appropriate response to others with whom one is linked. Compassion is based on a sense of interdependence and is concerned with the welfare of the other.[14] However, in Buddhism, compassion for others has such priority that another's deliverance is placed prior to one's own deliverance.[15] Buddhism also appears to suggest such an identification with others in their sufferings as to blur any distinction between self and others.[16]

Other Definitions of Compassion

Turning to *Webster's Third New International Dictionary Unabridged*, one finds that the word compassion is derived from two Latin words, "*com*" and "*pati*" which means to "bear with" or "suffer with." Compassion is there defined as a "deep feeling for and understanding of misery or suffering and the concomitant desire to promote its alleviation: spiritual consciousness of the personal tragedy of another or others and selfless tenderness directed toward it." However, Reich suggests that a more accurate translation of the Latin "*patior*" from which "*pati*" is derived is "suffering something to happen to oneself," or simply "to experience."[17] Etymologically, compassion is said to mean "to experience with."[18] Compassion "is

---

11. Becker, "Compassion: The Foundation of Care of the Sick."
12. Ibid.
13. *The Encyclopedia of Religion*, ed. Mircia Eliade, vol. 2 (New York: Macmillan, 1987), p. 269.
14. Ibid.
15. Ibid.
16. Ibid., p. 270.
17. Reich, "Speaking of Suffering," p. 84.
18. Ibid.

thus the virtue by which we have a sympathetic consciousness of sharing the distress or suffering of another person and on that basis are inclined to offer assistance in alleviating and/or living through the suffering."[19] In a recent article articulating a theory of emotions, Richard Lazarus defined compassion as something that "is experienced when one comprehends and reacts to someone else in trouble by wanting to ameliorate the suffering."[20]

Some of these definitions of compassion share elements with the various religious traditions mentioned earlier. Other definitions include the element of sharedness that is emphasized in the Judeo-Christian and Buddhist traditions, even though the religious bases of this sharedness are not emphasized. One example is the work of Justin Oakley who conceptualizes compassion as indicating our connectedness with others.[21] Laurence Blum referred to compassion as involving "a sense of shared humanity, of regarding the other as a fellow human being:[22] and as promoting equality because of this shared humanity.[23]

Compassion is a complex emotion that includes an affective element where one experiences the suffering with the sufferer. Additionally, compassion has a cognitive component in which comprehension is said to be one of the key elements of compassion.[24] The presence of both affective and cognitive elements is noted by Bernard Brown who described compassion as "To know feelingly with others."[25] Compassion also has a definite behavioral dimension in that it is always concerned with the alleviation of suffering. Most commonly, compassion is said to be addressed to suffering in others.[26] In the latter regard, Lawrence Blum noted that compassion is fundamentally other regarding as opposed to self-regard-

---

19. Ibid., p. 85.

20. Richard Lazarus, "Progress on a Cognitive, Motivational-Relational Theory of Emotion," *American Psychologist* 46:8 (1991), p. 821.

21. Justin Oakley, *Morality and the Emotions* (New York: Routledge, 1991), p. 39.

22. Lawrence Blum, "Compassion," in *Explaining Emotions*, ed. Amelie O. Rarty, (Berkeley: University of California Press, 1980), p. 509.

23. Ibid., p. 510.

24. Lazarus, "Progress on a Cognitive-Motivational Theory of Emotions," p. 822.

25. Bernard G. Brown, "The Problem of Compassion," *Criterion* 29 (1990), pp. 24-26.

26. Blum, "Compassion," pp. 507-516. Also Lazarus, "Progress on a Cognitive-Motivational Theory of Emotions."

ing.[27] Even though the other-centeredness of compassion is normally emphasized, it will be argued later that one must also be attuned to suffering in oneself and that such a notion is important to those who serve in the counseling field.

Compassion and Related Terms

There are a number of terms connected to compassion which provide some clues as to its structure. Love is one of those related terms that comes most readily to mind as compassion is love in action. The meaning of the root word from which compassion is derived refers to the deep love that one has for another. A related word is also used to speak of a mother's love for her nursing baby or can refer to a father's love.[28] In reference to God, compassion is rooted in his love and his grace. In keeping with such thinking, compassion has been described as a form of neighbor-love.[29]

Another term that is closely related to compassion is altruism. Blum has observed that "compassion is one among a number of attitudes, emotions, or virtues which can be called 'altruistic' in that they involve a regard for the good of other persons."[30] Morton Hunt uses the word altruism as a synonym for compassion.[31] As he recounts terms for altruism before the latter term was coined by Auguste Comte, Hunt mentions compassion as a basic human trait referring to altruistic actions in which kindness is demonstrated as being integral to human nature. For Hunt, altruism is the compassionate side of human nature.[32]

Hunt's definition of altruism suggests one way in which altruism and compassion are related. Altruism is generally defined as concrete behavior that is carried out to benefit another without regard to reward.[33] Hunt modifies this definition and suggests that altruism is "behavior carried out to benefit another at some sacrifice to oneself and without, or not primarily because of, reward from

---

27. Blum, "Compassion," p. 507.
28. Harris, Archer, and Waltke, *Theological Wordbook of the Old Testament*, p. 841.
29. Robert Campbell Roberts, "Compassion," *The Christian Century* 100 (1983), pp. 14-17.
30. Blum, "Compassion," p. 509.
31. Morton Hunt, *The Compassionate Beast* (New York: Doubleday, 1990).
32. Ibid., pp. 17-23.
33. Ibid., p. 18.

external sources."[34] The primary behavioral emphasis of altruism addressed generally to suffering leads us to suggest that altruism may be part of the behavioral component of compassion.[35] We say part, because altruism is generally translated into actions. A strict definition of altruism would expect some form of helping behavior, not just intentions or inclinations to help.

Additional terms that one must consider when trying to understand compassion are pity and sympathy. David Cartwright suggests that the three terms must be distinguished if one is to fully understand compassion. He observed that these words were all expressions of attitudes toward those who were suffering and were graded in terms of one's actual participation in, closeness to, or identification with the suffering.[36] He also suggested that pity was the most remote and was often a form of gloating in disguise.[37]

We would concur with Cartwright that pity is very remote from compassion even though the two terms are sometimes used synonymously.[38] Compassion is also to be distinguished from pity because it is focused upon the good of others and is therefore life-affirming and positive. In contrast, pity is focused upon the negative state of others and, hence, is judgmental and condescending.

In the minds of some people, sympathy is related to compassion in some manner. We deliberately write the words "in some manner" because there is a lack of consensus about the relationship of sympathy to compassion, or even about the nature of sympathy itself. Much of this requisite lack of clarity stems from the fact that social scientists have not accorded the construct of sympathy sufficient serious and sustained attention. It is probably true to assert, however, that sympathy is an affective state in which a person experiences the affects of another individual but still is conscious of his own identity.[39] Sympathy thus is a sensitivity to another person's affective state but is always one's own sensitivity rather than a plunge

---

34. Ibid., p. 21.
35. Ibid., pp. 35-36.
36. David Cartwright, "The Ethical Significance of Sympathy, Compassion, and Pity" (Ph.D. dissertation, University of Wisconsin, Madison, 1981), pp. 39-87.
37. Ibid., pp. 13-14.
38. Ibid., pp. 58-59.
39. For a brief review of some conceptualizations on this matter, see Arnold P. Goldstein and Gerald Y. Michaels, *Empathy* (Hillsdale, N.J.: Erlbaum, 1985), pp. 7-8.

into the sensitivity of another. This maintenance of the conscious duality of self as apart from the other in the act of extending sympathy to a person in distress is suggested by the etymological roots of the word sympathy, namely the Greek term to feel together with, to feel alongside of. (We should note, however, that the rooting of modern English terms totally in etymology can be overdone, since the Latin root for the English word compassion is also to feel together with, to feel alongside of. As we shall see in this chapter, compassion is much wider, much deeper, and much more behaviorally oriented than simply feeling with another person.)

Though sympathy is primarily affective in nature, it also contains some strands of cognition. Adrian Piper suggests that a valid definition of sympathy, although primarily emphasizing affect, also contains some cognitive elements so that one who "thinks" like another may also be said to be showing sympathy.[40]

Generally, the person to whom sympathy is given is an individual who is experiencing some distress, some need, some suffering. An elderly woman who has been subjected to serious verbal abuse from her daughter, a man who has lost his home because he could no longer pay the mortgage because of a job loss, a woman whose son died as a result of alcohol abuse—these are just a few of the kinds of clients to whom the religious counselor may extend sympathy.

Related to sympathy, but distinct from it, is the construct of empathy. Empathy is far deeper and more personalistic than sympathy which probably accounts for its being preferred over sympathy as a counseling tool by the overwhelming number of experts in the field. Empathy is that affective process in which a person vicariously experiences the feelings, thoughts, and to some extent the acts of another individual.[41] This feeling by the empathizer extends not only to the emotional state of the person in distress at this present moment, but also extends to that individual's past and present, according to Piper.[42]

In sympathy the religious counselor feels for the client but is

---

40. Adrian M.S. Piper, "Impartiality, Compassion, and Moral Imagination," *Ethics* 101 (July, 1991), pp. 726-757.

41. Jan I. Harman, "Relations Among Components of the Empathic Process," *Journal of Counseling Psychology* 33:4 (1986), pp. 371-372. Ezra Stotland, "Empathy," in *Encyclopedia of Psychology*, ed. Raymond J. Corsini (New York: Wiley, 1984), vol. 1, pp. 428-429.

42. Piper, "Impartiality, Compassion, and Moral Imagination," pp. 726-757.

consciously aware of his own separate identity. In empathy, however, the counselor plunges as far as possible into the selfhood of the suffering client so that the pain the counselor feels is the client's pain rather than his or her own pain. Of course this experiencing of the other person's distress is a vicarious form of experiencing. The counselor never existentially becomes the other. Nonetheless, in the act of empathy, the counselor plunges into the sea of the client's feelings of distress so that, as far as is humanly possible, the client's distress becomes the counselor's distress.

Because empathy is an act of the whole person, it necessarily includes a cognitive dimension as well. This cognitive dimension does not consist merely of facts—the sufferer's age, the details of the causes of the distress, the data on the particular kinds of suffering being experienced, and so forth. Even more saliently, the cognitive dimension of empathy consists of personalistically understanding the client in all relevant dimensions but most importantly as a unique human being.[43] Furthermore, empathy involves the use of a most important cognitive function, namely that of imagination. It is through the process of imagination that the counselor is able to intellectually reconstruct the suffering that the client is feeling. Creative imagination, and in this case creative imagination of a reconstructive kind, is a most important ally of the empathic counselor because it enables the counselor to transcend the spatiotemporal limitations of the present situation so as to imagine how the suffering must be and must have been.

While empathy involves the plunging of self into the person and the suffering of the individual in distress, nonetheless, empathy is not to be confused with identification. In empathy, the counselor does not appropriate the characteristics of the person in distress. The counselor's personal characteristics remain the same. What does happen in the act of empathy is that the religious counselor vicariously becomes, as far as possible, immersed in the suffering of the individual so as to feel this suffering much in the same way as the person in need is feeling it.

Empathy has become a staple in the counseling literature.[44] The

---

43. Lazarus, "Progress on a Cognitive Motivational-Relational Theory of Emotions."

44. Michael Barkham and David A. Shapiro, "Counselor Verbal Response Modes and Experienced Empathy," *Journal of Counseling Psychology* 33:1 (1986), pp. 3-4.

religious counselor seeking to be empathic toward the client in need of compassion must not only feel empathy for the client but must also communicate that empathy to the client. It must never be forgotten that the counseling process is essentially one of communication between the counselor and the client. No facilitation is possible without communication. Thus the religious counselor should not only strive to increase his or her own empathic feeling for the person in need, but, also and very importantly, act in such a way as to ensure that the client realizes and feels the counselor's genuine empathy.

While there is a certain commonality among sympathy, empathy, and compassion, nonetheless, there are important differences. Compassion is the broadest of these terms, including empathy as well as other elements. Reich[45] claims that both sympathy and empathy are embraced within the construct of compassion. Piper[46] asserts much the same thing, though with a different interpretation. Thus Piper states that "compassion involves modal imagination, empathy, sympathy, a disposition to render aid or mercy, and what I will describe as strict impartiality." Yet it is difficult to see how sympathy and empathy, which in a certain sense are at odds with one another in terms of a person's psychological affinity with the individual in distress, can both fall under the construct of compassion.

If intellectual understanding comprises the cognitive component of compassion, then empathy is the affective ingredient. This is not to say that the counselor's empathic feelings are without admixture from other human domains. After all, the counselor, as person and as facilitator, is a human being and thus functions holistically. Hence during the empathic act (whether as part of compassion or outside it), the religious counselor utilizes, though in a minor and supporting capacity, important correlative cognitive processes such as imagination when endeavoring to "feel into" the client's emotional dynamisms.[47]

As an affective process, empathy can be considered as an attitude, an emotion, or both. In the opinion of some, it is difficult to

45. Reich, "Speaking of Suffering," p. 85

46. Piper, "Impartiality, Compassion, and Moral Imagination," p. 727.

47. Oakley, *Morality and Emotions*; Reich, "Speaking of Suffering"; William T. Kirwan, *Biblical Concepts for Christian Counseling* (Grand Rapids, Mich.: Baker, 1984).

distinguish between emotion and attitude. Even in attitude research, it is the emotional aspect of attitude which is accorded special attention.[48] Others combine emotion and attitude and categorize compassion as an emotional attitude.[49] In our view, empathy—and therefore the empathic component of compassion—is indeed an attitude as well as an emotion. It is attitude which gives the empathic counselor a more or less permanent disposition toward the client in distress. And it is emotion which provides the empathic counselor with that temporary bond of strong feeling between the counselor and the suffering client.

Physical Elements of Compassion

Compassion also includes physical elements. These essential physical elements on the part of the counselor are both external and internal. They are external because they involve physically helping the client in some manner. We shall consider this in the next paragraph. The physical elements are internal because the compassionate counselor viscerally experiences some of the anguish and suffering of the person in need.[50] Thus the religious counselor who wishes to do his or her work in a deeply compassionate manner must not only have an affective approach to the facilitational process but must also have the fortitude for this kind of counseling. To share physically in the anguish and suffering of the client means that the counselor may also suffer physically during the counseling encounter. Consequently, compassionate counseling is not for everyone. Indeed, this kind of counseling can easily wear the counselor down since he or she physically suffers together with the clients year in and year out. But such is the high price of compassionate counseling, a price which some otherwise splendid pastoral counselors might wish to undertake only for a short period of their careers, occasionally, or never.

External physical elements are also central to compassion. By

---

48. Steven Breckler and Elizabeth C. Wiggins, "On Defining Attitude and Attitude Theory: Once More With Feeling," in *Attitude: Structure and Function*, ed. Anthony Pratkanis, Steen Brecklet, and Anthony Greenwald (Hillsdale, N.J.: Lawrence Erlbaum, 1989), pp. 407-428.

49. Blum, "Compassion," pp. 509-510.

50. Reich, "Speaking of Suffering," pp. 85-86.

external physical elements[51] here we mean actual concrete overt behaviors. Sympathy and empathy deal only with the counselor's affective sharing in the sufferings of the client in distress. Compassion, on the other hand, includes empathy but goes much further in that it also, and of necessity, includes activities in which the pastoral counselor will find ways to provide physical assistance to the client in need. Thus compassionate counseling is more holistic and more person-centered than sympathetic counseling or empathic counseling because compassionate counseling means that the totality of the counselor's personhood, physical as well as nonphysical, come into full play.[52] One can only wonder whether a counseling event which does not include the overt concrete behavioral element on the part of the counselor is really and truly person-centered, holistic counseling, since a key holistic and personal ingredient (overt behavior) is missing. Put differently, can a counseling event which is not compassionate be authentic counseling, or is it just advisement with feeling? One can also question whether the long-debated lack of treatment efficacy might, in part, be a function of the failure of counselors to incorporate the behavioral element in the counseling encounter. All this suggests that compassionate counseling requires a new, more vital role for the pastoral counselor. This role expands and severely challenges any bland view of counseling as passively sitting in an office placidly conversing individually or in a group setting with clients who verbally share innocuous problems or developmental concerns. We will return to this important issue later on in this chapter.

To what extent are sympathy and empathy intrinsically and causally linked to altruism?[53] Solid empirical research is inconclusive on

---

51. In using the terms internal and external, we do not mean to imply in any way a dualistic view of human nature. Every person acts holistically, and so really there is no such thing as "internal" or "external" as separate entities or functions. More precisely, there is less visible ("internal") and more visible ("external"). We use the terms internal and external not because we like these words — we do not — but rather because this is how many persons refer to these functions.

52. For a fine treatment of person-centered counseling and psychotherapy, see Nathaniel J. Rasken and Carl Rogers, "Person Centered Therapy," in *Current Psychotherapies*, ed. Raymond J. Corsini and Danny Wedding, 2nd ed. (Itasca, Ill.: Peacock, 1989), pp. 131-184.

53. Lauren Wispé, "The Distinction Between Sympathy and Empathy: To Call Forth a Concept, a Word is Needed," *Journal of Personality and Social Psychology* 50:2 (1986), pp. 314-321.

this question and suggests only that in some circumstances sympathy and empathy might give rise to altruism. But this cause, this motivation, is highly tenuous at best. Our previous analysis of sympathy and empathy has clearly shown that in themselves neither of these two constructs necessarily include overt concrete behavior, so that the best connection to altruism which these constructs can have would be in the motivational sphere.

To what extent is compassion intrinsically and causally linked to altruism?[54] Since there has been such a paucity of serious social-scientific research on compassion, it is not possible to say whether compassion is causally linked to altruism. However, we suggest that compassion is intrinsically connected with altruistic behavior because by its very definition, compassion encompasses concrete altruistic behavior. By this very inclusion, one can deduce that compassion must indeed be causally linked with prosocial behavior.

From our previous discussion of the nature and structure of compassion, it is evident that compassion, far more than sympathy or empathy, is functionally holistic. In order to be compassionate, the cognitive, affective, and overtly behavioral elements must not only be present and operative, but must flow together in concert, as appropriate. Cognitive understanding of the client's suffering is necessary but not sufficient for compassion. Affective empathy with the client's suffering is necessary but not sufficient for compassion. The inclination toward and the actual performance of a concrete overt behavior is necessary but not sufficient for compassion. To be necessary and also sufficient for compassion, the concrete, affective, and overtly behavioral components must be dynamically and harmoniously linked together if compassion is to be present.[55] These three components are linked together in terms of having a common source in the way a person actually functions. And the way a person actually functions is by a combination and linkage of cognition, affect, and overt behavior.[56] Compassion, in our view, is the full expression of genuine human love and authentic Christian love

---

54. Ibid., p. 318.

55. Oakley discusses this point well, but strictly in connection with emotions. What Oakley writes about emotions being linked to other elements also applies to compassion. See Oakley, *Morality and the Emotions*, pp. 7-16.

56. Kirwan, *Biblical Concepts for Christian Counseling*.

for the client, an expression far deeper and far more effective than sympathy or empathy. Giving, as well as receiving compassion, is an expression of the total self.

There has been a strong undercurrent of skepticism, if not outright fear, on the part of many pastoral counselors of bringing concrete overt behavior into the counseling process or even of closely linking religious counseling with overt behavior. Some of this skepticism and fear may flow from counselors' perceived adherence to one or another Rogerian, phenomenological, humanistic, transpersonal, and in a certain respect Jungian theories. Other roots of this skepticism and fear can be found in a kind of theological standpoint and attitude which profoundly distrusts the empirical axis of psychology because it is, in their view, insufficiently spiritual.[57] Additional grounds for this skepticism and fear lie in the belief that to make overt behavior a condition or even an important dimension of the counseling process would be to surrender abjectly to learning theory, to mechanistic positivism, to a hardened form of behavioral modification, or to other similar bogeymen of genuine pastoral counseling.

Let us consider the religious counselor's posture in regards to overt behavior. Richard, the client, was reared in a pious evangelical Protestant home. He met his wife, Nancy, during college and fell in love. Nancy was a devout Catholic and refused to marry Richard unless he converted to Catholicism and agreed to rear their children as Catholics. After considerable and anguished soul-searching, Richard converted and subsequently married Nancy. It was a happy marriage and within six years they had three children together. Richard took his new religion very seriously and attended Mass weekly. After their third child was born, however, Richard began to have severe guilt feelings about leaving the religion of his birth. He sought out a friendly mainline Protestant pastoral counselor who had the reputation for being compassionate. This counselor adhered to the humanistic school of psychology. Thus the axis of the counseling process consisted in helping Richard explore his feelings and gain insight about

---

57. Richard Gorsuch, "Psychology of Religion," in *Annual Review of Psychology,* ed. Mark R. Rosenzweig and Lyman W. Porter, vol. 39 (Palo Alto, Calif.: *Annual Reviews,* 1988), p. 204.

whether his conversion and subsequent life as a Catholic was helping or hindering the actualization of his full human potential.[58]
After a year of counseling, Richard's guilt feelings had not significantly receded. What should the counselor do now, and most
especially, what should the compassionate counselor do? Should
the counselor continue along the same track hoping that greater
progress will be made as Richard continues to explore his feelings as they relate to the actualization of his unique potential as a
person? Should the counselor subtly shift the focus of the counseling encounter to assist Richard in exploring his feelings of guilt
in themselves rather than get in touch with these feelings as they
relate to his affective awareness of his human potential? Or should
the counselor become more fully compassionate and suggest gen-
tly to Richard that he gain deeper oneness with the flow and eti-
ology of his guilt feelings by helping his parish priest teach a con-
firmation class and also to befriend Joe, an evangelical Protestant
who is attending this class with a view to becoming a Catholic?
Additionally, should the counselor herself occasionally accompany Richard and his wife to the convert class and to dinners which
Richard has at his home with Joe?

In some cases the compassionate counselor might be reluctant to
engage in overt behaviors. For example, Joe, a forty-five-year old
client, with feelings of negative self-esteem, contends that he des-
perately needs $3,000 to pay off chronic debts so that he can start
afresh and better deal with his feelings of worthlessness. The pastoral
counselor is a twenty-eight-year old man who has just received his
doctorate in counseling psychology and who owes $25,000 incurred
during his years of study. Obviously the counselor is in no position
to lend Joe any money. But in cases such as this, the truly compassionate counselor will endeavor to be as resourceful as possible.
Perhaps he can work with the local church cooperative to assist Joe
in paying off the loan. Or perhaps he can assist Joe in finding a
moonlighting job where Joe can earn additional money to pay off
the loan. What we are suggesting, then, is that the spirit and the
flow of compassion might possibly dictate, in appropriate circum-

---

58. On the relation of conversion and psychological processes, see Lewis R.
Rambo, "The Psychology of Conversion," in *Handbook of Religious Conversion*, ed. H.
Newton Malony and Samuel Southard (Birmingham, Ala.: Religious Education
Press, 1992), pp. 159-177.

stances, that the counselor leave the counseling office and concretely help the client to engage in those kinds of overt behaviors
which, when combined with the affective exploration of the client's
feelings, will enable the client to more nearly attain his or her
human potential.

Another reason why the compassionate counselor might be
unwilling to engage in overt behaviors on behalf of the client is
that some overt behaviors might violate some important aspect of
the sufferer, as for instance his or her autonomy. Personalistically oriented counselors may not wish to do anything which would violate
the autonomy of the client. They may perceive that concrete reme-
diation might seem to be superficially effective, but it would ultimately be ineffective and even harmful since it attacks the very selfhood and existence of the client-as-person. Still, the compassionate
counselor should not peremptorily rule out overt action or perceive it as a violation of client autonomy. The compassionate counselor should explore whether a possible overt behavior does indeed
violate the autonomy of the client or whether such a violation exists
only in the mind of the counselor. If the results of careful intro-
spection suggest that a particular overt behavior would violate the
autonomy and freedom of the client, the counselor should try alternative overt behavior which would not violate or otherwise negatively
impact upon the client's autonomy. The compassionate counselor
is one who places his or her total resources at the disposal of the
client, even if this requires great effort and sacrifice in and out of the
counseling office.

We have attempted to show in the foregoing paragraphs that
pastoral counselors cannot automatically rule out engaging in overt
behavior, or having the client engage in overt behavior, as part of the
overall counseling process. If indeed counseling is to be compassionate, then there must be some element of overt behavior on the
part of the counselor and client, since by definition counseling
includes overt behavior.

Compassion and Freedom

To what extent does the linkage of pastoral counseling with overt
behavior represent the diminishment of the client's freedom to be
and to become? The basic issue of human freedom was skillfully

addressed by Richard Williams.[59] We shall briefly summarize Williams' position not in an attempt to persuade pastoral counselors one way or another but rather to bring this frequently assumed but infrequently examined issue to their attention.

Williams views the issue of human freedom (and thus, by extension, the client's freedom in the counseling process) as being confused with two major issues, namely the issue of determinism versus indeterminism, and the issue of freedom-as-choosing-among-alternatives.

There is a growing body of empirical and philosophical evidence, Williams asserts, which strongly suggests that any explanation of human behavior as being determined by forces external or internal to the person is not only unhuman but is also unproductive.[60] On the other hand, Williams asserts that indeterminism leads to personal nihilism and social chaos because it suggests that human events lack meaningful antecedents and therefore cannot be adequately understood or predicted.

Williams also believes in the inadequacy of the conception of human freedom as choosing among alternatives. This notion of freedom is typically phrased as follows: "Human freedom exists when one could have done otherwise, all circumstances being the same." For Williams, this view of human freedom is unsatisfactory for three principal reasons. First, freedom of choice requires a person who chooses. But the nature and activity of such a chooser (agent) entails serious ontological problems in establishing the grounds on which the chooser can exercise free choice. In short, the grounds themselves determine the choice. Second, there is a major problem in establishing the grounds on which the chooser can make a free choice. Basically, the chooser often (always) does not choose the grounds; in a sense, the grounds choose the chooser.

59. Richard N. Williams, "The Human Context of Agency," *American Psychologist* 47:6 (1992), pp. 752-760.

60. Some of the sources Williams adduces include Abraham Maslow, *Toward a Psychology of Being*, 2nd ed. (New York: Van Nostrand, 1968); C. William Tageson, *Humanistic Psychology: A Synthesis* (Homewood, Ill.: Dorsey, 1982); Christopher M. Aanstoos, "Humanistic contra Mechanistic Psychology," *Humanistic Psychologist* 13:3 (1985), pp. 3-7; Paul Ricoeur, *Hermeneutics and the Human Sciences* (New York: Cambridge University Press, 1981); *Reconsidering Psychology: Perspectives from Continental Philosophy*, ed. James E. Faulconer and Richard N. Williams (Pittsburgh: Duquesne University Press, 1980), pp. 9-60.

Third, it is difficult to distinguish when a choice is a free choice and a random one, if one looks closely at a human act which is said to be free.[61]

Past rationales for the foundation and existence of authentic human freedom have been inadequate because they have not sufficiently incorporated philosophical insights into their social-scientific conceptions of freedom, Williams asserts. In an approach which will doubtless exert considerable appeal to many pastoral counselors, Williams claims that the question of freedom must be framed in such a way as to ask *how* the person is involved in the world truthfully. Drawing heavily on Martin Heidegger, Williams asserts that freedom "is not a quality people have nor a 'category' attached to humanity, but an activity, a way of being in concrete situations." Freedom is being in the world truthfully, because the essence of truth reveals itself in freedom. Truth in this sense is not cognitive or propositional but rather existential, namely the disclosure of a reality, an openness which reveals that reality to itself and to other realities. In the end, then, the issue of human freedom is not only what a person does but what that person is. The grounding of doing in being, at least the contextualizing of doing in being, has always been a position close to the hearts of quite a few pastoral counselors.

The issue of human freedom enunciated by Richard Williams can be fruitfully connected to some of the main points brought out by Barry Estadt in his William G. Bier Award Address to Division 36 of the American Psychological Association.[62] Estadt, a counseling psychologist specializing in pastoral psychology and pastoral counseling,[63] contends that a key axis in the pastoral counseling relationship is to assist clients in their ongoing striving for freedom. For Estadt, the client's psycho-existential and spiritual needs thrust that person forward to freedom in general and to freedom of opportunity in particular.[64] By freedom of opportunity Estadt means free-

---

61. This very brief summary does not really do justice to the sophistication and nuancing of Williams' critique.

62. Barry K. Estadt, "In Pursuit of Freedom," *Psychology of Religion Newsletter* 18:1 (1993), pp. 1-6.

63. Barry K. Estadt, ed., *Pastoral Counseling* (Englewood Cliffs, N.J.: Prentice-Hall, 1991).

64. In formulating this principle, Estadt relies on Joseph Nuttin, *Psychoanalysis and Personality*, 2nd ed. (New York: Omega, 1962); Abraham Maslow, *The Farther Reaches of Human Nature* (New York: Viking, 1971).

dom to fulfill one's human potential in the practical order, the ability to satisfactorily meet human needs without undue compulsion from within or unwarranted restraint from without. At the deepest level, human freedom involves what Estadt terms "flowing with the core of one's being."[65] Freedom is a key expression of the flow of one's being because freedom is not only actuality but also capacity—the capacity to be what we are and to be what we can become. Freedom is the existential potential and the existential realization of one's being, or more precisely, the flow of one's being in the practical order. Freedom is very deeply involved in the harmony of the flow of a person's being as this flow connects the person's being with practical affairs. The pastoral counselor should be exquisitely sensitive to the flow of the client's being, and should communicate to the client a sense of confidence both in that flow and in the client's ability to actualize the flow in freedom. A prime task of the pastoral counselor is to confirm the client's free existence, the being of the client for present and future freedom.

Compassion and the Role of Experience

Must one experience the same or similar sufferings of a sufferer in order to be compassionate? Doubtless, having the same or similar experiences to an object of suffering should help one to be compassionate. On the other hand, having the same or similar experience to the object of suffering may lead one to over-identify with the sufferer and lead to the kind of identity confusion that is not helpful.[66] Furthermore, the experience of suffering does not guarantee that one will be compassionate. Persons who suffer may become embittered or consumed with self-protection.[67] In order for personal suffering to be therapeutic, one must assimilate and accept those sufferings.[68] Suffering that is denied or minimized may not be therapeutic for another.

Although a personal experience with suffering may promote the development of compassion, it is not the only route to compas-

---

65. Here Estadt utilizes Mihaly Csikszentmihalyi, *Flow: The Psychology of Optimal Experience* (New York: Harper & Row, 1990).
66. Blum, "*Compassion,*" p. 511.
67. Roberts, "Compassion," pp. 14-17.
68. Ibid.

sion.[69] In cases where the compassionate person does not share the experience of suffering, it is the imaginative aspect of compassion that reconstructs what the person has experienced and leads to compassionate behavior.[70] Here is where the empathic dimension of compassion plays such a key role. Part and parcel of empathy is the vicarious plunging of self into the personhood of the other. Empathy is vicarious. Of course if the pastoral counselor has had an experience of suffering similar to that of the client, the empathy is quite possibly more reality-grounded and more shared than if the experience is vicarious. Furthermore in terms of communication, it may help the client appreciate the counselor's compassion for his or her suffering if the client knows that the counselor has undergone similar distress. But even here, the power of vicariousness is not necessarily diluted when compared with a real-life experience of suffering. Indeed, if the compassionate counselor is not careful, or fully in touch with self, he or she could distort the client's experience of suffering. In such a situation, the counselor is not plunging into the suffering of the client, but instead is plunging into his or her own suffering and attributing all or most of the general and specific features of that suffering to the client's suffering.

In enhancing the power and coloration of his or her abilities to experience the client's suffering in a vicarious manner, the counselor can engage in a wide variety of exercises. Some of these might include engaging in creative expressions which help move one out of self-centeredness into another reality. According to Piper, forms of creative expressions such as music, painting, fiction and first-person narrative accounts enhance one's ability to imagine modally another's state even when the compassionate person has not had the experience of the sufferer.[71] This occurs because such experiences provide fresh combinations of images, words, metaphors, and other material to aid reconstruction and enlarge one's range of emotional responses.[72]

---

69. Blum, "Compassion," p. 510.

70. Jerry M. Lewis, *To Be A Therapist* (New York: Brunner/Mazel), 1978. See also D. Corydon Hammond, Dean H. Hopeworth, and Veon G. Smith, *Improving Therapeutic Communication: A Guide for Developing Effective Techniques* (San Francisco: Jossey Bass, 1977).

71. Piper, "Impartiality, Compassion, and Moral Imagination," p. 739.

72. Gerard Egan, *The Skilled Helper*, 4th ed. (Pacific Grove, Calif.: Brooks Cole, 1990), p. 135.

Self-Compassion

We have suggested that compassion is primarily other-regarding rather than self-regarding.[73] Indeed, according to Blum, in compassion, one might act contrary to one's mood, feelings, or inclinations.[74] However, this does not necessarily rule out speaking about self-compassion. One might argue that, strictly speaking, compassion is addressed to suffering. Therefore, any object of compassion is a legitimate recipient of compassion. In many cases, the object of suffering may be another. At other times, the object of compassion may be one's own suffering. In such a case, self-compassion may be an appropriate response to such suffering.

Such a theme of self-concern or what is being called, self-compassion, is found in some religious writers on compassion. In an article about pastoral care for the sick, Becker noted that "while we respond with suffering compassion to the suffering of another, it is important that we are not overwhelmed by that suffering." Further, he noted that "if we are so overwhelmed, then we are impelled to deal with our own misery, and solve our own problems rather than being free to care for another."[75] In a similar vein, Brown noted that "the limits are real to what one may personally absorb and integrate through contact with those in extreme situations. It can quickly become a critical task for the one who is present with the suffering to establish boundaries to contain one's feelings, so that one doesn't disintegrate in the face of such demands for compassion."[76]

Other authors referring to self-compassion include Carl Goldberg who suggested that in addition to having compassion for client's suffering a therapist must also treat him or herself with liberal amounts of compassion.[77] He clearly spoke of two kinds of compassion; one toward clients and one toward self. Goldberg views both types of compassion as essential. Kirwan suggests that compassion toward ourselves is the first component in the restoration of

---

73. Blum, "Compassion," p. 509.
74. Ibid.
75. Becker, "Compassion: The Foundations of Care of the Sick."
76. Brown, "The Problem of Compassion," p. 25.
77. Carl Goldberg, "Understanding the Impaired Practitioner," *Psychotherapy in Private Practice* 4:3 (1986), pp. 25-34.

one's personal identity.[78] Such compassion is based on our sense of the compassion that Christ has for us.[79] In a compassionate relationship, one gains a sense of being accepted and thereby learns to accept oneself.

There is also biblical support for self-compassion. In the command to love our neighbors as ourselves, one owes no response of love to another that is not first owed to self. In fact, this verse suggests that one must first have a pattern for loving self which then becomes the pattern by which we love others. Compassion as a loving response to suffering is therefore appropriate even when self is the object of suffering. Furthermore, compassion for oneself is a basis from which one learns to be truly compassionate toward others. Reich supported this assumption when he stated that "unless we are compassionate with ourselves and receive compassion from others, we are not able to provide compassion."[80]

The notion of self-compassion is supported by the need for balance in compassion. According to Reich, compassion requires a balance so that the one who is the subject of compassion (that is, one who shows compassion) must also become the object of compassion.[81] Piper also contends that the notion of balance in compassion is important. He suggests that persons must have a level of involvement that respects both self and others.[82] Too much emphasis on self results in self-absorption. In contrast, too much involvement with others leads to "vicarious possession." The response that respects both self and others suffering is what Piper called compassion.[83] Compassion that is a balance between the demands of self and the demands of others fulfills the principle of "strict impartiality." In strict impartiality, one is neither biased toward oneself or toward others.[84] Piper also noted that "consistent application of the principle of rendering aid to the needy prohibits depleting or sacrificing one's resources so thoroughly that one ends up joining the ranks of the needy oneself."[85]

---

78. Kirwan, *Biblical Concepts for Christian Counseling*, pp. 114-115.
79. Ibid.
80. Reich, "Speaking of Suffering," p. 105.
81. Ibid.
82. Piper, "Impartiality, Compassion, and Moral Imagination," p. 734.
83. Ibid., pp. 744-745.
84. Ibid.
85. Ibid., p. 755.

Compassion as the balance between self-absorption or other-absorption is therefore attuned to both others (compassion in common parlance) and to self (self-compassion as we use the term). As noted earlier, self-compassion in the client has implications for the healing process. Self-compassion also has implications for the counselor in that its application will save one from burnout and other deleterious effects of caring-counseling with others.

Compassion and Suffering

One of the reasons for the relative neglect of compassion in the counseling literature is because of its link to suffering.[86] According to Reich,[87] we do not know what to think of suffering, would rather avoid it than face it and surely are not interested in explaining its meaning. He also suggested that an approach which experientially interprets suffering and the compassionate response to it is necessary to an understanding of compassion. In explicating an experiential approach to suffering, Reich suggested that there are three phases to suffering.[88] These, in turn, correspond respectively to three phases of compassion appropriate to a particular phase of the person's suffering. These phases of suffering and compassion are directly applicable to religious counseling. The first phase of suffering is labeled by Reich as "mute suffering."[89] In this phase, the suffering person is rendered speechless by either the magnitude or the precipitous nature of their suffering. By speechless, Reich[90] means that the individual is unable to communicate the suffering being experienced, or the feelings that go along with that suffering. Furthermore, even when the power of speech is present the suffering person may experience alexithymnia where it is impossible to fully communicate inner attitudes, feelings, and drives. In this stage of suffering, such persons lose a sense of autonomy and identity and are unable to find any meaning in their suffering.

The second phase of suffering, called "expressive suffering," is where the sufferer, in pursuit of understanding, finds some means

86. Reich, "Speaking of Suffering," p. 84.
87. Ibid.
88. Ibid., p. 86.
89. Ibid.
90. Ibid., pp. 86-87.

of communication. Generally such communication is expressed in lament, story (narrative), and interpretation. In lament, the person gives expression to suffering through complaint. In narrative, the persons begins a continual recounting of the story. Such continual narrative serves two purposes. First, the narrative serves the purpose of reconstructing the past suffering and providing a new perspective and some distance from the suffering. Second, the narrative is told in the hope that someone may affirm the sufferer in the search for a new story; a story that will account for and justify a new self that might emerge from the suffering. Finally, in interpretation, the expression of suffering is designed to find a language whereby the suffering can be interpreted. According to Reich,[91] this is often expressed through metaphor which pairs negative and postive images. For example, Reich[92] suggested that a sufferer may use the image of the victim. Paired to that victim metaphor, the caregiver may be seen as a victor. The second image suggests that one does not have to remain a victim of suffering but can overcome it. Therefore, the sufferer is led to see some possibility for change.

In the third phase of suffering, the sufferer finally finds voice for the suffering experienced and change takes place. According to Reich,[93] this change involves identification with a view of self that emerged from dialogue and reformulation of one's experience. The change is also facilitated by solidarity with a compassionate other.

Three Phases of Compassion

Corresponding to each of the three phases of suffering of individuals, there are also three phases of compassion. According to Reich,[94] the first phase (silent empathy, silent compassion) begins with empathy which leads to compassion and both of these begin with silence. In this phase, the compassionate person is silent in the face of suffering and is committed to being with and for the client and laying aside personal biases. Such silence in the face of

91. Ibid., pp. 89-90.
92. Ibid.
93. Ibid., p. 91.
94. Ibid., p. 93.

suffering throws the sufferer back upon himself and forces the individual to discover his own language for expressing his experiences. At the same time, the compassionate person demonstrates a caring receptivity.

A second phase of compassion, addressed to the second phase of suffering involves what Reich[95] called "expressive compassion." In this phase, the compassionate person assists the sufferer in finding a voice for the suffering. This phase also involves helping the sufferer to gain a broader perspective on the suffering. Additionally, this phase may be demonstrated through reformulation of the sufferer's story. According to Reich,[96] reformulation of the story can take several forms: First, reformulation may mean encouraging and not obstructing the sufferer's self-expression. Second, it can mean helping the client to make connections between aspects of the story and self. Third, reformulation may lead to translational statements whereby the compassionate person converts the sufferer's words into comprehensible language. Finally, reformulation of the story may take the form of an interpretative statement that promotes intellectual understanding and thus make sense out of the suffering.

A third phase of compassion is where the compassionate person also experiences some change through working with the suffering individual. Most obviously, that change involves having experienced the suffering of the person. Moreover, the compassionate person also identifies with the compassionate view of self that emerged from trying to alleviate the sufferings of another. At the same time, the compassionate behavior exemplified during work with the suffering persons reinforces the sharing of compassion. Finally, the compassionate individual experiences change in that he or she now has a larger repertoire of stories of pain and suffering from having empathically experienced sufferings. These stories or images then become affective and conceptual models whereby compassion can be shared yet again.

Compassion in Religious Counseling

We contend that religious counselors should incorporate compassion more directly into their ministry of counseling for several

---

95. Ibid., p. 94.
96. Ibid.

reasons. First, as persons who are part of God's created order pastoral counselors are called to imitate him in a variety of ways. Compassion is one of the ways in which we imitate him as we encounter suffering humanity. Second, our religious traditions serve as a reminder that as part of God's creation, we are inextricably linked to the rest of creation. Compassion is an appropriate response to the suffering persons to whom we are linked. It is indeed a heritage from creation.[97] Third, because of its religious origins, compassion is one of the unique theological concepts of our Judeo-Christian tradition. As religious counselors become more proficient in the use of counseling skills, they are more likely to replace theological concepts with psychological ones.[98] This is not to suggest that one ought not to be psychological, but religious therapists should retain and cherish theological traditions and concepts that may be a vital part of the therapeutic process.[99] Finally, the religious nature of compassion holds out therapeutic value both for counselors and clients. From the client's perspective, compassion serves as a reminder of the value of persons and that all persons are deserving of respect as we work with them. From the counselor's perspective, a compassionate view of persons may protect him or her from developing dehumanizing attitudes toward other persons.[100]

Some of the therapeutic qualities found in compassion include sensitivity to suffering; caring and acceptance of the one who is suffering; and a sense of fellow-feeling. Fellow feeling can help to promote a kind of equality that protects the counselor from condescension which is damaging to the therapeutic process. Goldberg suggested that compassion is potentially the therapist's most sensitive tool for attending to the client's suffering, and that compassion creates a vulnerability which facilitates an effective and meaningful rapprochement between the counselor and the client.[101]

---

97. Becker, "Compassion: The Foundation of Care of the Sick."

98. William Hulme, *Pastoral Care and Counseling* (Minneapolis: Augsburg, 1981). Also Paul Pruyser, *Minister as Diagnostician* (Philadelphia: Westminster, 1976).

99. Caroll Saussy, "How Do You Integrate Your Theology into Your Clinical Work," *Pastoral Psychology* 35:1 (1986), pp. 56-68.

100. Ayala M. Pines, Elliot Aronson, and Ditsa Kafry, *Burnout: From Tedium to Personal Growth* (New York: Free Press, 1981), p. 83.

101. Goldberg, " Understanding the Impaired Practitioner."

Counselor Compassion and Therapeutic Change

The primary purpose and goal of compassion is to attempt to alleviate suffering of another. Using the cognitive, affective, and overt behavioral dimensions previously described as components of compassion, we now explicate the purposes of compassion and indicate how compassion contributes to therapeutic change. We also discuss the contributions of compassion, beginning with the cognitive dimension since this is the genesis of the whole compassionate process.

In terms of alleviating the client's suffering, or at least as a key beginning stage of alleviating the client's suffering, the role and function of empathy is very important. Earlier in this chapter we defined empathy and discussed it in more or less general terms, with occasional allusions to the place of empathy in the pastoral counseling act. Now we wish to link empathy more closely with pastoral counseling with and for compassion.

Most counseling specialists hold that empathy is a valuable part of the therapeutic process and is both an attitude and skill which transcends counseling stages.[102] Its value lies in the several functions that it serves in therapeutic change. The counselor's appropriate empathic responding enables clients to appreciate that a caring person is with them and that they are understood.[103] From a self psychology perspective, contact with an empathic counselor leads to firm self-cohesion and positive self-esteem, while counteracting destructive attitudes toward self and others.[104] In addition, empathic responding also reduces clients sense of threat and helps to lower defenses. Moreover, empathy can foster rapport and build the counseling relationship. Empathy also can enhance the emotional growth and improvement of the client through the facilitation of self-exploration.[105]

In order for compassion to be appropriate to the object of suf-

---

102. See, for example, Samuel Gladding, *Counseling: A Comprehensive Profession*, 2nd ed. (New York: Macmillan, 1992), p. 193.

103. Lewis, *To Be a Therapist*. See also Hammond, Hopeworth, and Smith, *Improving Therapeutic Communication*.

104. Robert L. Randall, "Self Psychology in Pastoral Counseling," *Journal of Religion and Health* 28:1 (1989), pp. 7-15.

105. Ibid.

fering, empathy must not only be present, it must also be accurate.[106] The counseling literature speaks about two types of accurate empathy. In primary accurate empathy, the counselor is able to understand and communicate an understanding of the client's feelings, behaviors, and experiences.[107] In advanced empathy, the counselor is able to understand not only what the client states but also what is implied or stated incompletely.[108] The latter aspect of empathy appears closely related to what Reich described as expressive compassion.[109]

The importance of counselor accuracy in the empathic process is one which cannot be overestimated. The counselor's empathy is not empathy for its own sake, or empathy to make the counselor have warm feelings for the client. Rather, the primary and abiding purpose of the counselor's empathy is to enable the helper to better assist the client—and in the case of compassionate counseling, to better alleviate the suffering of the person in distress. Thus the pastoral counselor must always ask himself or herself during the empathic encounter: "Am I truly helping the client?" The counselor's task is to be empathic so that the client at this particular moment feels not only genuinely understood but also "felt with," understanding that his or her feelings are being genuinely appreciated and shared by the counselor without distortion in color or intensity.

Carl Rogers insightfully highlights the central role of counselor awareness and counselor "technique" during the therapeutic event. He underscores the fact that the conditions which lead to effective counseling results pertain to attitudes and not just to specific behaviors—or more accurately, we would say, to the enfleshment of attitudes in specific behaviors, to the flow of underlying attitudes in specific behaviors which the counselor employs with the client. Rogers speaks of these attitudes, not so much in terms of what social psychologists would technically define as attitude, but rather "a continuing set which consistently infuses all the different behaviors" in which the counselor engages. Thus—and this is so crucially important that we are italicizing it—"*the conditions [of effective ther-*

---

106. Piper, "Impartiality, Compassion, and Moral Imagination," p. 738.
107. Egan, *The Skilled Helper*, p. 87. See also Gladding, *Counseling*, pp. 193-194.
108. Ibid, pp. 195-196.
109. Reich, "Speaking of Suffering," p. 94.

apy] emphasize not what one does but how one does it."[110] Thus the counselor's empathic technique is vital and indispensable—not a mechanistic technique, not a wooden technique, not an artificial technique, not technique for technique's sake, but a flowing, harmonious way of being with the client. Thus the counselor's authentic empathic technique will center on and work through interpersonal qualities in an interpersonal encounter. So, Rogers adds, "Measurement of these conditions involves the defining of objective behavioral indices which are relevant to and indicative of subjective modes of personal response."[111]

We also must highlight the importance of accuracy in the counselor's empathic "feeling into" the affective state of the anguished client who needs compassion. If the client thinks or feels that the counselor's empathy is misdirected and inaccurate, then the client will tend to "turn off" the counselor rather than be helped by the facilitator. The client must perceive as fully as possible that the counselor truly feels for him and truly understands him. Inaccuracy in the counselor's empathetic responding destroys the bond the client is developing or has developed with the counselor. Indeed, if the client perceives that the counselor's empathy is inaccurate in terms of the sufferer's own feelings, the client will regard the counselor as just one more person who does not understand, as just one more disinterested individual, as just one more of those fakes and frauds who claims to want to help but who does not and maybe even will not.

In order to develop accuracy in the empathic encounter, the pastoral counselor would do well to display two qualities. The first of these is selflessness. If the religious counselor is selfish, if the religious counselor has entered the counseling profession and remains there primarily to solve his or her own problems, if the religious counselor has personal problems of such a magnitude and pervasiveness as to consume a considerable portion of his or her energy, then quite possibly he or she will not be sufficiently self-

---

110. Carl R. Rogers, "The Conceptual Context," in Carl R. Rogers, *The Therapeutic Relationship and Its Impact* (Madison, Wis.: University of Wisconsin Press, 1967), p. 11. We should add that Rogers also believed this to be a crucial point for all counselors. He italicized the words what and how in the quotation we cited in the body of the text.

111. Ibid.

less to engage in authentic empathy, even though the external trappings might be in place. In the empathic encounter the counselor must feel into the client, must become the client not on his or her own terms but on the terms of the client as the client has set these terms and as the client lives these terms.

The second quality is a continual, active awareness of what transpires during the counseling process. Self-awareness, plus awareness of the dynamics of the counseling process, is a crucial element for truly helpful empathy, for healing empathy, for compassionate empathy.

In contrast to empathy, sympathy is not well regarded by many experts in the counseling profession. Egan, for example, suggests that sympathy has much more in common with pity, commiseration, and condolence than with empathy.[112] Sympathy, it will be recalled from our earlier discussion, is more selfish and less sharing of self with the client since in sympathy the counselor is always aware of his or her own identity, whereas in empathy the counselor endeavors vicariously to plunge into the sea of the client's feelings as the client experiences these feelings.

Sympathy as a counseling tool might be ill-advised if it distorts the listening process and thus the stories that clients tell.[113] A second danger is that sympathy may emphasize awareness of feelings to such an extent that the counselor may become overinvolved in the feelings of the client.[114] Thus sympathy is seen as denoting agreement with others which can lead to over-identification and collusion with the client.[115] Empathy is preferred, since in contrast to sympathy it allows for better experiential understanding and the sharing of powerful feelings and experiences of others without being overwhelmed by them.[116] Archibald Hart, a noted Christian author, regards sympathy as being overly sentimental and suggested that one's compassion should not be dom-

---

112. Egan, *The Skilled Helper*, p. 139.

113. See Carl Schlauch, "Empathy as the Essence of Pastoral Psychotherapy," *The Journal of Pastoral Care* 44:1 (1990), pp. 3-17. Also, Seward Hiltner "Empathy in Counseling: We can feel our way into the experience of another only to the extent that we have felt at home with our own experience," *Pastoral Psychology* 1 (1951), pp. 25-30.

114. Reich, "Speaking of Suffering," p. 105.

115. Egan, *The Skilled Helper*, p. 119.

116. Reich, "Speaking of Suffering," pp. 104-105.

inated by sympathy but by empathy.[117]

It is not enough for the counselor to empathically share the feelings of the client. The facilitator should be able to overtly express these shared feelings in an appropriate manner to the client. A counselor who fails to effectively communicate the sharing of the client's feelings and experiential anguish is probably not "with the client" in the most intense sense of that term.[118] Lack of effective communication—which amounts to affective shallowness and possibly even affective fear—can possibly be eliminated or reduced when placed in the context of compassion which brings appropriate counselor sensitivity for the feelings of others into a preeminently behavioral mode.

Essential to compassion, and therefore for compassionate counseling, are overt behaviors which are geared toward the alleviation of suffering in the client. In compassionate counseling, then, the counselor must engage in activities which address the problems and suffering of the client. It is essential that counselors distinguish between their "regular" actions and the actions they will be taking as part of compassionate counseling. Regular counselor actions such as listening, attending, empathic responding, and the like, are important, especially when they are appropriately expressed to the client. They certainly are the underlying basis for effective counseling. But compassionate counseling necessitates more than this. It necessitates either the counselor suggesting that the client engage in concrete overt behaviors (preferably behaviors suggested by the client), or overt behaviors by the counselor during or sometime after the counseling encounter. For some counselors such a suggestion might raise serious ethical questions or be considered otherwise unprofessional. Certainly it is somewhat different from the normal run of much counseling, as for example traditional nondirective counseling. Thus pastoral counselors who wish to engage in compassionate counseling are challenged to ask themselves whether and how their counseling can be genuinely compassionate if they restrict their counseling efforts to the counseling office or restrict the client's activities to sharing his/her experiences and

---

117. Archibald Hart, *Counseling the Depressed,* in *Resources for Christian Counseling,* vol. 5 (Dallas: Word, 1990).

118. Egan, *The Skilled Helper,* p. 126.

stories. In like manner pastoral counselors of the more humanistic schools must confront the difficult question whether "regular" counseling functions fulfills the humanistic goals of compassionate counseling.

In dealing with the thorny and possibly controversial issue of the role of overt behavior in compassionate counseling, we must again highlight the issue of client autonomy since this issue often surfaces soon after overt behavior and counseling are linked. Whatever the role which overt behavior plays in compassionate counseling—from never to frequently—its use by counselors should avoid robbing clients of their autonomy. According to Reich, persons who are suffering have already lost some sense of their lives and are struggling to regain a sense or autonomy.[119] Counseling should be a process of liberation that frees up clients to be themselves and to move toward autonomy. From a religious perspective, counseling in the most basic sense involves helping persons to become all that God intended them to become. The counselor's compassionate actions should become a means whereby clients are empowered, liberated to be all they were intended to be and assisted in regaining some sense of control of their lives. As Egan rightly suggested, helping is ineffective and possibly dangerous if it leads to added feelings of powerlessness in clients. When client dependency is increased, counseling simply becomes another form of oppression.[120] This is especially true for clients who are by nature nonassertive and who readily acquiesce in the face of the counseling "expert" or "guru."

Conversely, the counselor must use power effectively for there is much in the counseling process that places it in his/her hands. Two examples illustrate the power base of the counseling relationship. First, the counseling relationship is rooted in the establishing of a power base that makes the counselor important to clients. This power base is important so that clients are more willing to listen to the suggestions of the counselor.[121] According to Egan, such a power base is seen in terms of the attractiveness, trustworthiness, and competence of the helper.[122] Closely related to the notion of a power base is the fact that counseling is a manifesta-

---

119. Reich, "Speaking of Suffering," p. 87.
120. Egan, *The Skilled Helper*, p. 12 ff.
121. Ibid.
122. Ibid., pp. 135-137.

tion of the social influence of the counselor on the client.[123] In addition to the obvious power of the counselor, Paul Hopkins suggested that the counselor's training and insight may increase the possibility of counseling becoming a process of oppression.[124]

These difficulties may be precluded by a pervasive sense of compassion in the counselor so that she or he is led to help in ways that do not oppress the client. Hopkins called this type of counselor the "compassionate oppressor." This is the counselor who is constantly aware of the possible unjust use of his or her power and authority and tempers the latter with compassion.[125] But how can one empower and facilitate clients' control of their lives? Egan suggests the following: that counselors use a participative rather than a directive model of counseling; that counselors accept helping as a natural two-way influence process; that they act as consultants to their clients; that counselors democratize the helping process, and finally, that they focus on the client's enlightened self-interest.[126]

Does all of this preclude counselor overt action following the counseling session? And does all of this preclude the counselor working with the client so that the latter will engage in overt action during or following the counseling session? These are questions which pastoral counselors who wish to engage in authentically compassionate counseling must ask themselves, keeping in mind that compassion necessarily includes overt action on the part of the compassioner.

Counselor Self-Compassion

All counselors must be self-compassionate. But, given the theological "baggage" that they bring to the counseling relationship, self-compassion is especially critical in religious counselors. Indeed, it is quite possible for religious counselors to become oversensitive to the suffering of others and thereby lose their sense of objectivity. This possible or potential oversensitivity to suffering likely stems from three sources. The first source is the Christian or other reli-

---

123. Ibid., pp. 131-132.
124. Paul E. Hopkins, "On Being A Compassionate Oppressor," *Pastoral Psychology*, 34:3 (1986), pp. 204-213.
125. Ibid.
126. Egan, *The Skilled Helper*, pp. 78-79.

gious value system that the pastoral counselor upholds. Many believers are likely (and appropriately so) to experience an inordinately strong desire to behave compassionately as an expression of their own personal and ecclesial relationship with God. A second source is the nature of the counseling profession itself which seems to require a heightened reactivity to the suffering in others. Third, those who enter the counseling profession tend to be particularly sensitive toward the needs of others.[127] Thus, the importance of compassion for others may be unduly and inappropriately overemphasized through a combination of the counselor's religious devotion, the perceived characteristics required by the counseling profession, and one's personal characteristics. Concomitant with the overemphasis of other-compassion, one is also likely to experience a reduction in self-compassion.

The lack of self-compassion is a deleterious outcome that may place counselors themselves in the ranks of the suffering. Lack of counselor self-compassion may manifest itself as overcommitment and overload which result in stress and burnout.[128] Can pastoral counselors truly be other-compassionate without first being self-compassionate? Can pastoral counselors adequately care for others if they themselves are experiencing great suffering due to being overloaded? And, is it ethical for counseling caregivers, even in the name of compassion, to subject themselves to such physical and emotional trauma that can potentially impair their judgment, skills, and overall ability to render aid? Such overextension, even in the name of compassion, is obviously harmful to the counselor. Ultimately, such overextension can also become harmful to the client in that it impairs the caregivers' therapeutic judgment and reduces the effectiveness of the care that is given.

Client-Self Compassion and Therapeutic Change

Counseling is a collaborative process that necessitates the participation of both counselor and client.[129] This suggests that it is not enough that pastoral counselors have compassion for clients. Of necessity, clients must also become more self-compassionate. Such

---

127. Pines, Aronson, and Kafry, *Burnout*, pp. 50-51.
128. Ibid, pp. 20-21.
129. Egan, *The Skilled Helper*, p. 78.

client self-compassion is positively related to therapeutic change.[130] Client self-compassion is therapeutic in that it revolves around clients' self-acceptance and leads to a sense of belonging. According to Kirwan, this is the first step in the restoration of client identity.[131] From our discussion of compassion as having cognitive, affective, and behavioral components, one would expect that client self-compassion would be expressed in each of these areas.

The client's own self-compassion should harmoniously integrate all the major elements of compassion, namely cognitive elements, affective elements, and overt behavior or lifestyle elements. The cognitive dimension of compassion, which in its finest form is understanding from experience, is important and necessary for therapeutic self-compassion because it is through understanding[132] that the client can gain fresh and deeper perspectives on his or her suffering. Indeed, all suffering, whether brought on by loneliness,[133] by the sudden death of a loved one, or by enduring terminal disease can, if properly understood, bring with it the potential for gaining deeper insights for personal growth. Additionally, the acquisition of a genuine understanding of their distress may well help clients to look at their whole existential situation in a new light. David Seamands calls this set of new perspectives "retrospection that reinterprets."[134] Or again, understanding of the "why" of his or her suffering might assist the client to fit together or at least make sense of what might seem to be discrepant aspects of his or her suffering.

The compassionate pastoral counselor can facilitate the client's gaining and increasing his own understanding of suffering by helping him to personalize the meaning of the suffering. As Robert Carkhuff has noted, the process of personalizing meaning is an important and essential step toward facilitating the client's under-

---

130. Kirwan, *Biblical Concepts*, pp. 105-109.

131. Ibid.

132. The importance of understanding is detailed in those psychological theories which emphasize the role of cognition in the facilitational process, such as Albert Ellis' emotive therapy, Aaron Beck's cognitive therapy, Donald Meichenbaum's cognitive-behavior modification, and the like. Interesting for counselors is the role which understanding is given in psychotherapeutic theories such as those of Sigmund Freud and Alfred Adler.

133. Samuel M. Natale, *Loneliness and Spiritual Growth* (Birmingham, Ala.: Religious Education Press, 1986).

134. This point was mentioned and elaborated by David Seamands in the Cessna Lectures delivered at Asbury Theological Seminary on April 2, 1992.

standing of where he or she is in relation to where that person wants to be or needs to be. The client personalizes meaning when the counselor shifts the interpretative ground from meaning as an objective cognitive grasp of why suffering is occurring to meaning as a personally significant event to the client. The counselor can facilitate the client's acquisition of personally significant meaning by helping the client internalize the suffering by linking it to personal accountability and responsibility.[135]

The affective dimension of compassion, namely empathy, should also be a prominent feature of the client's compassion for self. Cognition, even when such cognition is at the level of understanding, is not sufficient. This is especially apparent when clients understand their suffering and distress but, because they lack empathy for themselves, may feel that they deserve to suffer. Distortions in the affective dimension of awareness may take even more extreme forms in which the client indulges in unproductive, inappropriate, and neurotic self-punishment. In such situations, empathy toward self may help the client to become less blaming and less punishing toward self. This, in turn, might lead such persons to be more actively cooperative with their religious counselor and to participate more vigorously in their own healing.

If empathy is the affective plunge into another person's self with the intent of feeling the world as that other individual feels, how can the client have empathy for self? Technically, of course, empathy does mean the vicarious affective plunging into the life of another. Notwithstanding, a broader and more inclusive view of empathy surely includes the affective plunging into self. This kind of affective plunging was at the heart of many of the human potential movements of the 1960s and 1970s, virtually all of which held that before a person could come to wholeness that person had "to get in touch with self." Getting in touch with self, in this perspective, placed great emphasis on freeing the person to feel who he or she truly is, to be who he or she authentically is. (The reader may wish to reexamine the earlier comments on freedom by Richard Williams and Barry Estadt.) Most of these movements stressed that a major cause of all personality dysfunction, and even a major cause of the failure

135. Robert R. Carkhuff, *The Art of Helping*, 5th ed. (Amherst, Mass.: Human Resource Development Press, 1983), p. 117.

to reach one's full human potential, came from being out of touch with self and being alienated from self. Only by plunging into the sea of one's own feeling functions, only by becoming in unison with the affective dimensions of the self, can one truly be who one truly is. It is in this sense that it is accurate to refer to empathy as being an important feature of the client's self-compassion.

Clients can be significantly helped when they engage in those kinds of behaviors which help alleviate their suffering and distress. These kinds of behaviors are both less visible and more visible.[136] One dimension of the process in which the client engages in less visible behaviors is that these kinds of actions often involve gaining new perspectives, new insights, refashioning old feelings into more productive ones, and the like. Egan calls this kind of client action the heart of the helping process.[137] Thus, compassionate counselors must help clients to take responsibility for themselves and to participate in actions that will be therapeutic. When clients fail to act intelligently in their own behalf, the likelihood of real therapeutic gains is minimal.[138] When clients act on their own behalf they are likely to gain new perspectives on their sufferings and also to consolidate gains made during the therapy session.

By engaging in visible behaviors, in overt action, clients can relieve the pain and distress to a significant degree. This is especially true for altruistic behavior done on behalf of other persons. Joseph Canale suggests that such altruistic behavior is therapeutic for clients in that it gives them a meaningful opportunity to be of assistance to others and also leads to a sense of satisfaction and adequacy.[139] The same author quoted earlier research that showed that chronic patients in altruistic group therapy were discharged more quickly and had less hospital stay than patients in self-ori-

---

136. We write less visible and more visible to escape the false dichotomy of "inner" and "outer," a dichotomy which suggests a dualistic human being. Anything which an organism does is a behavior. A thought is as much a behavior as throwing a baseball. A big difference between these two is that one is less visible into the more visible, so that the client makes visible to the counselor his or her thoughts and feelings, and that reciprocally the counselor makes visible to the client his or her cognitive and affective proactions and reactions.

137. Egan, *The Skilled Helper*, p. 37.

138. Ibid, p. 85.

139. Joseph R. Canale, "Altruism and Forgiveness as Therapeutic Agents," *Journal of Religion and Health* 29 (1990), pp. 297-301.

ented groups.[140] In a similar vein, Hulme suggested that clients as recipients must also become givers.[141] According to him, one's self-image is elevated through both receiving and giving.[142]

Further support for the therapeutic nature of actions done on behalf of others can be found in the therapeutic approach of Alfred Adler and his concept of social interest. Social interest is expressed through an involvement in the lives of other persons and partly stems from one's sense of being related to the rest of society.[143] Adler's premise was that persons high in social interest were more likely to be psychologically healthy. This assumption has been supported by research indicating that social interest is positively correlated with adjustment and well-being.[144]

Viewed from the focus of compassion, it is obvious that clients engagement in compassionate behavior, both less visible and especially more visible, will facilitate their gaining experientially based insight as to the nature of their own suffering. Such insight can assist clients in dealing meaningfully with their own plight. And by engaging in overt compassionate behaviors, clients will be lead not only to intentionally place their own suffering into the much larger pool of the communion of saints, but also to gain that selflessness which both leads to personal change and which is quintessentially Christian. Let us say, for example, that a client is experiencing much pain and anguish caused by a serious disease. The physician at this point does not know if the disease is terminal. By visiting hospital patients in the latter stages of the disease, and by volunteering to help these patients by praying with them or by doing physical acts of help to them, the client can quite possibly gain more insight into pain and suffering, more self-empathy, more awareness of real physical pain, more of a disposition to offer his or her own pain to Jesus in union with the Lord's agony when he was on earth, and more of a focus on the plight of others than could be acquired in all the verbal therapy done in a counselor's office.

---

140. Ibid.

141. Hulme, *Pastoral Care and Counseling*, pp. 160-163.

142. Ibid.

143. Alfred A. Adler, *Social Interest: A Challenge to Mankind*, (New York: Capricorn, 1964). See also Lewis M. Way, *Adler's Place in Psychology* (New York: Collier, 1962).

144. Alfred A. Adler, *Superiority and Social Interest: A Collection of Letter Writings*, ed. H.L. Ansbacher and Rowena Ansbacher (New York: Viking, 1964b).

For compassion to be actualized, the cognitive, affective, and behavioral elements must be dynamically linked. Applied to what we have just said about compassion and therapeutic change, this suggests that both counselor and client must have each of these elements functioning and linked if true change is to occur. Stated otherwise, both counselor and client must experience empathy and sympathy and demonstrate behaviors that facilitate change. Failure in any of these elements in either the counselor or client can undermine the therapeutic process. This would suggest that the counselor and client's compassionate behaviors are linked in the collaborative therapeutic process. Both counselor and client must be compassionate for healing to occur.

Phases of Suffering, Compassion, and Counseling

Reich's treatment of the various phases of suffering and the corresponding phases of compassion suggest that a compassionate response must be appropriate to each phase of the suffering and must be addressed to the needs of that particular phase.[145]

In the first phase of suffering, the needs of clients are directed toward finding some means of giving voice to their suffering and regaining some sense of autonomy. What is the compassionate response to this phase? In some cases silence may be an appropriate lead, that is, a specific behavior in which counselors engage so as to bring about change in clients.[146] Silence as a leading response is particularly appropriate at the beginning of the counseling process.[147]

The phenomenon of silence in the face of suffering is common. Not only are some sufferers driven to silence, but those who aspire to alleviate the suffering are also driven to silence. When Job's friends attempted to comfort him, they eventually succumbed to silence. "When they saw him from a distance, they could hardly recognize him; they began to weep aloud, and they tore their robes and sprinkled dust on their heads. Then they sat on the ground with him for seven days and seven nights. No one said a word to him, because they saw how great his suffering was."[148]

---

145. Reich, "Speaking of Suffering," pp. 86-99.
146. Ibid. See also Egan, *The Skilled Helper*, p. 95 ff.
147. Ibid.
148. Job 2:12-13 (NIV), emphasis ours.

Conversely, in the face of suffering, some helpers are prone to think that they must say something that will be perceived as comforting. Many times, in so doing, a person says something that trivializes the pain and suffering of the sufferer. Counseling situations also present a similar dilemma. In the face of client suffering and the resulting silence, the compassionate counselor is likely to think that something must be said. Such a strategy may restrict sufferers from finding their own language for communicating their suffering. In addition, the counselor's discomfort with silence and subsequent attempts to address the suffering may trivialize the suffering of the client. Such premature communication by the counselor may also distort the suffering of the client, in that the language of suffering is not the client's but the counselor's. Clients at this stage of suffering have experienced a loss of autonomy. Premature communication may be a means of further reinforcing this sense of loss. This kind of communication may preclude the client's own expressions of suffering. Additionally, premature counselor communication may imply to the clients that they are inadequate to find their own voice. In so doing, one may help to create a sense of powerlessness in the client.

The value of silence is that it demonstrates respect for clients' sufferings.[149] Moreover, when silence is used appropriately, the compassionate person communicates a sense of caring receptivity to the sufferer.[150] Silence might also serve to communicate an understanding of the unspeakable nature of the suffering.[151] Reich has also noted that silent compassion throws the sufferer back upon himself and forces him to find a language for the suffering.[152] Similarly, Samuel Gladding noted that when the counselor is silent, the client will feel some pressure to continue and that he will choose how to continue with minimal input from the counselor.[153]

Mute versus Expressive Suffering

According to Reich, sufferers move from mute suffering toward expressive suffering. Expressive suffering often takes the form of

---

149. Reich, "Speaking of Suffering," pp. 86-87.
150. Ibid.
151. Ibid.
152. Ibid.
153. Gladding, *Counseling*, pp. 76-78.

lament, story, or interpretation. Expressive suffering or the symbolization of experience into words is what Katherine Clarke calls "creation of meaning."[154] The creation of meaning is formed by the interplay of experiencing and something that functions as a symbol, in this case, language. Through language, clients are able to reconstruct the meaning of their emotionally charged experiences. Essentially, the reconstruction process involves changing clients' perceptions of affect and cognition together in the sense that through symbolization, clients cognitively understand their emotions. Acquiring meaning through symbolization has been found to produce "greater portions of patient speech which contain a synthesis of readily accessible, newly recognized, or more fully realized feelings and experiences which produce personally meaningful structures or resolve issues."[155] Additionally, creation of meaning also produces "greater reduction of discomfort, greater clarity and feelings of strength and agency."[156]

Movement from mute suffering to expressive suffering is facilitated when sufferers are confronted with the possibility of change.[157] Often this possibility for change comes through some "contrast experience" whereby the sufferer is confronted with what may be and thus decides that the suffering should not continue.[158] Egan's model for movement in therapy includes a stage in which clients are challenged to face possibilities for change and to commit to such changes.[159] Counselors help clients with such contrast experiences by asking or getting clients to ask future oriented questions. Applied to suffering, the form of a future oriented question would be "what would the future look like if you were able to cope with this suffering?" Thus clients are invited to find contrasting images in which they see themselves as coping rather than being overwhelmed.

The appropriate response to expressive suffering is what Reich called "expressive compassion."[160] Clients need a supportive person who will help them tell their personal story so that they may gain

---

154. Katherine M. Clarke, "Creation of Meaning, An Emotional Processing Task in Psychotherapy," *Psychotherapy* 25:2 (1989), pp. 139-148.
155. Ibid., p. 147.
156. Ibid.
157. Reich, "Speaking of Suffering," p. 88.
158. Ibid.
159. Egan, *The Skilled Helper*, pp. 33-34.
160. Reich, "Speaking of Suffering," p. 94.

new perspectives and distance themselves from the old story.[161] Expressive compassion may also facilitate the creation of meaning.[162] Additionally, suffering persons need a compassionate supporter who will be able to affirm and assist them in the reformulation of a new personal story.[163] The telling of one's story and the reformulation of the same is very important in counseling. Gerard Egan's model of therapeutic change is based on the importance of clients telling their personal stories. Clients telling their stories forms the first stage of the Egan model. The second stage of Egan's model is referred to as developing a preferred scenario and essentially is what Reich means by the reformulation of the sufferer's story.[164]

Forms of Expressive Suffering

As noted earlier, the forms of expressive suffering are lament, story, and interpretation. Most clients have little trouble with the latter two but may struggle with the expression of lament.[165] As stated by Reich, caregivers are likely to perceive such lament or complaint as an annoyance.[166] However, the expressive compassionate response will allow for narrative, interpretation, and lament.[167] The religious counselor must be attuned to this need for lament as a legitimate expression of one's suffering and must see it as potentially beneficial in moving one through and beyond suffering. Religious counselors in the Judeo-Christian tradition have a model for such lament in the penitential psalms and in the book of Job. It is noteworthy that Job's first response after the silence is the lament.[168]

Besides allowing for lament, compassionate counselors must express compassion in other forms. According to Reich, compassion can be expressed by the very language of diagnosis.[169] Furthermore,

---

161. Ibid.
162. Clarke, "Creation of Meaning," pp. 141-142.
163. Reich, "Speaking of Suffering," pp. 94-95.
164. Egan, *The Skilled Helper*, pp. 151-152.
165. Yet the creation of meaning is more often precipitated in therapy by negative emotions such as one might see in lament. Cf. Clarke, "Creation of Meaning," p. 140.
166. Reich, "Speaking of Suffering," p. 89.
167. Ibid., pp. 94-95.
168. Job 2:12-13.
169. Reich, "Speaking of Suffering," p. 94.

expressive compassion may be demonstrated by story. Here, the counselor assists the client in the reformulation of his or her own personal story. This may be facilitated through encouraging but not disrupting the client's narrative; "helping the client elicit the realistic past"; providing insight into how various pieces connect; translating clients' suffering into intelligible language and providing meaning to the sufferer's experience through what Reich called the interpretative statement.[170]

Achieving a New Identity

Through the demonstration of expressive compassion, clients can be led to change and come to a new identity in their suffering. This comprises the third phase of suffering. According to Reich, a sufferer changes because of solidarity with compassionate others and because a new identity is gained through the reformulation of the story.[171] We take this to mean that the reformulated story provides an identity for the sufferer as one who is capable of coping or getting beyond the suffering. To borrow an image that Reich used and which is often found among suffering persons, clients move from being victims to persons who can be victors. In this image of the victor as opposed to the victim, one may find an answer to the initial dilemma of the sufferer. In the language of the potential victor, one finds the restoration of the language of autonomy, a regaining of control in one's life, and a move toward a new more autonomous self. From the dimension of Christian compassion, we can also ask whether a client who is in distress can ever be the victor when he or she only gets *an* answer. It seems to us that from a religious perspective, *the* answer comes from living rather than primarily letting. Thus, the answer to the client's suffering is more likely to be found when the client renders compassionate assistance to others.

One of the more dramatic notions in the therapeutic experience is that the person who renders compassionate aid also achieves a new identity.[172] During the establishment of a relationship between the sufferer and the compassionate caregiver, a change often results

---

170. Ibid., p. 97.
171. Ibid., pp. 98-99.
172. Ibid., p. 104.

in both persons. That caregivers also change is consistent with the view that counseling is a two-way influence process.[173] What are the changes that the compassionate counselor experiences? When caregivers respond compassionately and identify with their voice of compassion, the caregiver decides at a deeper level to be a compassionate person.[174] Additionally, the demonstration of compassion also serves to reinforce compassionate behavior in the caregiver. Finally, the caregiver is changed because contact with a sufferer also provides the former with new stories and images that again can reinforce the habit of compassion.[175]

Compassion in Various Keys

Other examples of counselors' compassionate responses may be illustrated by referring to the field of pastoral counseling. One primary compassionate response is active listening which is an attempt to enter the experiential world of the other. Counselors cannot read client's mind, so they must be very attentive to the content of verbal expression and the nuance of the nonverbal communication. When one can truly "hear" another person, there is a possibility for understanding. The reverence of attending to another is critical to the developing of trust and is essential to self-disclosure. By giving such attention, the pastoral counselor may be open to accepting the client. When the client is truly understood, the caregiver will be in the covenant of acceptance.

Appropriate scripture reading and prayer may also be helpful. When these religious resources are used, it is imperative that the client be treated with reverence and respect. Scripture improperly applied may serve to increase pain and alienation. When used appropriately scripture may be supportive and give permission for the client to own some unacceptable but human feelings, as, for examples, fear or doubt. Prayer is a significant religious resource when used with discretion. Formal prayer that is a customary part of a person's religious ritual is useful when requested by a patient or troubled person. Spontaneous prayer that focuses on the needs of the client in distress, not on the interests of the one praying,

---

173. Egan, *The Skilled Helper*, p. 144.
174. Reich, "Speaking of Suffering," p. 98.
175. Ibid., pp. 98-99.

can help articulate feelings that are difficult to express. Asking the suffering client whether he or she would like prayer, and asking what needs to be mentioned in the prayer shows a respect for a person's privacy. When a pastoral counselor expresses the feelings of the client in prayer, the client's level of trust and security is increased.

As the helping person identifies with the client in need, prayer can become an authentic and intimate act of concern and caring. Through the act of compassionate identification, prayer is a means of overcoming isolation and alienation. Prayer then becomes a humbling act of egalitarian identification hence breaking down the partitions that separate people. By expressing the empathic realities in prayer, care becomes an act of religious acceptance and reassurance of God's presence.

Similar to prayer, guided imagery may be helpful in expressing religious compassion. Through the careful utilization of guided imagery, a person can be aided in experiencing a new level of spiritual openness. The openness of one's spiritual pilgrimage may afford the helper important key images or metaphors that facilitate the act of caring and healing. Exposing the basic images of a person-in-need provides a bridge of compassion between people.

The use of traditional sacraments can be a very helpful expression of compassion when utilized in an appropriate contextual manner. The rites of religious tradition are intended to facilitate a rite of passage from one condition or role to another. For example, the Sacrament for the Sick, used in many of the liturgical Christian churches may offer comfort for those taken with illness and confirm the person in the sick role. Confession of one's transgressions can be most relieving of guilt when appropriate penitence is prescribed followed by the rite of absolution. This confirms the person in the forgiven role. The employment of any sacrament must be dictated by the person-in-need and by the clear understanding of the emotional context when these are used.

Because compassion necessarily involves overt behavior, we believe that the compassionate counselor should do whatever possible and appropriate to ensure that the client engages in some productively healing form of overt behavior as part and parcel of the overall counseling process. Praying with the client, as we have already mentioned, is one form of overt behavior. Sacramental participation, again which we have just recommended when appropriate, is another form of bringing overt behavior into the counseling encounter.

Conclusion

Compassion is the underlying dynamic in Jesus' teaching regarding the final judgment.[176] The final judgment will be based on one's living out the admonition to love one another which is the compassionate response to the needy. The King will reply, "I tell you, whenever you did this for one of the least important of these brothers/sisters of mine, you did it for me."[177] In religious counseling, one must be willing to give oneself on behalf of another. It is in the giving of oneself to meet the needs of another that one truly finds oneself. Religious counseling in the family of God should be a microcosm of compassionate relationships. This enables the counselor to become real in the spirit/actions of compassion. Compassion is a very difficult command to actualize in daily living as it involves respecting the integrity of the other and relating respectfully to the needy person.

There are many creative ways to manifest compassion when the counselor is willing to do the hard work of entering the frame of reference of the client. Compassion requires the emotional identification with the client coupled with an act of disciplined use of religious resources. The New Testament concept of self-giving love, "*agape*," sets the stage for the intentional involvement with others. Compassion, then, is an act of one's will, thinking, and emotions. The self-sacrifice required will afford significant life changes for the religious counselor acting with compassion as well as the client who experiences the compassion.

---

176. Mt 25:41-46 (RSV).
177. Mt 25:40 (RSV).

6

Compassion in Religious Instruction

JAMES MICHAEL LEE

"What is compassion if it is not taking its object
in its hands and cradling it?"
Antoine de Saint-Exupéry[1]

Introduction

The two most important functions of every religion are worship
and religious instruction. History shows that no religious group
has lasted long or has made a genuinely significant impact on its
adherents if either of these two essential activities were missing or
weak.

In terms of compassion, the worship services of virtually all religions combine the celebration of the compassion of God with rit-
ualistic petitions to the deity to help the worshipers increase the
depth and range of their own compassion. In like fashion, the religious instruction efforts of all religions, in varying degrees of inten-

---

1. Antoine de Saint Exupéry, *Citadelle*, en *Les Oeuvres completes d'Antoine de Saint-Exupéry* (Paris: Gallimard, 1950), XXVI, 57-58 (p. 518), trans. mine.

sity and awareness, aim or would like to aim in one way or another to assist learners to become more compassionate.

In the formal field of education, instruction is a synonym for teaching. Like the word teaching, instruction explicitly denotes the intentional facilitation of desired learning outcomes. And like the word teaching, the term instruction does not directly or indirectly connote any particular form or procedure of teaching such as didactic teaching or group discussion or role playing. And again, like the word teaching, the term instruction is not bound to any particular setting such as the classroom, the home, or the playground. Instruction takes place in all types of settings both formal and informal. And yet again, like the word teaching, the term instruction is not linked to any one age group such as children but applies to learners of every age from infancy through old age.

The Content of Religious Instruction

There are two primary, essential, and always coexistent contents found in every religious instruction act, namely substantive content and structural content.

Substantive content is the subject matter or substantive zone of instructional activity. Structural content is instructional practice itself, including both the process of pedagogical enactment itself and the conditions attendant upon the here-and-now process of pedagogical enactment. In terms of teaching learners to be more compassionate, the substantive content is compassion while the structural content is the way in which compassion is taught (including the conditions attendant upon the actual teaching).

Giving the name structural content to instructional practice points to the very important fact that teaching procedure is not just a way of facilitating substantive content, but in fact is a content in its own right. *Empirically*, studies confirm the common observation that how a substantive content is taught is also what is taught.[2] For example, there is a great deal of difference in the learning outcome when compassion is taught in a compassionate manner and

---

2. See, for example, Herbert J. Wahlberg, "Synthesis of Research on Teaching," in *Handbook of Research on Teaching*, ed. Merlin C. Wittrock, 3rd ed. (New York: Macmillan, 1986), pp. 214-229; Jere Brophy and Thomas L. Good, "Teacher Behavior and Student Achievement," in ibid., pp. 328-375.

when compassion is taught in an uncompassionate manner. Or again, there is a significantly different learning outcome when compassion is taught using cognitive teaching practices and when compassion is taught using affective instructional procedures. *Ontically*, the religious instruction act as a whole is not substantive content plus structural content, but rather a fundamentally new mediated entity formed by the subsumptional fusion of substantive content and structural content.[3] The overall content of the religious act, therefore, necessarily contains, in mediated form, structural content as well as substantive content. By virtue of its ontic mediatorship, compassion changes in the act of teaching it.[4]

Definition of Compassion

Compassion has no ontic existence of its own. On the contrary, compassion has mental existence only. Specifically, compassion is a construct, namely a kind of concept which is deliberately invented or constructed for the express purpose of enhanced usefulness. As a construct, compassion is a mental abstraction which synthesizes and places into one general unified category a large number of discrete but related specific human behaviors.

There is a lack of complete agreement, and in some cases of substantial disagreement, by lexicographers[5] and by social scientists[6] on the exact meaning of compassion and of its two most closely

---

3. For an amplification of this point, see James Michael Lee, "The Authentic Source of Religious Instruction," in *Religious Education and Theology,* ed. Norma H. Thompson (Birmingham, Ala.: Religious Education Press, 1982), pp. 165-177.

4. George Albert Coe, *What Is Christian Education?* (New York: Scribner's, 1929), p. 23.

5. See, for example, *Webster's New Dictionary of Synonyms* (Springfield, Mass: Merriam, 1973, p. 818; S. I. Hayakawa, *Use the Right Word: Modern Guide to Synonyms and Related Words* (New York: Funk & Wagnalls, 1948), p. 284; *The Oxford English Dictionary,* corrected edition (Oxford: Clarendon, 1933/1978), vol. II, p. 714, and vol. X, pp. 368-369.

6. These disagreements occur not only between clinicians and nonclinicians, but also between some clinicians and other clinicians as well as between some nonclinicians and other nonclinicians. For fine reviews and also fine advocacies of these disagreements, see Lauren Wispé, "The Distinction between Sympathy and Empathy: To Call Forth a Concept, A Word is Needed," *Journal of Personal and Social Psychology* 50 (February, 1986), pp. 314-321; Nancy Eisenberg and Janet Strayer, "Critical Issues in the Study of Empathy," in *Empathy and its Development,* ed. Nancy Eisenberg and Janet Strayer (New York: Cambridge University Press, 1987), pp. 3-13; Arnold Goldstein and Gerald Y. Michaels, *Empathy: Development, Training, and Consequences* (Hillsdale, N.J.: Erlbaum, 1985), pp. 4-11.

related constructs, namely sympathy and empathy. My definitions and elaborations of these constructs are what I regard as the best available. Notwithstanding, there is room for legitimate disagreement with these definitions and their extensions because these constructs have not been researched with requisite depth or explored carefully over the long term by social scientists. Indeed, disagreements on the nature and force of sympathy, empathy, and compassion are evident even in the present volume, which illustrates the relative infancy of sophisticated research and painstaking elaboration of these important constructs.

Sympathy is that affective condition in which a person is vicariously and indirectly part of but separate from the feeling functions experienced by an individual in distress.[7] My definition reflects the Greek etymology of sympathy, namely *sympatheia*, which means suffering or feeling with. In German, this is *Mitleid*, or more to the point of this discussion, *Mitfühlung*. A key element in this definition is the phrase "part of but separate from." This phrase indicates that while the sympathizer feels along with the individual in distress, nonetheless the sympathizer's affects are his/her own and not those of the individual in need.[8] In the act of sympathizing, the sympathizer is aware that his/her identity and affects are separate from the identity and affects of the individual in need.[9] The pain of the sympathizer and the pain of the sufferer are different. In the act of sympathizing, the sympathizer is conscious of the parallelism or even the dualism between his/her affects and those of the person in need. Thus, the sympathizer is not so much involved with the objective reality or the subjective suffering of the other person as with an analogy, similarity/paral-

---

7. In any discussion of sympathy, empathy, and compassion, it is well to keep in mind what cultural anthropologist Ronald Cohen remarks, namely that "as an anthropologist I am continually struck by the cultural limitations of our ideas of empathy and sympathy." For me, this does not mean cultural relativism or cultural determinism. Rather, it means that social scientists (and also theologians and philosophers, and so forth) should always be expanding their horizons and their constructs by examining how other cultures construe phenomena. Ronald Cohen, "Altruism: Human, Cultural, or What?" in *Altruism, Sympathy, and Helping,* ed. Lauren Wispé (New York: Academic Press, 1978), p. 95.

8. Lauren Wispé, "Sympathy and Empathy," in *International Encyclopedia of the Social Sciences,* ed. David L. Sills, vol. 15 (Macmillan, 1968), p. 441.

9. Goldstein and Michaels, *Empathy: Development, Training, and Consequences,* p. 8.

lelism between his/her affects and those of the other individu-al.[10] Sympathy is more than just vicarious sharing of the affects of an individual in distress. Sympathy means that the sympathizer feels positively for the other individual's suffering and might even do something eventually to relieve that suffering. In contrast, nonsympathetic vicarious participation in the affects of an individual in distress might cause the nonsympathizer to harbor negative affects of antipathy or disgust at the person in distress, leading possibly to unsympathetic judgments (such as, "Why doesn't that wino in the gutter get up and find a job?") and avoidance behaviors (such as shielding one's eyes to avoid the unsightliness of an individual in need).[11]

Empathy is that affective condition in which a person is vicariously and directly part of and united with the feeling functions experienced by another individual. My definition reflects the Greek word *empatheia* which was virtually coined in 1909 by Edward Titchener[12] as a translation of the then relatively new German word *Einfühlung* which means feeling into. A key element in this definition is the phrase part of and united with. This phrase indicates that the empathizer not only feels along with the other individual but also merges into the affects of that individual.[13] Empathy is the active experiencing of the affects of another person. It is the vicarious but still dynamic introjectory "experiencing within oneself of what actually belongs to the other perceived persons or objects."[14] Empathy is a vicarious response which relates more to someone else's situation than to one's own situation.[15] In empathy, a person

---

10. Robert L. Katz, *Empathy: Its Nature and Uses* (New York: Free Press, 1963), p. 8.

11. Ezra Stotland et al., *Empathy and Birth Order* (Lincoln, Neb.: University of Nebraska Press, 1971), pp. 1-2.

12. Edward Bradford Titchener, *Lectures on Experimental Psychology and Thought Processes* (New York: Macmillan, 1909), pp. 21-22.

13. Thus Arnold Bucheimer states that "empathic behavior suggests a convergence in the behavior of two individuals [while] sympathetic behavior suggests a parallelism." Arnold Buchheimer, "The Development of Ideas about Empathy," *Journal of Counseling Psychology* 10 (January, 1963), p. 63.

14. Gardner Murphy, *Personality* (New York: Harper, 1947), p. 496 (see also p. 985).

15. Martin Hoffman, "Development of Prosocial Motivation: Empathy and Guilt," in *The Development of Prosocial Behavior,* ed. Nancy Eisenberg (New York: Academic Press, 1982), p. 281.

takes on and becomes the affect—and to some extent the role—of the person in distress.

Whereas the object of a person's sympathy is necessarily an individual in distress, the object of a person's empathy does not have to be an individual in distress. Empathy is that affective condition in which a person feels into another individual regardless of whether or not that other individual is in distress. Thus one can empathize with the happy feeling-tone of another as well as with the other individual's feeling-tone of distress. Although common parlance, clinical usage, and counseling/psychotherapeutic discussion usually link empathy with the affective sharing of personal distress, such linkage is not inherent in the construct. Indeed, one indispensable key to successful friendships and successful marriages is that each partner is part of and directly united to the happy as well as to the sad feeling functions of the other.

Compassion is that affective and concrete helping condition in which a person is not only vicariously and directly part of and united with the feeling functions experienced by an individual in distress but also comes to the appropriate concrete assistance of that individual.[16] Compassion embraces the full sweep and depth of empathy but is more focused and goes much further than empathy. Compassion is more focused than empathy because it is directed only at a person in distress. Compassion goes much further than empathy because it necessarily includes concrete action, namely rendering appropriate tangible assistance to the other individual. While empathy might possibly lead to appropriate concrete assistance on the part of the empathizer,[17] compassion necessarily

---

16. Because compassion has neither been examined with requisite care in the Western world nor has been subjected to rigorous sustained empirical research, both social scientists as well as persons outside the social sciences tend to define compassion differently and often idiosyncratically — when they do consider the construct of compassion. One unfortunate outcome of this conceptual and investigative confusion is that explanatory, verificational (validational), and predictive measures are often not reliable, to say the least. See Ted Landsman and Linda Clawson, "A Compassion Checklist for Children," *Academic Psychology Bulletin* 5 (June, 1983), pp. 281-287. By linking my definition of compassion with the definitions of sympathy and empathy, I hope to advance the clarity and convergence of the construct of compassion.

17. The issue of whether empathy (or sympathy) leads to the concrete assistance of the suffering person in need is unclear. Indeed, the alleged positive correlation between sympathy/empathy and prosocial behavior is more often assumed than

includes such assistance. It should be underscored that empathy is a necessary dimension of compassion. Rendering assistance to a person in distress because it is one's religious or social duty, because it is the humane thing to do, or because one has pity on the suffering individual—these are not acts of compassion because they lack the deeply affective empathic "feeling into" the other individual. It should also be underscored that the assistance rendered to the other individual in the compassionate act is at once concrete and appropriate. The assistance is concrete because the compassioner does something specific, immediate, and tangible for the person in distress rather than just feel togetherness for that person or even feel sorry with that person. The assistance is also appropriate because it is directed toward alleviating the sufferer's distress as that individual is experiencing that distress, as contrasted with alleviating what the commiserator thinks or imagines ought to be best for the sufferer. Empathy, the becoming of the other's feelings on the other's own terms rather than on my terms, enables the compassioner to take action which is appropriate to alleviating the sufferer's distress rather than being locked into his/ her own ideas or hopes or agendas for the person in need.

Compassion has at least seven major characteristics.

First, compassion is affective. It is the vicarious, active, affective participation in and unity with the feeling functions of the other individual as that individual experiences these functions.

Second, compassion is concrete action. It necessarily includes at its core the giving of concrete and appropriate assistance to the individual in distress.

Third, compassion is psychomotor. It is psychomotor because the compassioner to some extent enters into the physical suffering of the person in distress, sharing and experiencing a psychomotor reaction to the physical suffering of the other individual or at least having a psychomotor reaction to the misfortune of the

---

proved in the psychological literature. (Prosocial behavior is the technical social-science term for voluntary assistance of any sort.) Summarizing the pertinent empirical research, Nancy Eisenberg and Janet Strayer conclude that while sympathy and empathy are positively correlated with prosocial behavior, they do not always lead to prosocial behavior or even to the desire to concretely help the individual in distress. Eisenberg and Strayer, "Critical Issues in the Study of Empathy," pp. 10-11.

other individual.[18] Compassion is also psychomotor because the compassioner endeavors as far as possible to come to the physical and material assistance of the person in need.

Fourth, compassion is cognitive. It is cognitive in a minimal, accompanying, supportive, but still important sense. Every activity which is human is fundamentally holistic, and therefore compassion includes cognition. One of the most important functions of cognition in the act of compassion is to intellectually interpret the variety of cues which the person in distress gives forth. The compassioner combines his/her cognitive interpretation of these cues with affective awareness of the cues, and places both at the disposal of the primarily affective and conduct components of compassion. Though cognitive interpretation does indeed accompany the compassionate act, it is more probable that cognition plays its major role as a consequence of compassion rather than as an accompaniment of compassion. In other words, cognition interprets what happened rather than constituting a key part of what happened. Indeed, it often occurs that a person is moved to compassion on deeply affective grounds despite warnings from the cognitive side of one's personality that the compassionate act might not be in the best interests of the compassioner. Of signal practical importance to the religious educator seeking to be compassionate is one review of the pertinent research which found that those who emphasize the role of cognition in empathy tend to view neutrality and detachment as important characteristics of the successful empathizer.[19] In contrast, those who emphasize the role of affect in empathy tend to view a positive disposition toward the other person and also a personal attachment to the other individual as important characteristics of the successful empathizer.[20] It should be noted that medical research tends to support the contention that neutrality and detachment

18. Though Bernard Rosenthal seems to confuse compassion in some respects with sympathy, he nonetheless does recognize the psychomotor dimension of compassion, as well as the fact that there are different degrees of compassion. Bernard G. Rosenthal, "The Psychology of Compassion," *Human Context* 4 (Fall, 1972), pp. 600-607, especially p. 603.

19. Ezra Stotland et al., *Empathy, Fantasy and Helping* (Beverly Hills, Calif.: Sage, 1978), pp. 14-15.

20. Mark H. Davis, "The Effects of Dispositional Empathy on Emotional Reactions and Helping: A Multidimensional Approach," *Journal of Personality* 51 (June, 1983), pp. 167-184.

are not nearly as successful—and are often quite deleterious—as personal attachment and affective warmth not only in enhancing the patient's psychological well-being but in bringing about desired physical results as well.[21]

Fifth, compassion is personal. It is the personal act of one person feeling into and concretely acting to help another person. Thus it is very difficult if not impossible for a group or society to be compassionate as a group or as a society. Compassion is fundamentally a one-on-one matter.

Sixth, compassion involves sacrifice. The lesser dimension of this sacrifice occurs when the compassioner goes out of self affectively in order to participate in and become directly united with the sufferer on that individual's own terms. The greater dimension of this sacrifice occurs when the compassioner goes to the concrete appropriate assistance of the other individual, assistance which is often difficult, inconvenient, and time-consuming for the compassioner.

Seventh, compassion is loving fellowship. Whereas other forms of love are more often than not based on affective unity with the beloved,[22] compassion is based on loving fellowship exclusively toward those who are suffering, who are deficient, or who are weak.[23]

Compassion in itself is superior both to sympathy and to empathy. Compassion is superior to sympathy because sympathy contains a significant tinge of egoism in that sympathy focuses on the affects of the sympathizer rather than on the affects of the person in distress. Compassion, on the other hand, is altruistic in that it focuses on the affects of the person in distress as that other person is experiencing his/her affects. Compassion is also superior to sympathy in that while sympathy might eventually give rise to assisting concretely a person in distress, compassion includes as part of its very nature the concrete appropriate assistance of a person in need. To be sure, it often happens that an individual is sympathet-

---

21. A classic and still widely cited studies in this connection is René A. Spitz, "Hospitalism: An Inquiry into the Genesis of Psychiatric Conditions in Early Childhood," in *The Psychoanalytic Study of the Child*, vol. 1 (New York: International Universities Press, 1945), pp. 53-74.

22. For a concise treatment of the major types of love from many complementary perspectives, see James Michael Lee, *The Content of Religious Instruction* (Birmingham, Ala.: Religious Education Press, 1985), pp. 229-244.

23. On this last point, see Robert C. Roberts, "Compassion," *Christian Century* 100 (January 5-12, 1983), p. 14.

ic to the plight of a person in distress but never goes to the concrete assistance of that individual. Compassion is superior to empathy because empathy does not include coming to the active concrete assistance of the person in distress. Empathy might eventually result in concrete assistance, but such assistance is not an integral part of empathy.

While compassion in itself is indeed superior both to sympathy and empathy, this does not mean that the religious educator should strive only to be compassionate and never sympathetic or empathic. As a social-scientific practitioner, the religious educator must weigh whether in this particular instructional situation with this particular learner or group of learners, sympathy, empathy, or compassion will likely be the most effective in bringing about the desired learning outcome. In religious instruction, like all other forms of facilitation, what is objectively superior might not necessarily be the wisest and most effective pedagogical course in action in a particular instance.

Of the many ways in which religious educators can proactively enhance their capacity for appropriate compassionate behavior toward learners, three might be briefly mentioned at this juncture.

First, religious educators should strive to heighten their sensitivity to the affective states of other persons. Religious educators who are exclusively or even mostly concerned with their own feelings, with their own path to salvation, and what is worse with their own political or ideological agenda, will never develop the sensitivity and awareness of the other person's affective state which is so essential for compassionate behavior.

Second, religious educators should strive to become increasingly open as persons. Religious educators must be free and open enough as persons to allow feelings of compassion to well up in their own selves. The importance of this principle is heightened by the fact that compassion is not always under the control of the compassioner.[24] If religious educators are not free and open enough to let compassion happen to them, then indeed compassion will happen to them seldom if at all.

Third, religious educators should strive to increase their per-

---

24. This is true of empathy, and probably is also true of compassion. See Stotland et al., *Empathy, Fantasy and Helping*, p. 13.

ceptivity of the entire context of the instructional event. All learning, and indeed all human behavior, necessarily occurs in a context, in an existential situation. The religious educator's compassionate behavior is triggered by a wide variety of cues occurring in the ongoing dynamic of the instructional event. If religious educators are not habitually attentive to these cues, they will miss valuable opportunities to exercise appropriate compassionate behavior.[25]

Compassion in Religious Instruction Literature

Compassion is almost totally neglected in the professional literature on religious instruction. Several reasons can be advanced to explain this abject inattention. First, some religious educationists such as Gabriel Moran[26] and Thomas Groome[27] are highly cognitive

25. What Harold Burgess's careful research investigation found in 1975 still holds true today, namely that religious educationists who contend that religious instruction is a branch of theology give scant attention to situational variables in the teaching event, whereas religious educationists who believe that religious instruction is a mode of social science give considerable attention to these situational variables. Harold William Burgess, *An Invitation to Religious Education* (Birmingham, Ala.: Religious Education Press, 1975), pp. 50, 83-84, 119-120, 154-158.

26. Gabriel Moran is primarily concerned with language, meaning, and power, none of which is inherently related, to say the least, with compassion. Also Moran's highly cognitive stance toward religious education leaves little room for considerations of love, compassion, or empathy. See Gabriel Moran, *Religious Education as a Second Language* (Birmingham, Ala.: Religious Education Press, 1989); Kenneth Barker, *Religious Education, Catechesis, and Freedom* (Birmingham, Ala.: Religious Education Press, 1981), pp. 128-159.

27. That the pedagogical method of "shared praxis" concocted by Thomas Groome is extremely cognitive cannot be legitimately debated. First, Groome clearly and unambiguously labels his method as "a way of knowing." Second, in his description of how "shared praxis" is supposed to work, Groome's total emphasis is on cognitive activity during the instructional event. Noncognitive contents such as affect and lifestyle are not incorporated as parts of the religious instruction act itself. Third, the way in which "shared praxis" is enacted by the teacher and learner is, for Groome, totally verbal, with no intrinsic inclusion of nonverbal content. It is well known from the research that verbal content is highly correlated with cognition, whereas nonverbal content is highly correlated with affect and lifestyle. Fourth, Groome asserts that of all the psychological bases and axes of instruction available to him, "shared praxis" is most congenial to David Ausubel's advance organizer model. Ausubel's advance organizer model is one of the most highly cognitive models ever proposed; indeed it is exclusively cognitive. Fifth, in dealing with the nature of will (conation) in his "shared praxis" method, Groome asserts that all-important will is a form of cognition, a view which philosopher Vernon Bourke states is the most intellectualist position one can take about will, and a position which breaks down the integrity of will and makes it into a form of knowing. Sixth, as Groome takes pains to point out, the inspiration and overarching ratio-

in their views of religious education. For these intellectualists, not only is compassion ignored, but the whole domain of love is given virtually no attention. Second, some religious educationists such as William Bean Kennedy[28] see the process of religious teaching as a political activity seeking to accomplish political agendas. Politics is ultimately about power, and in such a scheme, compassion is weakness and hence has no real place in religious instruction.[29] Third, some religious educationists such as Robert O'Gorman[30] and Richard Osmer[31] think that the teaching of religion is a form of theology and is basically a theological act. Because the theological act is always cognitive in character—the word reflection typically follows the word theological when referring to what a theologian does when theologizing and what theology is all about—the role of compassion is negligible.[32]

---

nale for "shared praxis" is the extremely cognitivist position advanced by the neo-Marxist Frankfurt School of Critical Theory. Thomas H. Groome, *Christian Religious Education* (San Francisco: Harper & Row, 1980), pp. 165-323; Thomas H. Groome, *Sharing Faith* (San Francisco: Harper & Row, 1991), pp. 26-32; Vernon J. Bourke, *Will in Western Thought: An Historico-Critical Survey* (New York: Sheed and Ward, 1964), pp. 29-51.

28. William Bean Kennedy, "Ideology and Education: A Fresh Approach for Religious Education," *Religious Education* 80 (Summer, 1985), pp. 331-344.

29. I should note that there does surface from time to time an occasional liberationist religious educator who accords welcome emphasis to the role of compassion in the religious instruction act. One such is Daniel S. Schipani, *Religious Education Encounters Liberation Theology* (Birmingham, Ala.: Religious Education Press, 1988), pp. 220-221.

30. Robert T. O'Gorman, "The Search for Usable Knowledge in Religious Education: Educating Reflective Practitioners," *Religious Education* 82 (Summer, 1988), pp. 323-336.

31. Richard R. Osmer, "Teaching as Practical Theology," in *Theological Approaches to Christian Education*, ed. Jack L. Seymour and Donald E. Miller (Nashville: Abingdon, 1990), pp. 216-238.

32. Of telling interest in this connection is Daniel Schipani's accurate statement that in liberationist religious instruction, theological reflection is inspired and oriented by (Schipani's own words) compassion. Schipani's views on the reactive axis of theology concur with the position taken by the father of liberation theology, Gustavo Gutiérrez, who writes: "Theology *follows:* it is the second step. What Hegel used to say about philosophy can likewise be applied to theology: it arises only at sundown. Theology does not produce pastoral activity; rather, it reflects upon it." I should note that both Schipani and Gutiérrez are careful scholars. Schipani, *Religious Education Encounters Liberation Theology,* p. 220; Gustavo Gutiérrez, *A Theology of Liberation*, trans. Caridad Inda and John Eagleson (Maryknoll, N.Y.: Orbis Books, 1973), p. 11. See also Lee, *The Content of Religious Instruction*, pp. 758-759.

Can Compassion Be Taught?

Can the religious educator teach learners to be compassionate? And can the religious educator, in turn, be taught to be a compassionate teacher?

On both theoretical and empirical grounds, the answer to both of these questions is a resounding yes.

On theoretical grounds, compassion is primarily a learned behavior[33] and thus is the result of teaching in one form or another. All human behavior is either instinctual or learned. There is nothing in the theory of human psychology, or in the research evidence which contributes to that theory, to suggest that compassion is instinctual. Anything which is learned not only has been successfully taught but can be taught over and over again in the future.

It should be underscored that teaching is not just talking to a learner or group of learners. Far more importantly, teaching essentially consists in structuring those conditions which facilitate the acquisition of a learning outcome.[34] There are four basic conditions of learning present in each and every teaching act. These four basic conditions—or molar variables as they are often called—are the teacher, the learner, the subject-matter content, and the environment. It is by structuring and restructuring these four variables into various changing patterns and arrangements that the educator brings about the desired learning outcomes during the enactment of the here-and-now instructional dynamic.[35] From this all-too-brief description it can be easily seen that teacher talk represents only one small part of overall instructional procedure. And because teacher talk makes minimal use of the full scope and power

---

33. When I write phrases like "compassion is a behavior" and the like throughout much of the remainder of this chapter, it must be kept in mind that compassion is technically a construct and not a behavior. As noted earlier, compassion is a mental synthesis of a bundle of specific related behaviors. I am using terms like "compassion is a behavior" because of its linguistic simplicity and because readers of this chapter know how to interpret phrases and terms and sentences like this.

34. James Michael Lee, "The *Teaching* of Religion," in *Toward a Future for Religious Education,* ed. James Michael Lee and Patrick C. Rooney (Dayton, Ohio: Pflaum, 1970), pp. 55-92; Robert Glaser, "Components of a Psychology of Instruction: Toward a Science of Design," *Review of Educational Research* 46 (Winter, 1976), pp. 17-21.

35. James Michael Lee, *The Flow of Religious Instruction* (Birmingham, Ala.: Religious Education Press, 1973), pp. 223-248.

of all four molar variables, it tends to be among the least effective of all pedagogical devices. I underscore this last point because some religious educators, especially those who hold that religious instruction is a branch of theology, erroneously identify the whole of the teaching process with teacher talk, or at the very least think that teacher talk constitutes the primary form of instructional practice.[36] To paraphrase Ronald Habermas and Klaus Issler, telling does not mean learning; it only means telling. Sometimes teacher talk results in learning outcomes which are quite different and sometimes opposite of what the religious educator intended.[37]

On empirical grounds, compassion can be taught because there is overwhelming empirical evidence to suggest that compassion has indeed been successfully taught. Strong evidence comes from Buddhist sources, from psychotherapeutic sources, and from empirical investigations in nonpsychotherapeutic fields including instruction.

Compassion lies at the very center of classical Buddhism. Indeed, no major world religion places more emphasis on compassion than does classical Buddhism. Not only does classical Buddhism hold as a pivotal tenet that persons must learn to be compassionate, but also its educational efforts in formal and informal environments are geared to deliberatively teaching its devotees to be more and more compassionate.[38] Though there are no rigorous empirical data (in the Western sense) to support the millennium and a half contention that Buddhist teaching has effectively facilitated compassionate behavior, nonetheless the empirical testimony of Buddhist teachers and learners down through the centuries attest to the fact that Buddhism has indeed been successful

---

36. Possibly the classic and most clearcut example of this is Josef Goldbrunner, "Catechetical Method as Handmaid of Kerygma," in *Teaching All Nations: A Symposium on Modern Catechetics,* ed. Johannes Hofinger, rev. and partly trans. Clifford Howell (New York: Herder and Herder, 1961), pp. 111-112. See also Alfred McBride, *Catechetics: A Theology of Proclamation* (Milwaukee: Bruce, 1966), pp. vii, 150. For a critique of this position, see Lee, *The Flow of Religious Instruction,* pp. 188-194.

37. Ronald Habermas and Klaus Issler, *Teaching for Reconciliation* (Grand Rapids, Mich.: Baker, 1992), pp. 102-103.

38. Natalie Maxwell, "Great Compassion: The Chief Cause of the Bodhisattvas," (Ph.D. dissertation, University of Wisconsin-Madison, 1975); Harvey Bear Aronson, "Love, Sympathetic Joy and Equanimity in Theravada Buddhism", (Ph.D. dissertation, University of Wisconsin, 1975), pp. 244-255.

in teaching compassion to those who wish to learn it.[39]

Compassion thus far has received very little attention in psychology. However, the construct of empathy has received more attention, particularly in depth psychology and in psychotherapy. Since compassion fully incorporates empathy (while adding the dimension of concretely coming to the assistance of a person in distress), the empirical research on the teaching of empathy can legitimately be extrapolated to the question of whether or not compassion can be taught. Consequently research studies on the successful intentional facilitation of empathy apply directly to compassion even though they do not explicitly use the word compassion.

Empirical research investigations have also concluded that empathy can be taught to a wide variety of professionals and others working in nonpsychotherapeutic settings as well as in depth psychology milieux. To be sure, empathy as a skill has been successfully taught to teachers,[40] to married couples,[41] to social work students,[42] to first-year university students in world literature,[43] and to mentally retarded children,[44] to name just a few of the many studies which show that empathy can be successfully taught.

In short, controlled empirical research of divers kinds, plus the evidence of human experience over the centuries, clearly suggests that compassion (1) is teachable and (2) has been successfully taught over and over again in a wide variety of cultures to a wide variety of people.

---

39. In Buddhist ordination services conducted in China, monks make four lifelong vows, including the vow of learning from teachers in such a way that they can become more compassionate and so attain the highest glory which is bodhisattvahood.

40. Donald Benjamin Gregg, "An Investigation of the Development of Empathic Communication through a Sensitivity Training Experience" (Ph.D. dissertation, Lehigh University, 1968).

41. Harry Mark Flapan, "A Study to Determine Effective and Reproducible Conditions for Increasing Empathy in Marital Relationships" (Ph.D. dissertation, University of Chicago, 1957).

42. Clara Louise Myers, "An Experiment in the Development of Measurement of Empathy in Social Work Students" (Ph.D. dissertation, Washington University, 1966).

43. S. Natale, *An Experiment in Empathy* (Slough, England: National Foundation For Educational Research in England and Wales, 1971), pp. 44-73.

44. Loraine Pilkey, "Role Playing as a Technique for Increasing Empathic Ability of Mentally Subnormal Adolescents" (Ph.D. dissertation, University of Missouri at Kansas City, 1959).

Substantive Content

Substantive content is absolutely essential in the teaching of compassion because substantive content is the basic subject matter[45] of that which is being taught. There can be no teaching in the absence of substantive content. In teaching compassion to learners, the substantive content is compassion.

The first four chapters, plus some of the present chapter, have delineated the nature of compassion. Thus there in no need to repeat what has already been treated. I would like to underscore, however, that compassion is a religious entity and not a theological entity. Compassion is something which is lived in the here-and-now concrete order, as is true with every religious act. Theology, on the other hand, is the cognitive examination of the compassionate act. Thus in teaching religious compassion, the religious educator should focus primarily on the act of compassion itself rather than chiefly on the theology, philosophy, or psychology of compassion. In terms of teaching religious compassion, the proper role of theology, biblics, philosophy, and so on is not to serve as a substitute for the compassionate act but rather to provide necessary cognitive knowledge about the nature and structure of compassion. The theology of a religious act is not that religious act. The theology of compassion is not compassion. The study of a reality is in no way the same as that reality or the practice of that reality.

Structural Content

Structural content is absolutely essential in teaching compassion because structural content is the set of teaching procedures which the religious educator uses to facilitate compassion in learners. From the religious instruction standpoint, it is not enough for the teacher to know the nature of compassion, to feel compassion, or even to engage in overt compassionate behaviors. For religious instruction to take place, the educator must actually facilitate com-

---

45. My use of the term subject matter in no way suggests or implies that substantive content is equivalent to or is derived from school-based topics. Subject matter is the topical content facilitated by the educator regardless of whether this facilitation occurs in formal or informal settings.

passionate behaviors in learners. Hence structural content is of paramount importance.

Earlier in this chapter I demonstrated that the substantive content of compassion has received virtually no attention from religious educationists. The situation is no less lamentable with respect to the abysmal lack of attention accorded to structural content by the overwhelming majority of religious educationists. Only an exceedingly few religionists are genuinely conversant with the nature, structure, dynamics, and varieties of instructional procedure. This pathetic situation is exacerbated by many religious educationists who, in their ignorance, actually believe that emphasis on instructional procedure is unimportant to the real task of religious education,[46] is destructive of the basic reality of religious education,[47] or sets inappropriate norms for the instructional behavior of religion teachers.[48] Because of the prevalent lack of familiarity with and feel for structural content, the field of religious instruction is easy prey for all manner of hucksterism, faddism, and gimmickry. This regretful situation must come to a rapid halt if religious educators are to successfully teach compassion or any other substantive religious content. As facilitators, religious educators must have an adequate working knowledge of the nature and dynamics of structural content, as well as the skill to blend this knowledge into their actual teaching activities. The remainder of this chapter will offer some general instructional principles and specific procedures to assist religious educators to heighten their effectiveness in teaching compassion to learners of all ages and circumstances.

---

46. Two unassailable facts bear out this contention. First, religious educationists accord very little space in their books and articles discussing instructional procedure. And even these relatively rare forays into instructional practice typically are more of a commonsense or empirically unverified variety rather than permeated with the relevant empirical research and pertinent theory on the teaching act. Second, the graduate university and seminary programs operated by religious educationists typically give very little place in their curricula to the study and practice of theory and procedure even though they claim to be preparing students to improve their teaching skills or at least their understanding of the educational process. The exception to this statement consists in a handful of graduate programs situated in a few Evangelical Protestant institutions of higher learning.

47. Probably the clearest formulation of this viewpoint remains Goldbrunner, "Catechetical Method as Handmaid of Kerygma," pp. 108-121.

48. Karen B. Tye, "Those Who Teach: The Local Church School Teacher's Perspective on Being a Teacher," *Religious Education* 83 (Summer, 1988), pp. 338-339.

General Principles

I will briefly describe some general instructional principles which will enable religious educators to enhance the effectiveness of their efforts to teach learners to be more compassionate.

Teaching as the Essence of Religious Instruction. The single most important general principle undergirding the effective teaching of compassion is the unremitting attention by the religious educator to the dynamics of the instructional act. The essence of religious instruction, the thing which makes religious instruction distinctive among all church and individual ministries, is that religious instruction essentially consists in teaching. Other ministries might involve facilitational activities of one sort or another; only religious instruction can be completely and essentially equated with the teaching process. Religious instruction, in short, is teaching.

Teaching as an Art/Science. All teaching, including teaching for religious compassion, is a compound of the artistic and the scientific realms of life.[49]

Teaching is an art because it is an enactment, because it is doing something in a purposeful deliberative fashion. Teaching for religious compassion, then, is the active, skillful, and artistic fashioning of scientific principles and data into a form which yields the desired results.[50] Generically, and therefore inclusively, art is an activity whereby something is made, produced, or performed.[51] This has been the meaning of art since the time of Aristotle.[52] Hence the all too prevalent contemporary conception of art as restricted solely to the fine arts is unduly narrow.

---

49. For a discussion of this point, see Lee, *The Flow of Religious Instruction*, pp. 215-221.

50. This fashioning is not a mechanistic application of scientific principles and data. Rather, it is the dynamic admixing of these scientific realities with the religious educator's own vision, personality, and enactment skills which forms the artistic shape into which the scientific principles and data are incorporated.

51. Etymologically, the English word art derives from the Latin *ars* which most broadly means making or doing. *Ars* also means a trade or a profession, two life-works which center around the production of something. *Artes liberales* (our modern day liberal arts) for Cicero meant honorable occupations (as opposed to sitting around idly and speculating). It should also be noted that one important meaning of ars is theory, further illuminating the view that all art is based on theory, that all art in one large sense consists in the enactment of theory (theory being the scientific foundation appropriate for the activity in question).

52. Aristotle, *Physics*, B. 8, 199a, 17-19.

As an artistic activity, teaching for religious compassion is first and foremost the deployment of a technical skill. It is the fluid, concrete, here-and-now enactment of a set of instructional practices which the educator predicts will result in the attainment of compassionate activity. To highlight the fact that teaching is undeniably a technical skill is not to assert that teaching is somehow anti-human. Because it is an activity performed by a human being, teaching must necessarily be human. The degree to which it is human depends both on the way the teacher enacts the instructional event and the degree to which the goals of the instructional event correlate with human values and aspirations. And to highlight the fact that teaching is undeniably a technical skill is not to assert that teaching is therefore shallow and mechanistic.[53] Technical skill is not shallow because technical skill makes it possible for human beings to become deeper, more fully functioning, and more effective persons.[54] Technical skill is not mechanistic because all the available empirical research clearly reveals that mechanistic deployment varies inversely with instructional effectiveness.[55] At bottom, technical skill in religious instruction, as in all forms of education, means the actualized process by which the educator communicates effectively to learners. For example, Carl Rogers remarks that in the facilitational arts, it is not enough to emphasize and care for learners. What is necessary, Rogers stresses, is that the facilitator effectively communicate this empathy and care to the learner,[56] else the learner will never learn that he/she is cared for and will never subsequently engage in those

53. Karen Tye and some other religious educationists, notably Dwayne Huebner and his students, appear to hold the position that technical equals mechanistic. See Tye, "Those Who Teach," pp. 338-339; Dwayne E. Huebner (with William B. Kennedy), "From Theory to Practice: Curriculum," *Religious Education* 57 (July-August, 1982), pp. 372-373. See the response to the above by Lee, in *The Flow of Religious Instruction*, pp. 393-394.

54. John Julian Ryan, *The Humanization of Man* (New York: Newman, 1972), pp. 13-25.

55. Kathy Carter, "Teachers' Knowledge and Learning to Teach," in *Handbook of Research on Teacher Education*, ed. W. Robert Houston, Martin Haberman, and John Sikula (New York: Macmillan, 1990), pp. 297-299.

56. Carl R. Rogers, *On Becoming a Person* (Boston: Houghton Mifflin, 1961), pp. 51, 284, 342-344. Though Rogers is dealing specifically with psychotherapy, nonetheless his empirically based statement, as noted in the body of the present text, can be legitimately extrapolated to all forms of facilitation, since facilitation necessitates and involves communication.

behaviors which are a consequence of the facilitator's care.

Teaching is a science because (1) its theory and its enactment rest upon a scientific base; (2) its theory and its enactment are thoroughly permeated in whole and in each part by scientific conceptualizations and findings; (3) its enactment in an important sense is a set of scientific findings which are interactively fashioned and refashioned by and in artistic activity.

A science of teaching has three basic functions, namely to explain, to predict, and to verify instructional activity. Each of these is absolutely essential if the religious educator is to teach compassion effectively. The science of teaching gives the religious educator the basic explanations of instructional activity so that he/she can know *why* a particular pedagogical procedure is likely to work or to fail.[57] The science of teaching provides the religious educator with reliable hypotheses, clues, and information upon which to reliably predict which teaching procedures are likely to work in a certain situation and which are likely to fail.[58] Finally, the science of teaching enables the religious educator to adequately verify if and to what extent the learners have actually acquired the desired learning outcomes on compassion.

In the absence of a scientific base and scientific permeation, religious instruction for compassion necessarily consists of hopeful hunches, well-meaning guesses, chancy processes, hit-or-miss behaviors, and seat-of-the-pants activity. In the presence of a scientific base and scientific permeation, religious instruction for compassion consists in deliberatively selecting those teaching procedures which have been reliably shown to enjoy a good probability of success in a given situation.[59]

As a general rule, the greater the artistic achievement, the more it is consciously based on and permeated with scientific theory and findings. The fine arts amply illustrate this fact. Not only did great all-around artists like Leonardo da Vinci and Michelangelo

57. The religious educator cannot know the *how to* of teaching activity without first understanding explicitly or implicitly the *why of* teaching.

58. James Michael Lee, "Prediction in Religious Instruction," *Living Light* 9 (Summer, 1972), pp. 43-54; James Michael Lee, "How to Teach Foundations, Process, Procedures," in *Handbook of Preschool Religious Education*, ed. Donald E. Ratcliff (Birmingham, Ala.: Religious Education Press, 1988), pp. 183-185.

59. N.L. Gage, *The Scientific Basis of the Art of Teaching* (New York: Teachers College Press, 1978), p. 41.

Buonarroti deeply know and utilize scientific findings on perspective, pigmentation, surface, and the like, but they also devoured all the latest relevant scientific information they could obtain. Thus Leonardo illegally examined the anatomy of corpses,[60] and Michelangelo examined the anatomy of the Belvedere Torso over the course of many years.[61]

To be valid, reliable, and therefore useful, the science of teaching must be rooted in the appropriate form of science. It is obvious that the appropriate form of the science of teaching is social science since social science has as its purview the theoretical and empirical investigation of social and behavioral interactions of persons. All teaching, including the teaching of religion, primarily consists in the social and behavioral interactions of persons, educators and learners alike. Other important forms of science such as theology, philosophy, history, literature, natural science, and the like, do not provide the appropriate grounding for religious instruction since these forms do not frontally concern themselves with investigating the teaching act.[62]

To assert that religious instruction for compassion is an art/science is to concomitantly assert that the religious educator is necessarily a procedurist and a procedurologist. The religious educator is a procedurist because he/she engages in the art of enacting instructional procedure. The religious educator is a procedurologist because the instructional procedure which is enacted is based on and permeated with the science of teaching.[63]

The scientific dimension of the religious educator's work is enhanced by ongoing *behavioral analysis* of what is actually happening during the instructional event.[64] Various forms of interaction

---

60. Elmer Belt, *Leonardo the Anatomist* (New York: Greenwood, 1955).

61. The influence of the anatomy of the Belvedere Torso is evident in Michelangelo's sculptures, and in the frescos in the Sistine Chapel. See Charles H. Morgan, *The Life of Michelangelo* (New York: Reynal, 1960), p. 101.

62. For a more detailed discussion of this seminal point, see Lee, *The Shape of Religious Instruction*, pp. 101-257; Lee, "The Authentic Source of Religious Instruction," pp. 100-197; Timothy Arthur Lines, *Systemic Religious Education* (Birmingham, Ala.: Religious Education Press, 1987), pp. 211-243.

63. James Michael Lee, "Procedures in the Religious Education of Adolescents," in *Handbook of Youth Ministry*, ed. Donald E. Ratcliff and James A. Davies (Birmingham, Ala.: Religious Education Press, 1991), p. 217.

64. Lee, *The Flow of Religious Instruction*, pp. 280-286.

analysis such as that devised by Ned Flanders[65] can help the religious educator be a more acute observer of his/her instructional behavior. Observation generated by interaction analysis systems is especially helpful to the religious educator because it offers the teacher a nonimpressionistic and data-based view of what is really and truly occurring in the course of his/her teaching activity.[66] When inserted into the overarching framework of instructional theory, the fruits of this ongoing behavioral analysis will suggest general and specific prescriptions for the improvement of one's teaching procedures.

The artistic side of the religious educator's work is enhanced by ongoing *behavioral control* of his/her teaching skills during the instructional event. Microteaching is one proven way of effectively improving the religious educator's mastery of various teaching skills.[67]

The implementation of a parish, interparish, and diocesan/judicatory Teacher Performance Laboratory would go a long way toward enhancing significantly the religious educator's functions as an artist.[68]

Teaching as Structuring the Learning Situation. In every religious instruction event there are four molar variables which are always present, regardless of the age-level of the learners or the setting. These four molar variables are the teacher, the learner, the subject-matter content, and the environment. Thus all effective religious instruction, including teaching for compassion, consists in so structuring the dynamic interaction among these four molar variables that the desired learning outcome is thereby achieved.[69] Teaching, then, is not standing in front of a group of learners and talking. Rather, as just noted, teaching can be defined as structuring the situation in such a manner that the desired learning outcome is brought about. The importance of this concept of teaching for

---

65. Ned A. Flanders, *Interaction Analysis in the Classroom: A Manual for Observers* (Ann Arbor, Mich.: School of Education, University of Michigan, 1966).

66. Nicholas Hobar and Debra K. Sullivan, "Systematic Observation of Instruction: Genesis, Research, Practice, and Potential," *Journal of Classroom Teaching* 19 (Summer, 1984), pp. 26-34.

67. Dwight Allen and Kevin Ryan, *Microteaching* (Reading, Mass.: Addison-Wesley, 1969).

68. Lee, *The Flow of Religious Instruction*, pp. 288-289.

69. Ibid, pp. 233-240.

the effective facilitation of religious compassion cannot be overemphasized.

All professionally informed practice, including that of religious instruction, is centrally concerned with what Herbert Simon calls design, namely the process of "changing existing situations into preferred ones."[70] Neglect of structural design, neglect of seeing the facilitational act primarily and holistically as structuring the learning situation, leads to that kind of practice which is nonreflective, chancy, and cookbooky. Such a Mr. Fix-It mentality, such a cookbook outlook to facilitational practice flows from a combination of an antitheoretical bias toward facilitation,[71] and what Donald Schön contends is a view of practice rooted in positivistic epistemology.[72]

The recognition of the fact that religious instruction consists essentially of structuring the learning situation accentuates the previously discussed view that the teaching process is necessarily and always an art/science. The art of skillfully and harmoniously adjusting the four molar variables in a constantly changing fashion is based on the religious educator's ever-present awareness of the scientific principles and data about what constitutes the effective facilitation of learning.

The central fact that every religious instruction act is composed of four interactive variables shows that teaching for religious compassion is essentially contextual in nature. All four variables operate in a somewhat different fashion depending on the here-and-now interactive context in which they occur. This context consists of the four interactive variables as a dynamic whole.

Teaching Holistically. All effective teaching is necessarily holistic[73] because the learner is a whole person in whom psychomotor, cognitive, affective, and lifestyle operations intermingle and work as a

---

70. Herbert Simon, *The Science of the Artificial* (Cambridge, Mass.: MIT Press, 1972), p. 44. See also Donald Schön, *The Reflective Practitioner* (New York: Basic Books, 1983), p. 55.

71. Lee, *The Flow of Religious Instruction*, pp. 149-205.

72. Schön, *The Reflective Practitioner*, p. 46.

73. To affirm holism is to affirm that the human being operates as a system, namely a unified and integrated entity which operates as a whole. Thus a change in any one of the person's domain-oriented activities impacts the other systemic domains. Lines, *Systemic Religious Education*, pp. 49, 112-113, 149-151, 192-193, 221-224.

whole in virtually every human activity.[74] Depending on the subject-matter content of the religious instruction event, one or another human domain will predominate. Nonetheless all are present, if
only to a very minimal extent.

The effective teaching of religious compassion, therefore, must
be holistic. The lifestyle and affective domains have to be present
and active, because they constitute the essence of compassion and
hence are the two most important operative domains in the compassionate act. Without the flow of overt activity there is no compassion, and without empathic behavior accompanying this flow
of overt activity there is no compassion. Psychomotor behavior,
though of lesser importance in the compassionate act, nonetheless is very important and must be given a significant place in the religious educator's efforts to teach compassion. The cognitive domain
is also present in the compassionate act, though to a somewhat
minimal extent. Consequently, in teaching for compassion, the religious educator should restrict cognitive content just to what is necessary for the compassionate act, which is often quite little. The
relatively small (in relation to the other contents taught) amount of
cognitive content should be focused on understanding and on intuition. Understanding is the critical ratiocinative component of the
compassionate act because the experiential center of the process of
understanding enables the compassioner to grasp as far as is intellectually possible the existential condition of the person in need.[75]
Intuition is a very helpful cognitive component of the compassionate act in that intuition enables the compassioner to gain immediate intellectual apprehension of the existential state of the person
in need without the intervention of any (inhibiting and braking) rati-

---

74. As June Lowenberg points out, holism, or basically integrated unity, is the
opposite of viewing the person from a mechanistic perspective. And as she also
observes, even medical science is moving toward a holistic approach since the
data increasingly reveal that illness (and wellness) is a consequence of the interaction among all major human domains. Stress is a clearcut example of this fact.
June S. Lowenberg, *Caring and Responsibility: The Crossroads between Holistic Practice
and Traditional Medicine* (Philadelphia: University of Pennsylvania Press, 1989),
pp. 18-25.

75. Lee, *The Content of Religious Instruction*, p. 178; John of St. Thomas, *The
Gifts of the Holy Ghost*, trans. Dominic Hughes (New York: Sheed and Ward, 1951)
IV. 1-10, pp. 123-128; Leonard Allen, "Toward a Ministry of Compassion," *Christian
Ministry* 11 (January, 1980), p. 30.

ocinative processes.[76] The cognitive dimension of compassion is given far less attention than the affective and lifestyle dimensions by the religious educator because there is a sense in which compassion involves the suspension of ratiocinative cognition. By this I mean that it often happens that being compassionate in a given situation is to be unreasonable, makes no ratiocinative sense, and often goes against what reason tells us is in our own best interests.

The importance of teaching religious compassion holistically while downplaying much of ratiocinative cognition is well illustrated in what is probably the most famous experimental study ever conducted on religious compassion, and probably one of the most celebrated studies in the annals of social psychology itself.[77] In this extremely well-conducted research investigation, participating groups of students attending a prestigious mainline Protestant seminary on the East Coast were given the parable of the Good Samaritan (Lk 10:29-37). The seminarians were asked to deliver a three to five minute religious education speech on this parable. This speech would be recorded on tape. The seminarians were told that they would not be allowed to use any notes while delivering their religious education talk, thus directly indicating that they should cognitively prepare themselves well to insure a meaty speech. After they had studied the parable for some minutes, they were informed that the recording session would take place in a nearby building. A portion of the seminarians were told to hurry right over to the nearby building since they were already late for the recording session there. The other group of seminarians did not receive instructions that they should hurry. As the seminarians hurried or walked to the nearby building, they passed through an alley in which a victim was sitting slumped in a doorway, head down, eyes closed, and not moving.[78] The research investigation found

76. On the nature and thrust of intuition, see Lee, *The Content of Religious Instruction*, pp. 156-157.

77. John M. Darley and C. Daniel Batson, "From Jerusalem to Jericho," *Journal of Personality and Social Psychology* 27 (July, 1973), pp. 100-108. In my discussion of this superb and rich experimental study, I am only highlighting some of its many significant facets.

78. The Darley and Batson experimenters gave the following instructions to the "victim." As the seminarian passed by, the "victim" was to cough twice and groan, keeping his head down. If the seminarian stopped and asked if something was wrong, the "victim," acting startled and somewhat groggy, was to say: "Oh, thank

that 60 percent of the seminarians in both groups did not even minimally offer direct or indirect assistance to the victim[79] even though they were even at that moment cognitively reflecting on the parable of the Good Samaritan. The investigation found that variables other than cognitive reflection on religious compassion seemed to be more potent in determining the amount and degree of the seminarians' helping behavior. Thus seminarians in a hurry were less likely to offer help to the victim than seminarians not in a hurry. The Darley and Batson study concluded that whether or not a seminarian was cognitively reflecting on the religious education speech he was preparing to give on the parable of the Good Samaritan did not significantly influence his own compassionate behavior.[80]

Teaching as Deliberate Intentionality. An essential characteristic of all teaching is that it is carefully targeted toward the attainment of general and specific learning outcomes. If religious educators are to successfully teach for compassion, therefore, they should make compassion a conscious goal and a conscious objective. Compassionate learning outcomes do not just happen willy-nilly. Religious educators have to work deliberatively and systematically to ensure that their instructional efforts do indeed bring about these outcomes. Religious educators who rely solely or primarily on the Holy Spirit to directly produce compassionate outcomes in learners as if by magic[81] will soon discover that the Spirit historically has

---

you [cough]. . . . No, it's all right. . . . [Pause] "I've got this respiratory condition [cough]. . . . The doctor's given me these pills to take, and I just took one. . . . If I just sit and rest for a few minutes, I'll be O.K.. . . . Thanks very much for stopping though" [smiling weakly]. If the seminarian persisted, insisting on taking the "victim" inside the building, the "victim" was instructed to allow the seminarian to do so, and to thank the seminarian.

79. Indirect assistance was operationalized in this study as not helping the victim concretely but rather telling the person making the audiotape that there was a victim in the alley.

80. Another finding of this study should give religious educators pause to think, namely that the seminarians' type of religiosity was not significantly correlated to the degree or amount of his helping behavior.

81. Curiously, and sadly, a large segment of American religious educationists and educators historically have taken the position that the Holy Spirit is the only real religion teacher and that the human religious educator really has nothing much to do with bringing about religious outcomes in learners. I have labeled this view the "blow theory" of religious instruction since it takes its inspiration, falsely, I believe, from Jn 3:8 which states that the Spirit blows where it wills and no

exhibited a consistent tendency to bring about learning outcomes in direct proportion to the conscious intentions and deliberative efforts of the religious educator. The Holy Spirit does not work on demand or in an *ex machina* fashion as was claimed for the gods in certain primitive ancient religions. Rather, the Holy Spirit typically works in and through the nature, laws, and regular operations of that world which the triune Godhead created once and continues to create. As Lois LeBar observes, instructional procedure "is simply finding out how the Spirit works and working with him rather than against him."[82] It is my firm conviction, buttressed by a wealth of historical evidence, that the religious educator best discovers how the Spirit works instructionally by examining what in fact has worked instructionally and by seeing what instructional theory predicts will work.

The intentionally based actual facilitation of every learning outcome, including that of compassion, has two antecedent dimensions, namely goals and objectives. While they are indeed antecedent, nonetheless goals and objectives are alive, directive, and corrective during the enactment of the religious instruction event. Religious instruction goals and objectives are basically statements of the intended outcomes of that instruction. They refer to what should be brought about by deliberatively planned and carefully deployed instructional procedure.[83]

---

person can contain it. The blow theory, which represents a form of theological Occasionalism, results ultimately in a denial of human efficacy and in the final analysis reduces the role of the religious educator basically to nil, to just waiting around and piddling with what are fundamentally superficial facilitational procedures until the real action which comes with virtually total unpredictability, namely the Spirit which blows where it wills. Interestingly enough, those religious educationists who are the strongest advocates of the blow theory are usually the very ones who make sure that teachers follow all sorts of direct pedagogical prescriptions (often of the highly constricted cookbook variety) to make sure that their instructional efforts do indeed bring about the desired learning outcomes. For a description of the blow theory, see Lee, *The Flow of Religious Instruction*, pp. 174-180. For some advocates of the blow theory, see Wayne R. Rood, *The Art of Teaching Christianity* (Nashville: Abingdon, 1968), pp. 74-202; William J. Jacobs, "The Catechist as Witness," in *Catechetics Reconsidered*, ed. J.T. Dillon (Winona, Minn.: St. Mary's College Press, 1968), pp. 85-89.

82. Lois E. LeBar, *Education That Is Christian* (Old Tappan, N.J.: Revell, 1958), p. 241.

83. Robert Gagné, Leslie J. Briggs, and Walter W. Wager, *Principles of Instructional Design*, 3rd ed. (New York: Holt, Rinehart and Winston, 1988), p. 41.

Goals are necessary but by no means sufficient for teaching compassion successfully. Because they are general statements, goals are inherently unteachable. To be teachable, goals must be placed into the form of specific instructional objectives which indicate how the religious educator goes about ensuring that the general goal is actually achieved by the learner.[84]

Objectives make an invaluable contribution to the way in which religious educators in formal and informal settings achieve pedagogically desirable continuity, sequencing, and timing during the enactment of the religious instruction event. Furthermore, instructional objectives are necessary if both the religious educator and the learner are to validly ascertain whether and to what extent the desired learning outcomes have actually occurred.[85]

Perhaps the most important advantage of instructional objectives is that they clearly, precisely, and unambiguously tell both the religious educator and the learners what the learners will be doing during the course of the instructional event.[86] Consequently, instructional objectives are preeminently learner-centered since they place emphasis on learner activity. Such emphasis is helpful to the religious educator during both the design phase and the enactment phase of religious instruction. During the design phase, instructional objectives enable the religious educator to determine and restructure which conditions of learning should characterize the religious instruction event.[87] During the enactment phase, instructional objectives serve to help the religious educator focus constantly and directly on those teaching activities which are directly related to

---

84. Anna Carol Fults, "Compassion: A Characteristic of Teachers," *Delta Kappa Gamma Bulletin* 47 (Summer, 1981), p. 28.

85. Benjamin S. Bloom, J. Thomas Hastings, and George F. Madaus, *Handbook of Formative and Summative Evaluation of Student Learning* (New York: McGraw-Hill, 1971), pp. 30-40.

86. Jon Wiles and Joseph Bondi distinguish between a general objective and a specific objective. For them, a general objective is a statement of the overall process or flow whereby a goal is translated into an objective. A specific objective is a statement placed in performance terms of what is to be learned. In this chapter I deal with performance objectives rather than what Wiles and Bondi call general objectives. Jon Wiles and Joseph Bondi, *Curriculum Development: A Guide to Practice*, 3rd ed. (Columbus, Ohio: Merrill, 1989), pp. 94-95. On performance objectives, see A.J. Romiszowski, *Designing Instructional Systems* (London: Kogan Page, 1981), pp. 43-64, 80-94.

87. Gagné et al., *Principles of Instructional Design*, p. 123.

producing the desired outcome of compassion.

How does the religious educator go about constructing an instructional objective in general, and an instructional objective for compassion in particular? Many fine guidelines have been offered by specialists in instructional design.[88] All these guidelines have two things in common: they emphasize the conditions of learning and they specify what the learner will be doing as he/she engages in the instructional dynamic. The most influential of all guidelines on the construction of instructional objectives remains that of Robert Mager. *First,* the religious educator identifies the terminal performance by name, that is, specify the particular kind of performance of compassion which will be accepted as evidence by both learner and religious educator that the learner has successfully achieved the objective. *Second,* the religious educator defines the desired performance outcome further by describing the important and significant conditions under which the performance of compassion can be predicted or expected to occur. *Third,* the religious educator specifies the criteria of acceptable performance of compassion by describing the level of performance which is considered acceptable both by the religious educator and the learner.[89]

Throughout the history of general education and of religious education, significant theoretical and procedural advances have almost always met with initial opposition. Thus it is hardly surprising that the advocacy of performance objectives by religious educationists and educators who are seeking to clarify religious instruction purposes and who are endeavoring to make teaching procedures more effective has met with stiff resistance in some religious education quarters. In general, this resistance is based on a lack of knowledge of the nature and structure of the educational process[90]

---

88. Thus, for example, Robert Gagné and his associates maintain that the ideal instructional objective comprises five components. For these educationists, the five-component objective "specifies the situation in which the performance is performed; the type of learner capability; the object of the performance, the specific action the learner takes in employing the capability; and the tools, constraints, and special conditions associated with the performance." Ibid., pp. 123-126.

89. Robert F. Mager, *Preparing Instructional Objectives* (Palo Alto, Calif.: Fearon, 1962).

90. See, for example, Richard P. McBrien, "Toward an American Catechesis," *Living Light* 13 (Summer, 1976), p. 175.

or on a system of somewhat hardened ideology[91] rather than grounded in solid research evidence or in a careful analysis of what actually
occurs during the religious instruction act itself. As Thomas Walters
remarks, every religious educator who teaches automatically has
an instructional objective, however intentional or however inchoate
that objective might be. It is impossible to begin or continue teaching religion without having a performance objective of one kind or
another. To paraphrase Walters, instructional objectives are not
something religious educators can choose to have or not to have. If
religious educators do not have performance objectives, they cannot even begin the teaching process. As soon as the religious educator thinks "I would like to . . . ", he or she has already adopted an
instructional objective.[92] What proposals about instructional objectives offered by persons like Robert Mager do is to help religious educators sharpen and make more teachable their goals for teaching
religious compassion.

Teaching as Behavioral Specificity. For any procedure to be even
minimally effective, it is absolutely necessary that there be behavioral
specificity at every stage of its planning and enactment. This
irrefutable fact holds true for religious instruction procedure in
general and for teaching compassion in particular.

Compassion is a construct, as was shown earlier in this chapter.
Thus compassion does not have real existence; it has mental existence only. Compassion is the name we give to a particular set or formation of specific human behaviors in order to distinguish in our
minds that set from other sets of interactive human behaviors such
as care, pity, joy, sadness, and so forth. Thus it is impossible to teach
compassion as such. We can teach the construct of compassion to
learners, but we cannot teach them to be compassionate because
compassion (and thus being compassionate) is a mental entity and
not a real entity. The only way in which a religious educator can
teach learners to be compassionate is to teach that repertoire of
specific behaviors which go to form the particular interactive set

---

91. See, for example, Padraic O'Hare, "Learning Objectives in Religious
Education: The Ideological Context," *PACE* 18 (October, 1987), pp. 25-29.
92. Thomas P. Walters, "Educational Objectives, Catechesis, and the Future,"
Religious Education 85 (Winter, 1990), pp. 84-91. This article ranks as one of the finest
down-to-earth, commonsense, and informed expositions of the absolute necessity and great usefulness of performance objectives in religious instruction.

of specific human behaviors we call compassion. When learners successfully acquire those specific behaviors which, in concert, go to make up the construct compassion, they will thereby become compassionate.

In order to teach compassion successfully, the religious educator should begin by identifying those specific behaviors which are subsumed and abstracted by the construct compassion. These specific behaviors fall under the psychomotor, cognitive, affective, and lifestyle domains of human living. Once the religious educator has identified these specific behaviors within each domain, he/she should place them into performance objectives so as to help ensure that they will be effectively learned. After that has been done, the religious educator can structure the four molar variables involved in all teaching in order to optimally situate the performance-phrased specific behaviors into an overall harmonious flow of successful instruction.

In their commendable zeal to teach, some religious educators become impatient with unremitting attention to specific behaviors, preferring instead to concentrate on such lofty rallying cries as "heralding the Good News" or "winning souls for Christ." As a result, specific teaching/learning behaviors are woefully neglected, and in the end these religious educators' efforts become garbled and ineffective. "Heralding the Good News" is a nice slogan,[93] but it is not even an instructional goal much less a statement of an instructional objective. These religious educators would do well to examine specifically and behaviorally what it is that they are doing or should be doing when they are engaged in the nitty-gritty of heralding the Good News or winning souls for Christ, just as an artist must give constant attention to the specific details of the painting he/she is executing. Focused attention to what is actually taking place in the here-and-now instructional dynamic when one is heralding will clearly show that heralding is actually composed of a whole series of specific behaviors on the part of the religious educator and the learners. Only when these behaviors are identified, carefully attended to, and systematically taught will the results of the heralding match the zeal of the herald.

---

93. On the topic of slogans and ceremonial language replacing instructional effort, see Lee, *The Content of Religious Instruction*, pp. 316-318.

Constant and unremitting attention to specific behaviors before and during the religious instruction act is not easy. In fact, such attention is one of the most difficult and most painful of all the religious educator's tasks. Christians all bear crosses depending on their nature and circumstances. Crosses are difficult to endure, and so it is understandable that religious educators tend to resist being crucified on the cross of specificity. But it is this kind of crucifixion which brings about the resurrection of results. What Mies van der Rohe once said about architecture also holds true of religious instruction, namely that God lies in the details. And, I might add, the devil lies in the neglect of details.

Specific Procedures

Instructional theory is where the ultimate action is in religion teaching.[94] General instructional principles are where the penultimate action is in religion teaching. Specific instructional procedures are where the immediate action is in religion teaching. Instructional theory and general instructional principles exist in order to make specific instructional procedures effective. Thus the specific instructional procedures which the religious educator enacts during the here-and-now pedagogical dynamic are of great importance in teaching religious compassion.

To acquire and reinforce a proper appreciation of the centrality of specific procedures in the concrete here-and-now enactment of teaching, the religious educator should keep five things in mind.

First, to successfully teach compassion, it is absolutely essential for the religious educator to possess both adequate procedural knowledge[95] and effective procedural skills in order to intentionally facil-

---

94. Fruitful and valid instructional theory necessarily includes substantive and structural content.

95. Dona Kagan's review of the pertinent empirical research concludes that when faced with students having little academic motivation and a tendency toward misbehavior, novice teachers possessing inadequate procedural knowledge tend to become quickly disillusioned and grow increasingly authoritarian and custodial. This finding can be legitimately extrapolated not only to religious educators operating in formal settings such as Sunday school and parish religious education (formerly called CCD), but also to religious educators in informal settings such as parents in the home. Dona M. Kagan, "Professional Growth Among Preserviced and Beginning Teachers," *Review of Educational Research* 62 (Summer, 1992), p. 145.

itate a wide variety of deeply religious outcomes.[96] Religious educators who do not pay sufficient attention to developing requisite mastery of procedural knowledge and specific procedural skills are thereby dooming themselves to instructional mediocrity at the very best and in all likelihood to pedagogical failure.

Second, specific teaching procedures do make a distinct and definite difference not only in determining whether learning takes place at all but also in determining what particular kind of learning takes place.[97] The facilitation of desired learning outcomes is a procedural art, and all effective long-lasting art occurs only when the artist knows which specific procedures to employ and how to employ them. The effective religious educator is one who is deeply committed to the crucial importance of instructional procedure, who is aware of the vast repertoire of specific instructional procedures which are available, and who is able to select from this vast repertoire that particular instructional procedure which research and experience suggest is the most likely to produce the desired learning outcome.

Third, there is no one best specific instructional procedure which the religious educator can use to effectively facilitate all of the myriad different kinds of learning outcomes. Each discrete cluster of the huge mass of different kinds of learning outcomes is facilitated by a different specific instructional procedure. Cognitive outcomes are facilitated by cognitively oriented specific instructional procedures, affective outcomes are facilitated by affectively oriented procedures, and the like. Furthermore, each of the numerous forms of cognitive outcomes is successfully taught by using a different kind of cognitively oriented instructional procedure. This principle also holds true for the many different forms of affective learning outcomes and lifestyle outcomes. The entire mass of specific teaching procedures constitutes a collection of precise instructional tools,

---

96. Iris V. Cully, *Education for Spiritual Growth* (San Francisco: Harper & Row, 1984), pp. 147-165. For an earlier and widely used compendium of procedures geared to foster progressively deeper spiritual growth, see Adolphe Tanquerey, *The Spiritual Life*, 2nd ed., trans. Herman Branderis (Westminster, Md.: Newman, 1930).

97. N.L. Gage, *Hard Gains in the Soft Sciences: The Case of Pedagogy* (Bloomington, Ind.: Phi Delta Kappa, 1985), pp. 1-24; Jere Brophy and Thomas L. Good, "Teacher Behavior and Student Achievement," in *Handbook of Research on Teaching*, 3rd ed., ed. Merlin C. Wittrock (New York: Macmillan), pp. 328-375.

each of which, in the hands of a skilled religious educator possessing adequate theoretical and procedural knowledge as well as procedural skill, yields a specific learning outcome which differs from
other types of learning outcomes. The empirical research on all of
this is so widespread and so well known that it is very difficult to
imagine that anyone even remotely familiar with instructional practice is unaware of it.[98]

Fourth, it is important to know prior to the deployment of any
specific facilitational procedure what are the probable learning
outcomes which this procedure will likely yield. Let us say, for example, that a religious educator wishes to use a specific deindividuation
procedure[99] to help learners become more compassionate. The
religious educator knows that the research suggests that deindividuation in the presence of appropriate eliciting cues has been
shown to increase positive social behavior, including compassionate
behavior.[100] But the religious educator is also aware of the empirical
research which suggests that deindividuation procedures have been
found to also increase aggressive behavior in persons on whom this
procedure has been used. Thus the religious educator desiring to
use deindividuation techniques to teach compassion will do so in
such a fashion as to maximize the probability that compassionate
behaviors are learned and to minimize the possibility that aggressive

---

98. Regretfully over the years a few publishers—and recently one in particular—
of Christian religion textbook series for children and youth in classroom settings
try by every means at their disposal to persuade religious educators that the specific
instructional procedure or set of procedures enshrined in their textbook series is
either the finest universal instructional device or what is worse the only truly effective instructional device. Claims such as these are flatly and palpably untrue, and
go counter to everything which research and experience has discovered, as these
publishers should know and quite possibly do know. Religion curriculum textbook publishing is a huge and profitable business running into the hundreds of mil-
lions of dollars. The stakes are as high as they are competitive. But this fact surely does not justify the attempts on the part of some publishers to hoodwink religious
educators into believing in the existence of an instructional magic wand which, if
waved over the learners, will produce any and all kinds of results. Fortunately publishers of this ilk are in the very small minority of Christian textbook series publishers.

99. J.T. Tedeschi, "Deindividuation" in *Encyclopedia of Psychology*, ed. Raymond
J. Corsini, vol. 1 (New York: Wiley, 1984), p. 351.

100. Robert Dennis Johnson, "The Divergent Effect of Increasing Level of
Deindividuation in the Presence of Aggression/Compassion Eliciting Cues" (Ph.D.
dissertation, University of Georgia, 1975, pp. 70-71).

behaviors are learned, unless these aggressive behaviors are such that they can beneficially promote the increase of compassion.

Fifth, the effectiveness of any specific teaching procedure is significantly enhanced or diminished to the extent to which it is harmoniously integrated into the religious educator's generalized teaching style. Teaching style is the overall, processive, and fluid way in which the religious educator integrates various instructional strategies, methods, and techniques in the here-and-now deployment of the instructional act.[101] Teaching style involves the religious educator's whole personality structure, attitudes, values, theories, generalized ways of behaving, and so forth.[102] It is the religious educator's personalized teaching style which helps prevent the enactment of specific instructional procedures from becoming mechanical, wooden, and lifeless.[103] To deploy specific instructional procedures in the most effective possible manner, the religious educator should (1) explore the range of possible, available, and suitable teaching styles; (2) identify his/her own present teaching style; (3) see where, how, and to what extent his/her present teaching style fits within the whole range of teaching styles proposed for or used in instructional activity; (4) work on improving his/her own teaching style in the light both of research on the effectiveness of this kind of teaching style and of how this particular teaching style meshes with many other types of teaching style available to religious educators; (5) endeavor to harmoniously integrate specific instructional procedures into the teaching style which he/she is enacting in the instructional event.[104]

Psychomotor Domain. Like all forms of human behavior, compassion involves a certain amount of psychomotor activity. In essence, human psychomotor activity consists of physical movement of one

---

101. Lee, *The Flow of Religious Instruction*, p. 34.

102. Louis J. Rubin, *Artistry in Teaching* (New York: Random House, 1985), pp. 19-20.

103. Allan C. Ornstein, "Teacher Effectiveness Research: Theoretical Considerations" in *Effective Teaching: Current Research*, ed. Hersholt C. Waxman and Herbert J. Wahlberg (Berkeley, Calif.: McCutchan, 1991), pp. 72-74.

104. Timothy Lines has done a superb job in identifying ten global teaching styles available to religious educators. He also shows how a religious educator's teaching style really forges his/her own personal and professional identity as a religious educator. Timothy Arthur Lines, *Functional Images of the Religious Educator* (Birmingham, Ala.: Religious Education Press, 1992).

sort or another.[105] Because the act of compassion, particularly in its lifestyle dimension, usually involves physical action of the compassioner to help the person in need, the religious educator would do well to teach learners how to (1) deepen the intensity and (2) enhance the effectiveness of their compassionate behavior through the skillful use of those physical movements which tend to be correlated with one or another aspect of compassion.

Through the use of compassion-related motor activities, the compassioner will come to feel increased compassion for the person in need since there is a demonstrated correlation between psychomotor activity and affective states. For example, a flowing, bending postural movement by the compassioner toward the individual in need will likely result in the compassioner feeling more personalistically oriented toward and caring of the person in need. And through the use of compassion-related motor activities, the compassioner will communicate to the person in need that the compassioner really cares and really feels compassion. For example, the research has shown that a flowing, bending posture by one person toward another communicates to the other individual a sense of personal involvement, care, and concern on the part of the person making the postural movement.[106]

In religious instruction, psychomotor activity becomes especially helpful when it is thought of as nonverbal behavior.[107] There are many forms of nonverbal behavior which the religious educator can teach learners in order to help them feel and be more compassionate toward persons in need. Posture is one of these. This topic was briefly discussed in the previous paragraph. Another important nonverbal behavior linked to compassion is paralanguage, namely those vocal characteristics occurring during speech which are nonverbal in form and structure. Examples of paralanguage include voice, tone, pitch, loudness, accent, and the like. A compassioner who speaks in a soft, low, unhurried, rhythmic man-

---

105. Anita J. Harrow, *A Taxonomy of the Psychomotor Domain* (New York: McKay, 1972), pp. 1-20.

106. Lee, *The Content of Religious Instruction*, pp. 438-441.

107. Despite the enormous importance of nonverbal behavior in religious and liturgical life, virtually no religious education writer has given sustained, careful, and scholarly attention to nonverbal communication. The lone exception to this valid generalization is James Michael Lee, *The Content of Religious Instruction*, pp. 378-474.

ner will tend to convey more warmth and feeling to the person in need than one who speaks in a loud, high, hurried, and pause-filled fashion.[108] Smiles and gaze have been shown by the research to communicate warmth, acceptance, concern, and personal involvement.[109] Head nodding conveys a positive concern and regard for the other person.[110] Touching has been shown to convey a sense of personal involvement, liking, and personal concern.[111] Open arms suggest that the person is open to the needs and interests of the other, as contrasted to folded arms.[112] These are just a few of the many ways in which the compassioner can nonverbally communicate compassion to the person in need.

Cognitive Domain. Since cognition does play a role, albeit minor, in compassion, religious educators should include it in their efforts to teach learners to be compassionate. This statement has two implications. First, religious educators should make sure that cognition plays a minor rather than a major part in their overall efforts to teach learners to be compassionate. Second, religious educators should as far as possible avoid heavily cognitive teaching procedures such as lecture or telling which contribute relatively little to the understanding or practice of compassion[113] while utilizing those instructional procedures which are correlated to a deeper understanding of the nature and process of the compassionate act.

As was noted toward the beginning of this chapter, understand-

108. Ibid., pp. 400-404.

109. Albert Mehrabian, *Nonverbal Communication* (Chicago: Aldine, 1972), pp. 12, 21.

110. Albert Mehrabian, *Silent Messages* (Belmont, Calif.: Wadsworth, 1971), p. 61.

111. Ashley Montagu, *Touching: The Human Significance of the Skin* (New York: Columbia University Press, 1971).

112. John Spiegel and Pavel Machotka, *Messages of the Body* (New York: Free Press, 1974), pp. 193, 202, 220.

113. Thus Matthew Fox can rightly state that the university at this stage in history "is not a worthy place to go to learn compassion" because the university system typically uses the lecture method exclusively — and, I might add, is almost wholly based on a cognitive axis. Compassion in Fox's view, and mine as well, is a way of living and "cannot be taught without living or trying to live it." What Fox is stating here is that more than anything else, compassion is a lifestyle and hence can only be taught adequately by using lifestyle-oriented instructional procedures. Matthew Fox, *A Spirituality Named Compassion*, (Minneapolis: Winston, 1979), p. 235. The experimental research I presented earlier in this chapter, "From Jerusalem to Jericho" highlights the very weak correlation between lecture and cognitive activity on the one hand and compassionate deeds on the other hand.

ing consists in a deeper grasp of the penultimate principles of reality. Unlike knowledge, which can be gained by study and by hearing a lecture, understanding can be acquired only by personal firsthand experience. One instructional procedure for helping learners come to an understanding of compassion is guided experiential discovery.

Guided experiential discovery consists in placing learners in that kind of a situation which contains a variety of natural or prepared stimuli which are directly or indirectly connected to the desired outcome.[114] By use of the inductive method of instruction, the religious educator guides the learners to discover for themselves the general principles and penultimate explanations underlying and unifying the stimuli which they are experiencing in the situation.

Guided experiential discovery is of two varieties, namely lightly structured and heavily structured.

Lightly structured discovery procedures are usually used in informal or natural settings such as a playground, home environment, street setting, and the like. In a lightly structured discovery procedure, for example, the religious educator might go with learners to a hospital in which persons are visibly suffering from a painful incurable disease such as terminal cancer. The learners personally experience a variety of related stimuli in that situation. Through probing questions and reflective statements made by the religious educator, the learners come to understand the nature and meaning of compassion for persons in need.

Heavily structured discovery procedures are usually used in formal or artificial settings such as a classroom or church. In a heavily structured discovery procedure,[115] materials about human suf-

---

114. Guided experiential discovery, as its name implies, lays heavy stress on the learner personally experiencing in a physical or nonphysical manner the stimuli at hand. In contrast, guided nonexperiential discovery procedures stress an almost exclusively cognitive approach. Thus, for example, Muska Mosston and Sara Ashworth propose a guided discovery procedure which consists totally of conceptual questioning in which the educator uses a series of highly structured questions asked in small incremental steps to guide learners to discover for themselves the basic principles underlying a reality such as compassion. Muska Mosston and Sara Ashworth, *The Spectrum of Teaching Style* (New York: Longman, 1990), pp. 193-217.

115. This procedure was developed by Richard Suchman for use in teaching the natural sciences. It has applications and usefulness in teaching all kinds of substantive content, including religious compassion. Suchman calls his procedure

fering and misery are given to learners wishing to come to an understanding of compassion. These materials are print, media, specimens, realia, and the like. The materials are such that their message about suffering and compassion seem to be somehow contradictory, puzzling, or otherwise out of harmony. Through the inquiry method, the religious educator leads learners to explore in depth this lack of harmony. Learners ask questions of each other and of the religious educator, all the while seeking to discover a unifying set of principles by which to understand the situation. The religious educator, in turn, asks probing "Why?" questions. Eventually learners are led to discover for themselves the penultimate principles and explanations by which they can understand the bases of the stimuli which they experienced in the prepared environment.

Affective Domain. True and effective compassion necessarily includes a great deal of empathy and other appropriate kinds of feeling tone. Affectivity precedes and accompanies concrete assistance given by the compassioner to the person in need. Concrete assistance given with little or no preceding and accompanying affect is not compassion but rather a form of welfare, the dole, or do-goodism.

Every religious educator is well aware that affect can be successfully taught to persons of all ages. Earlier in this chapter I showed conclusively that persons of varying ages and circumstances have been taught to be empathic. One use of all instruction, including religious instruction, has classically been that of socialization.[116] One review of the pertinent empirical research[117] suggests that children (and I should add, youth and adults) can be socialized in such a way as to contribute to the acquisition and enlargement of their empathy.

Two instructional procedures for helping learners become

---

the inquiry method, suggesting its cognitive axis. The original study was J. Richard Suchman, "The Elementary School Training Program in Scientific Inquiry," Report of the U.S. Office of Education, Project Title VIII, Project 216, 1962. See also J. Richard Suchman, *Inquiry Development Program* (Chicago: Science Research Associates, 1962).

116. As I point out elsewhere, religious instruction as socialization includes, but by no means is restricted to socialization into a particular institutional church society or ecclesiastical culture. Lee, *The Shape of Religious Instruction*, pp. 24-27.

117. Carolyn Zahn-Waxler and Marian Radke-Yarrow, "The Origins of Empathic Concern," *Motivation and Emotion* 14 (June, 1990), pp. 107-130.

empathic and increase their positive feeling functions for persons in need are affective sensitivity exercises and role playing.

Affective sensitivity exercises can contribute significantly to deepening empathy and making more immediate the other affective dimensions of compassion.[118] As I am using the term here,[119] an affective sensitivity exercise is an unstructured, intensely affective, small group situation which uses group dynamics procedures in such a way that deeper personal feelings and interpersonal relationships are openly explored and encountered for self and others to experience. Affective sensitivity exercises are typically conducted in a social laboratory milieu[120] rather than in a natural setting. In many instances affective sensitivity exercises take place in a tightly compacted time frame such as a few days or a week rather than over a longer duration.

The dual purpose of affective sensitivity exercises is to produce a heightened, feeling-full awareness of the affects of self and others in an interpersonal situation and to show how affect can be communicated and received in an authentic and effective manner.

Affective sensitivity exercises are not only used in group counseling and psychotherapy, but also in humanistic education.[121]

------

118. Donald G. Gregg, "An Investigation of the Development of Empathic Communication through Sensitivity Training Experience" (Ph.D. dissertation, Lehigh University, 1968). This study was conducted on preservice teachers.

119. There is considerable lack of consensus on the meaning and scope of sensitivity exercises and affective procedures related to sensitivity training in one way or another. Some of these related procedures, each of which purports to have a somewhat different form and emphasis, are the T-group, encounter group, sensitivity awareness group, Gestalt group, personal expression group, and human potential group, to name just a few. See Carl R. Rogers, *Carl Rogers on Encounter Groups* (New York: Harper & Row, 1970), pp. 4-11.

120. Some specialists contend that laboratory education is the genus for all these kinds of intensive affective exercises, while sensitivity experiences, T-groups, encounter groups, and the like are all types of laboratory work. Arthur Blumberg, "Laboratory Education and Sensitivity Training," in *Sensitivity and the Laboratory Approach*, ed. Robert T. Golembiewski and Arthur Blumberg, 3rd ed. (Itaska, Ill.: Peacock, 1977), pp. 14-24; Gerard Egan, *Encounter: Group Processes for Interpersonal Growth* (Belmont, Calif.: Brooks/Cole, 1970), pp. 4-11.

121. Humanistic education is a term which means education deliberately aimed at enabling the learner to become as fully human as possible. Religious instruction, obviously, seeks the same goals as humanistic education in that it endeavors to assist learners to become their full selves in order to foster their own personal and religious development. For two classic books on humanistic education, see George Isaac Brown, *Human Teaching for Human Learning* (New York:

Role playing is an instructional technique which can successfully produce a wide variety of affective learning outcomes, including empathy[122] and other feeling functions which are part of compassion in one way or another. Much of the power of role playing to produce and deepen affective outcomes such as empathy stems from the fact that role playing consists of active, personal, and affective involvement on the part of each role player. This power is magnified because the role player takes the other's role as the other experiences it—not a generalized other but a very individual other.[123] This dual aspect of role playing, namely (1) active personal affective involvement (2) which is directed toward a particular person makes this instructional technique an especially valuable one for broadening and deepening the affective dimension of the learner's compassion since compassion is always a personal act, always an affective act, and always an act of an individual.[124] Like every religious instruction procedure, role playing is not intrinsically or automatically effective. Thus the religious educator must carefully plan, implement, and follow up the roleplaying activity in order to achieve the desired learning outcome.

Lifestyle Domain. Lifestyle refers to the overall pattern of a person's activities. It consists of the way in which persons organize their self-system and live out their own life. It is a personal pattern of living.[125]

Viking, 1971); Harold C. Lyon Jr., *Learning to Feel—Feeling to Learn* (Columbus, Ohio: Merrill, 1971).

122. Natale, *An Experiment in Empathy,* pp. 41-42; Helen Lucille Davis Dell, "The Evaluation of Teaching Procedures Designed to Increase Empathy Ability" (Ph.D. dissertation, Ball State University, 1967).

123. James Michael Lee and Nathaniel J. Pallone, *Guidance and Counseling in Schools: Foundations and Processes* (New York: McGraw-Hill, 1966), pp. 328-329.

124. Though role playing is especially valuable for producing affective learning outcomes, it also yields cognitive insights into the situation being enacted, as William Pearlman observes. These cognitive insights are typically in the areas of cognitive understanding and other more generalized kinds of thinking. Phyllis Kitzerow reports that two or three years after participating in a role-playing situation which she structured, the participants forgot virtually all of the cognitive details of the event but remembered the generalized cognitive dimensions and affective aspects of the role which they enacted. William D. Pearlman, "Psychodrama: Discovering New Meaning in Personal Drama," *New Directions for Adult and Continuing Education* 55 (Spring, 1990), pp. 27-36; Phyllis Kitzerow, "Active Learning in the Classroom: The Use of Group Role Plays," *Teaching Sociology* 18 (April, 1990), pp. 223-225.

125. For a more detailed treatment of lifestyle content in religious instruction, see Lee, *The Content of Religious Instruction,* pp. 608-735.

Technically, lifestyle is not so much a separate domain as it is the holistic functionalistic integration of all domains.

Since I have already discussed the psychomotor domain, the cognitive domain, and the affective domain, this short section will focus on the other major ingredient of lifestyle, namely conduct or overt behavior. Indeed, conduct or overt behavior is the most distinctive and recognizable aspect of lifestyle. In discussing this salient feature of lifestyle, however, it should be kept in mind that psychomotor activities, cognitive activities, and affective activities are co-present with overt behavior, even though I might not mention them explicitly.

Compassion does not exist in the absence of concrete assistance given to the person in need. In order for an act to be compassionate, it is necessary but not sufficient that cognitive understanding of and feelingful empathy with the suffering individual also be present. Concrete assistance to alleviate the individual's distress is also necessary if an act is to be compassionate. Such alleviation should not be such that it simply assuages the suffering. Rather, this alleviation should also and necessarily include the promotion of relevant and appropriate growth of the individual in need. The assuaging of present suffering and the promotion of relevant appropriate growth are vitally important factors in determining how long and in what way the compassioner comes to the concrete assistance of the individual in need.[126]

Two instructional procedures for helping learners develop and increase their concrete overt behavior toward persons in need are establishing a compassionate instructional environment and simulation.

Because it is one of the four molar variables present in every teaching act, the instructional environment is a powerful force shaping and coloring the learning which takes place. Instructional environment consists both of the immediate physical surroundings and the psychosocial climate in which the teaching/learning act occurs.[127] In teaching for compassion, the religious educator should structure the situation in such a way that the environmental

---

126. Nel Noddings, *Caring* (Berkeley, Calif.: University of California Press, 1984), p. 16.

127. Lee, *The Flow of Religious Instruction*, pp. 65-72.

variables themselves promote an understanding of, empathy with, and actual overt action toward the person in need.

There once was a student in a midwestern Lutheran school who was undergoing radiation treatment for cancer. One result of this treatment was that the student lost all his hair. This hair loss proved to be a source of considerable psychological distress to the student. The teacher and his classmates decided to have compassion on the student undergoing radiation by having their own heads shaved. This act created a distinctly different instructional environment than that which had previously existed. The new environment communicated very effectively to the student in distress that his classmates really had compassion since they overtly sacrificed themselves to be in the same unfortunate situation as he. And the students who had their heads shaved gained a real understanding of and empathy with the student undergoing radiation. There is the possibility that this compassionate learning environment brought into existence by their own overt action of having their heads shaved was a powerful stimulus to them to engage in concrete overt compassionate behaviors in the future toward persons in need.

Simulation is another effective instructional procedure for teaching learners to utilize and expand their overt behavior in the act of compassion.[128] The religious educator can structure a simulation in which learners encounter a person in distress, and only through the use of overt action can this distress be noticeably alleviated. For example, in a family-based religious instruction situation, a slovenly dressed and dirty looking woman with several ragged children pulling at her skirt knocks on the door of the home in which the religious instruction group is meeting. When the door is opened, the woman asks for money and a place where she can sleep for the night. Then she faints and falls to the floor. Her children begin crying. What will the learners do? They certainly will have to act in an overt manner if the woman and her children are to be helped, if compassion is to be exercised.

It should be emphasized that like all instructionally effective simulation games, simulations like the one mentioned above should be

---

128. Simulation gaming is a rich and wide-ranging instructional procedure in that it can facilitate psychomotor, cognitive, affective, and lifestyle outcomes.

carefully structured and possess the requisite degree of specificity.[129]

Limits of Compassion

In addressing the question of whether compassion is absolute
or whether there are limits to compassion, it might be helpful to consider the following three cases.

A slightly swaying man in tattered clothing and smelling of alcohol stands on the sidewalk twenty yards from a tavern and bel-
ligerently presses a passerby for money. Does the passerby show a
lack of compassion by not giving money to the panhandler?

A homeless woman smelling faintly of urine and dressed in filthy
clothing enters a restaurant, sits on a stool at the counter, and
attempts to intercept the change which the waitress is giving to a
diner who has just paid his bill. Does the diner show a lack of compassion by preventing the woman from taking his change?

A student attending a midwestern university goes to Florida and
frolics in the sun with his friends the week before his final term
paper is due. Upon his return, he tells the professor to be compassionate to him because he has not completed the assigned paper.
Does the professor show a lack of compassion by giving the student
a grade of zero on his term paper?

The answer to the three questions posed in the previous paragraphs is an emphatic no. Compassion is not an absolute to be
given to all persons in all circumstances. Compassion is dependent
upon whether the act of helping a person in distress will actually help
that person's growth or hinder it. Compassion, after all, consists
essentially in helping the other person as a person. In all three
cases mentioned in this section, rendering assistance to the persons in distress would in all likelihood hinder their growth, and
hence would not be compassion.

Compassion is not do-goodism. Do-goodism is giving indiscrim-
inate aid to everyone with no regard as to whether this assistance in
practice will help or hurt the recipient.

---

129. For a helpful example of a simulation game which integrates cognitive,
affective, and lifestyle behaviors see Kathleen V. Cairns, J. Brian Woodward, and
John Savery, "The Life Choices Simulation," *Simulation and Games* 20 (September,
1989), pp. 245-271.

Compassion is not leniency. Leniency is a suspension of justice whereas compassion is the fulfillment of love. And love in its finest form always seeks the good in and for the other person.[130]

In 2 Chr 36:15-17 we read that out of compassion God sent his messengers to his chosen people. The Israelites proceeded to mock the messengers of the Lord and also mistreated his prophets. As a result, God withheld his compassion and delivered up the Israelites into the hands of the king of the Chaldeans. The message is clear. God's initial assistance hindered the religious growth of the Israelites and therefore he later withheld his compassion from them.

In helping learners to become compassionate, the religious educator should endeavor to teach them to assess for themselves whether or not a particular act is truly compassionate or whether it masquerades as compassion. Such masquerades often vitiate and do the opposite of what genuine compassion can accomplish.

Conclusion

I would like to conclude this chapter by highlighting two central axes of the act of compassion.

The first of these axes has to do with the role which compassion plays in the life of the compassioner.

Compassion is always deeply personal. It is the act of an individual. It is never the act of an institution. This personal act always entails sacrifice. Compassion as a deeply personal act involving sacrifice is nicely illustrated in a passage from the Babylonian Talmud.[131] In this lovely excerpt, the saintly rabbi Joshua ben Levi questions the prophet Elijah on how we can find the Messiah when he arrives.

"Where," Rabbi Joshua asked, "shall I find the Messiah?"

"At the gate of the city," Elijah replied.

"How shall I recognize him?"

"He sits among the lepers."

"Among the lepers!" cried Rabbi Joshua: "What is he doing there?"

---

130. Lee, *The Content of Religious Instruction*, pp. 233-235.

131. Babylonian Talmud, Sanhedrin, 98a, as discussed and quoted in Ronald Green, "The Perspective of Jewish Teaching," *Religious Education* 83 (Spring, 1988), pp. 228-229.

"He changes their bandages," Elijah answered. "He changes them one by one."

The second of the two axes of compassion which I would like to highlight in this concluding section has to do with the role compassion plays in a person's relationship to God.

Compassion occupies a very special place in the web of a person's religious relationships. The Jewish writer Samuel Dresner[132] put it this way:

> "*Prayer* is the way God enters our life
>   in terms of a person's relation to heaven.
> *Humility* is the way God enters our life
>   in terms of a person's relation to self.
> *Compassion* is the way God enters our life
>   in terms of a person's relationship with other human beings."

---

132. Samuel H. Dresner, *Prayer, Humility, and Compassion*, (Philadelphia: Jewish Publication Society of America, 1957), p. 183.

PROFILES OF CONTRIBUTORS

DIANNE BERGANT is Professor of Old Testament Studies at Catholic Theological Union in Chicago. Having completed five years as the editor of *The Bible Today*, she continues to serve on its editorial board as well as that of *Biblical Theology Bulletin*. Three of her many books include: *Job & Ecclesiastes* (Glazier), *Common Lectionary* (Church Hymnal), and "The Wisdom Books," in T*he Catholic Study Bible* (Oxford University Press). Dr. Bergant also has written numerous articles and conducted workshops in the areas of biblical interpretation, biblical spirituality, and social issues such as ecology, feminism, and peace.

WAYNE WHITSON FLOYD JR. is Assistant Professor of Religion at Dickinson College in Carlisle, Pennsylvania. He is a native of Mississippi and is an Episcopal layperson. Dr. Floyd received a Master of Divinity degree and his Ph.D. in Theology from Emory University in Atlanta. He is the author of two books, *Theology and the Dialectics of Otherness* (University Press of America) and *Bonhoeffer Bibliography: Primary Sources and Secondary Literature in English* (American Theological Library Association). He is the editor of the forthcoming English Edition of Dietrich Bonhoeffer's *Act and Being* in the series *The Works of Dietrich Bonhoeffer* (Fortress). His articles have appeared in *Modern Theology, The Journal of the American Academy of Religion, Philosophy and Theology,* and *Union Seminary Quarterly Review.* Dr. Floyd has taught at Gettysburg College, Lebanon Valley College, The University of the South, Lehigh University, and Lafayette College.

DONALD RATCLIFF is an Assistant Professor of Psychology and Sociology at Toccoa Falls College in Georgia. He holds an undergraduate degree from Spring Arbor College, a Masters from Michigan State University, and a Specialist in Education from the University of Georgia. He has published numerous articles in professional journals and has conducted research on using play in preschool religious education. His books include *Handbook of Preschool Religious Education* (Religious Education Press), *Handbook of Youth Ministry* (Religious Education Press), and *Handbook of Children's Religious Education* (Religious Education Press).

ANTHONY HEADLEY is an Assistant Professor of Counseling at Asbury Theological Seminary. He recently completed his doctoral studies at the University of Kentucky, majoring in Medical Behavioral Science. He received several scholastic awards, and he currently is a member of the International Society of Theta Pi. Dr. Headley taught in the Caribbean Graduate School of Theology, The University of Kentucky, and the Christian Union Bible School. An emerging scholar, this chapter is among the first of his major publications.

JOE BOONE ABBOTT is the corporate Vice President, Pastoral Care and Counseling Medical Centers, Birmingham, Alabama. In addition to his administrative duties he directs a large pastoral counseling training program and is a pastoral counselor in private practice. He is active in numerous national professional and AMC organizations, and he is an ordained Southern Baptist minister. He received his doctorate from Columbia Theological Seminary. Dr. Abbott is listed in *Who's Who in the South and Southwest* and *Who's Who in Religion*.

GARY L. SAPP is Professor of Education at the University of Alabama at Birmingham where he directs the Office of Educational Research. He is a native of Illinois and is a Southern Baptist layperson. He received his doctorate in Educational Psychology from the University of Tennessee. His books include *Perspectives in Educational Psychology* (MSS Educational Publication Company) and the *Handbook of Moral Development* (Religious Education Press). His numerous research articles have appeared in *The Journal for the*

Scientific Study of Religion, Counseling and Values, Journal of Psychology, and *Psychological Reports.* Dr. Sapp has taught at Tennessee Technological University, The University of North Carolina - Greensboro, and Chulalongkorn University, Bangkok.

JAMES MICHAEL LEE is Professor of Education at the University of Alabama at Birmingham. He was born is Brooklyn and is a Catholic layperson. He received his doctorate from Columbia University. Three of Professor Lee's many books are his trilogy, *The Shape of Religious Instruction* (Religious Education Press), *The Flow of Religious Instruction* (Religious Education Press), and *The Content of Religious Instruction* (Religious Education Press). His articles have appeared in many journals including *Herder Korrespondenz, Religious Education,* and *Living Light.* Dr. Lee has taught at the University of Notre Dame, Hunter College of the City University of New York, and St. Joseph's College. He was the recipient of a Senior Fulbright Research Fellowship to Germany and also a Lilly Endowment Fellowship. Dr. Lee is listed in *Who's Who in America, Who's Who in the World,* and *Who's Who in Religion.*

Index of Names

Index of Subjects

Absence of compassion, 95-96, 103, 109, 141-143
 solution for, 101, 104, 109, 111-117
Acculturation of compassion, 112-113
Active listening in therapy, see Compassionate responding
Affect, compassion as, 42-44, 129-130, 134-137, 151, 159-161, 163, 171, 193-195, 201, 209-210
Affective domain, 209-211
Affective sensitivity, 210
Affective sensitivity exercises, 209
Agapan, 45
Agape, 44-45, 170
Agapesis, 45
Ageism, 102
Allah, 59
Allport, Vernon, and Lindzey Scale, 85
Altruism, 64-65, 74, 76, 78, 81, 85, 91, 93-94, 130-131, 136-137, 179, 189-190, 198
 behavior as, 46, 64, 130, 161
 definition of, 130-131
 motivation, as, 78, 83-90, 93-94, 131-133, 138-139
Altruistic group therapy, 160
America 2000, 117-118
Analogia relationis, 41, 51
Anglican articles of religion, 53
Apostasy, Israel's, 17
Assumptions of compassion, 65-66
Attribute of God, compassion as, 127
Autonomy, 108

Axes of compassion, 306
Babylonian exile, 24
Babylonian Talmud, 36, 205
Balance in compassion, 146
Basis for morality, compassion as, 70-74
Batson model, 86-90
Behavior, compassion as, 44-46, 48-52, 57-58, 65, 67, 76, 78, 118-119, 129, 131-132, 135, 137-138, 140, 151, 155-159, 162, 169-170, 176-179, 193-195, 199-201, 206, 217, 222, 226, 230-232, 240-243, 287-290
Behavioral component in counseling, 137-138
Behavioral psychology, 105
Behavioral specificity, teaching as, 200-202
 see also Instructional principles, gen eral
Beten, 14
Biblical compassion, 9-34, 124
Biblical interpretation, types of, 16-17
 contemporary literary–critical method, 16-17
 historical-critical method, 16-17
Biblical metaphors, 11-12
Biblical view of compassion, 9-34, 16-17
 apostasy, Israel, of, 17
 Babylonian exile, 24
 Book of consolations, 19
 Buddhism, 9-10
 Canticle of Mary, 29

227